SUSTAINING FAITH TRAI

MW01093470

Diego —

To a wonderful student!

Carolyn Weber

Sustaining Faith Traditions

Race, Ethnicity, and Religion among the Latino and Asian American Second Generation

Edited by Carolyn Chen and Russell Jeung

NEW YORK UNIVERSITY PRESS
New York and London

NEW YORK UNIVERSITY PRESS
New York and London
www.nyupress.org

References to Internet websites (URLs) were accurate at the time of writing.
Neither the author nor New York University Press is responsible for URLs that
may have expired or changed since the manuscript was prepared.

Library of Congress Cataloging-in-Publication Data
Sustaining faith traditions : race, ethnicity, and religion among the Latino and Asian
American second generation / edited by Carolyn Chen and Russell Jeung.
p. cm.
Includes bibliographical references and index.
ISBN 978-0-8147-1735-6 (cl : alk. paper) -- ISBN 978-0-8147-1736-3 (pb : alk. paper) -- ISBN
978-0-8147-1737-0 (ebook) -- ISBN 978-0-8147-7289-8 (ebook)
1. United States--Religion. 2. Latin Americans--Religion. 3. Asian Americans--Religion. I.
Chen, Carolyn, 1971- II. Jeung, Russell, 1962-
BL2525.S87 2012
200.89'00973--dc23
2011052271

New York University Press books are printed on acid-free paper,
and their binding materials are chosen for strength and durability.
We strive to use environmentally responsible suppliers and materials
to the greatest extent possible in publishing our books.

Manufactured in the United States of America

c 10 9 8 7 6 5 4 3 2 1
p 10 9 8 7 6 5 4 3 2 1

We dedicate this book to our families:

*Joan Jie-eun Jeung, Bethsy Lal Rin Tluang,
Bonny Lal Tha Zual, and Matthew Kim Jeung,*

and

*Dylan Penningroth, August Craig,
and Julien James Chen-Penningroth*

CONTENTS

ACKNOWLEDGMENTS

We would like to express our deep appreciation to all the contributors for their strong contributions, as well as to our editor at New York University Press, Jennifer Hammer. We are grateful for the support and feedback from colleagues from the Asian Pacific American Religions Research Initiative and the Asian American Studies Department of San Francisco State University.

CHAPTER 1

Introduction

Religious, Racial, and Ethnic Identities of the New Second Generation

RUSSELL JEUNG, CAROLYN CHEN, AND JERRY Z. PARK

It's like regardless of your race or background, everybody comes. You see—well, there's not too many whites, [but] you know, we had that Bosnian guy, he came. And we have some African Americans, we have a whole lot of Arabs and people from the Indian subcontinent. We have an Indonesian guy who comes. . . . It's just everybody comes together. We come and pray together, and it's just awesome. . . . It's— we're all equal, all standing in line together, we're all praying to the same Lord, and we're all listening to the same speaker. It's unreal.
—Shaheed, second-generation Pakistani Muslim, describing how his university's Muslim Student Association transcends race and ethnicity

I think that Nueva Esperanza is what our people have been look- ing for, for years. And I think that if these folks stay on track, the Latino community is going to have a voice like never before over the next ten years. I think the black church is organized; I think that African Americans in this country have organized. It's time for our people to organize! You know, we're the least respected, least educated, most impoverished, and I think that that season and that age is changing now with organizations such as Nueva Esperanza.
—Pastor Francisco, a second-generation Puerto Rican evangelical, describing how his national organization mobilizes Latino religious leaders

Race and religion matter enormously for the new second generation, the children of post-1965 immigrants. They are negotiating who they are and where they belong in a United States that has transformed with contem- porary immigration. In the epigraphs, Shaheed delights in how his Mus- lim identity transcends ethnic and racial differences; for Pastor Francisco, on the other hand, religion offers a way to mobilize Latino solidarity and

organization toward social justice. What accounts for such different manifestations of their religious traditions?

This volume investigates the intersecting relationships between race, ethnicity, and religion in the lives of second-generation Asian Americans and
Latinos, examining how faith traditions transform in the American context.
The diversity of religious traditions held by Asian Americans and Latinos—
including evangelical Protestantism, Catholicism, Buddhism, Islam, Hinduism, Judaism, and ethnic popular religions—provides potential resources for
reconfiguring racial and ethnic relations in the United States today. Faith traditions are sources of innovation and self-determination.

This book engages with the influential thesis on religion and ethnicity that
social theorist Will Herberg proposed 50 years ago. Building on the traditional view of assimilation at that time, Herberg argued that commitment
to national and ethnic heritage would decline for the descendants of immigrants. He went on to argue that religious affiliation—as Protestant, Catholic,
or Jew—would become their primary source of social identity in the United
States. He explained, "The newcomer is expected to change many things
about him as he becomes American—nationality, language, culture. One
thing, however, he is not expected to change—and that is his religion. And
so it is religion that with the third generation has become the differentiating
element and the context of self-identification and social location" (Herberg
1955, 23). Herberg's theories, however, were based on the experiences of the
descendants of European immigrants at a time when mass immigration to
the United States had halted for over 30 years. Like other social theorists of
the time, Herbert did not account for race in a manner that would be largely
taken for granted by observers today. To Herberg, race was less relevant to
the immigrants he saw; religion instead constituted their main identity, especially after the first generation. Notably, race was important for black and
Asian (then sometimes called "Oriental") Americans, who sustained a permanent inferior status. Other European-origin Americans who held on to
their national (i.e., ethnic) culture risked similar marginalization. But they
could maintain their religious identity permanently and without social penalty because Protestantism, Catholicism, and Judaism reflect American "spiritual" values of democracy and the dignity of the individual. Indeed Herberg
argued that adherence to other religions such as Buddhism and Islam identified an individual as non-American.

In this volume, we examine religion, race, and ethnicity among Asians and
Latinos, the largest ethnic/racial groups among contemporary immigrants to
the United States. Much has changed since Herberg penned his treatise. We
argue that in light of critical social and demographic changes, ethnicity does

not become eclipsed. Instead, the experience of race and ethnicity not only foregrounds but shapes the religious experiences and identities of the new second generation. To answer the questions of "Who am I?" and "To which group do I belong?" the second generation today does not look merely to religion, as Herberg claimed, but to religion, race, and ethnicity simultaneously. The core motivating question for this volume, then, is, How does the second generation negotiate these three different forms of competing and possibly conflicting claims on identity and belonging in America?

Four Trajectories of Race, Religion, and Ethnicity

The second generation may be seen as negotiating race, religion, and ethnicity in four different ways: (1) religious primacy, (2) racialized religion, (3) ethnoreligious hybridization, and (4) familistic traditioning. Latino and Asian American evangelical Christians who belong to multiethnic congregations, Muslims, and Asian American Jews are examples of members of the new second generation who practice religious primacy and prioritize religious identities over all others. For those who practice racialized religion, religion does not transcend race and ethnicity but rather affirms racial boundaries that are a product of the racialized experiences of Asian and Latinos in the United States. Both Latino faith-based organizations and Latino gang ministries are examples of racialized religion. Ethnoreligious hybridization describes the processes by which second-generation groups such as Korean American evangelicals and Filipino Catholics employ multicultural discourse to reinvent religious traditions and to combine ethnic and religious identities. And finally, noncongregational religious and spiritual traditions that are domestic and kin centered fall into the category of familistic traditioning. Practices such as Chinese popular religion, Vietnamese ancestral veneration, and Indian American Hinduism are often not identified as "religions" by practitioners, but they are family traditions that affirm identification with and belonging in an "ethnic" family.

The four religious trajectories of the new second generation are structured by three factors that have emerged since Herberg's time of writing. First, the racial composition and economic opportunities of the American population have shifted as the new post-1965 immigrants have primarily been people of color. Their assimilation has been segmented, so that they do not necessarily adopt a singular "American Way of Life," nor do they have equal access to upward mobility, as Herberg described. Second, much of American discourse now embraces a racialized multiculturalism, in which both ethnic and racial identities are valued. Consequently, religious mobilization along these identities has been legitimated and even prized, which Herberg could not have foreseen when he predicted that assimilation must occur exclusively on religious grounds. Finally, the religious landscape in the United States has radically changed, so that the public authority and institutional role of religion in constructing individuals' and groups' identities has altered. These socioeconomic and cultural changes thus provide the context for the religions of the new second generation.

The Effect of Race and Class on Religious Identities

With the passage of the 1965 Immigration Act and the 1990 Immigration Act, newcomers from Latin America and Asia have significantly changed the racial make-up of the United States (Rumbaut and Portes 2001). Overall, in the 2010 U.S. Census, Latinos made up 16.3% of the population (50,477,594), and Asian Americans were 4.8% of the population (14,674,252). Their children—the new second generation—are now coming of age and compose significant proportions of America's youth and emerging adult populations. Their religious socialization and affiliation signal social change unlike any other in this nation's history. These demographic shifts, in turn, are also shaping the new religious landscape of America (Foley and Hoge 2007; Lorentzen et al. 2009; Min 2010; Raboteau, Dewind, and Alba 2008).

The new second generation, which currently makes up nearly 11% of the U.S. population, is made up of primarily people of color, whose racialization marks them as "ethnic" Americans. Given the current anti-immigrant political context of the United States, their opportunities to assimilate into mainstream American denominations are mixed, at best. As seen in figure 1.1, over half of the new second generation is either Latino or Asian American: 29% of the new second generation is from Mexico, 18% is from Asia, and another 16% is from other countries in Latin America. Members of the second generation who have parents from Europe or Canada make up one-third of this subpopulation. We note that while this latter group is significant in size, its members are generally much older than are the Asian Americans and Latinos in the second generation. According to analyses by the Migration Policy Institute, using data from the Current Population Surveys of 2005–2006, the European- and Canadian-origin second generation has a median age of 54, while the median age of the Mexican-origin second generation is 12 years, of other Latin American origin (13 years), and of Asian origin (16 years)—all below 18. Put differently, the non-European-origin second generation surveyed in 2006 has a median birth year between 1990 and 1994, whereas the European- and Canadian-origin second generation has a median birth year

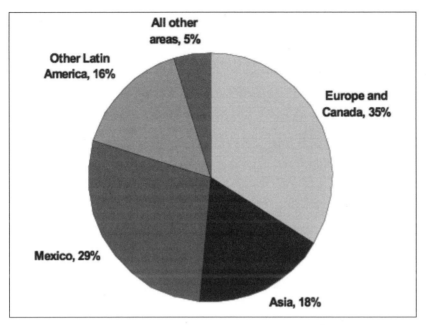

Figure 1.1. Background of the New Second Generation, Current Population Survey, 2006 (Dixon 2006)

of 1952. We can safely presume that the majority of the members of today's nonwhite second generation are the children of immigrants who arrived as a result of changes in immigration policy since 1965.

Thus, the new second generation will change the racial composition of the United States, as well as its religious landscape. By 2050, Latinos, as the largest minority group in the nation, will compose 29% of the population, and whites will be a minority (Fry 2008). The Asian American population will grow to make up 9% of the U.S. population. Neither white nor black, the racialization and Americanization of Latinos and Asian Americans will chart race relations for decades to come, as they adapt to a globalized, segmented economy in the United States.

Although Herberg argued that religious identity is primary, segmented assimilation theorists privilege the structural factors of race and class in the adaptation of the new second generation. They note that post-1965 immigrants differ from prior groups because the former are nonwhite and incorporated into a more multicultural, racialized society and into a postindustrial, segmented economy (Rumbaut and Portes 2001, 2006; Zhou 2009).

Both race and class prominently structure the religious experiences of the new second generation—not only the context in which individuals live out their religion but also in how theologies, institutional forms, and identities become established. The second generation's concrete material conditions frame the context in which members produce their theologies, build their congregations, and experience their religious traditions. Globalization and the concomitant restructuring of America's industrial base have led to an hourglass-shaped economy, with a large pool of service-sector jobs, little union-wage manufacturing work, and increased demand for high-tech professionals. Without the availability of the kind of union-waged jobs that were afforded previous immigrants, the new second generation has much more limited economic opportunities. Many low-income immigrants remain trapped in underclass neighborhoods, and their children may adopt values and practices of oppositional culture. On the other hand, professional immigrants can bypass urban centers and move straight to suburbs with significant concentrations of middle-class racial minorities, or ethnoburbs, where their children can maintain their privilege by attending better schools and utilizing professional ethnic networks.

Members of the new second generation therefore do assimilate but enter a segmented economy in which their opportunities for economic and social integration into the American middle class differ. Recent research shows patterns of segmented assimilation, in which educational attainment and income of the new second generation are shaped by structural factors such as race, class, and ethnic networks (Rumbaut and Portes 2001, 2006; Zhou 2009). Likewise, these structural factors continue to shape the second generation's religious affiliations in segmented trends.

An explicit comparison of different classes of the Asian American and Latino second generation highlights how segmented assimilation shapes religious traditions. In this volume, both the chapter by Milagros Peña and Edwin I. Hernández and the chapter by Edward Flores analyze how some Latino ministries clearly develop theologies and programs around the impoverished neighborhoods where they are based. As Flores demonstrates, "color-blind racism" has created racial inequalities that are addressed by these Latino ministries. Similarly, the children of Vietnamese refugees in Linda Ho Peché's chapter and the children of Toisanese working-class parents in Russell Jeung's chapter do not assimilate into the white middle class and their religions. Instead, they are much more likely to maintain their ethnic popular religious practices than are their Asian American upper-middle-class counterparts.

In fact, middle-class Latinos and Asian Americans have more ethnic options available to them than low-income Latinos and Asian Americans have (Waters 1990). Gerardo Marti in his chapter examines mostly middle-class Latinos, who are able to become "ethnic transcendent" as they enter multiethnic congregations in which their religious identities are primary. The Asian Americans in Sharon Kim and Rebecca Y. Kim's chapter, as well as those in Jerry Z. Park's chapter, are also upwardly mobile, but they utilize their class resources in a different trajectory. They choose not to assimilate religiously but instead to hybridize their ethnic and religious identities and to maintain ethnic solidarities. Not only have the racial demographics and economic opportunities of the new second generation shifted, but so has the dominant American discourse on race relations.

Racialized Multiculturalism

In contrast to the triple melting pot that Herberg described in the mid-20th century, American social institutions today may establish contexts in which racial differences and ethnic culture may be prized. Those who favor American multiculturalism not only acknowledge but celebrate ethnic, racial, and religious diversity. The term racialized multiculturalism highlights the twin discourses that now shape the religious trajectories of the new second generation.

Through racialization—the process of categorizing by race or extending racial meanings to practices or groups—the categories of Asian American and Latino have become taken-for-granted communities in the United States (Omi and Winant 1994). The United States employs a multicultural discourse that normalizes five major racial labels: white, black, Hispanic, American Indian, and Asian American (Hollinger 1995). Seen as neither whites nor blacks, post-1965 immigrants from Asia or Latin America face a cultural context that symbolically and structurally minimizes significant political-national differences in favor of these panethnic racial constructions that position them.

Beyond establishing panethnic groupings, racialization also creates a racial hierarchy in the United States, with Asian Americans and Latinos positioned in between African Americans and whites (Bonilla-Silva 2003; C. Kim 2003; Lee, Ramakrishnan, and Ramirez 2007; Light and Bonacich 1991). Because of their physical characteristics, geopolitical positioning, class backgrounds, and historical racial discourses, Latinos and Asian Americans are racialized on a nativist dimension and stand apart from both whites and blacks. Members of the new second generation are often considered outsiders and foreigners. In fact, the process of Americanization and determination of who is considered authentically American requires the creation of a deviant, non-American grouping. In the anti-immigrant sentiment of the times, Latinos and, to a lesser degree, Asian Americans become portrayed as "illegal aliens" and "suspect foreigners." Thus racially oppressed, the new second generation maintains ethnic and racial groupings out of reactive solidarity, despite the claims of new assimilation theorists (Alba and Nee 2005; Kasinitz et al. 2008).

Asian Americans and Latinos, including those involved with faith-based organizations and congregations, have taken these racial categories and rearticulated them as self-determined, empowered racial identities (Espinosa, Elizondo, and Miranda 2005; Jeung 2005; Park 2008). Religious leaders and institutions have also mobilized around these identities to build their congregations, to relate to other groups, and to engage their sociopolitical environment. Indeed, if the multiculturalist discourse were to be believed, being black, white, Asian, or Latino is as "American" as being Protestant, Catholic, or Jewish was in Herberg's frame.

Beyond these racial categories, individual ethnic groupings such as Mexican American or Pakistani American are also reinforced by dominant institutions in society. Multiculturalism, albeit sometimes superficial, prizes all forms of diversity, especially ethnic and cultural (Hollinger 1995; Taylor 1992). Politics, popular media, education, and even capitalist markets now may support the maintenance of ethnic groups to target. Indeed, multiculturalism is a preferred ideology used to reject racism, with its insistence that everyone's heritage and background be recognized equally (Darder and Torres 2004).

Although Herberg argued that religion was the only social identity legitimated by the government during his time, the multiculturalism of today acknowledges several identities. For example, hate-crimes legislation protects individuals against bias based on race, religion, disability, ethnic origin, or sexual orientation. Similarly, multicultural education policies, approved in some communities across the United States, promote the understanding of different cultural groups and the appreciation of these groups' values and differences.

While the extent to which religious groups acknowledge ethnic heritages differs, few openly espouse the denial of one's heritage and culture. Given the broadened acceptance of these new identities, members of the new second generation have generally embraced and integrated their ethnic backgrounds with their religious identities by fusing or hybridizing the two, as Hammond and Warner (1993) described in their typologies of the relationship between ethnicity and religion. Ethnic fusion entails the subsuming of religious culture into one's ethnic culture (Hammond and Warner 1993; Min 2010). Ethnic hybridization, on the other hand, is the innovative process of combining elements of religion and ethnicity to create two types of new subcultural identity, either ethnic religion or religious ethnicity.

The ethnographies and interview studies in this volume illustrate how these discourses operate. For example, Peña and Hernández describe the panethnic, Latino mobilization of Christian ministries. They do not necessarily emphasize denominational differences but do explicitly recognize the role of racial dynamics and racialization in the creation of faith-based organizations. Joaquin Jay Gonzalez III describes how Filipino Americans adopt multiculturalist viewpoints in "filipinizing" congregations. In a desire to maintain their ethnic heritage, second-generation Filipino Americans are more likely to establish and congregate in hybridized congregations than to enter white, mainstream ones.

The Changing American Religious Landscape

Just as racial and ethnic discourses—and the very populations themselves—have shifted in ways unforeseen by Herberg, the American religious landscape has also dramatically altered in two major ways. It has become religiously pluralistic, while concurrently the public influence of its religious institutions has dramatically declined. In consequence, the new second generation of Latinos and Asian Americans have greater religious options than before, including the option of being spiritual but not religious.

Immigrants have transformed not only the racial and ethnic landscape of America but also its religious composition. This shift has furthered the gradual de-Christianization of American religion. While the numbers of Buddhists, Muslims, Hindus, and members of other non-Judeo-Christian faiths make up only about 3% of the American population, their institutional presence and influence stand out (Eck 2002; Foley and Hoge 2007). For the second generation, these new religious spaces provide opportunities to preserve culture, to socialize with coethnics, and to develop identities distinct from white Americans (Chen 2008; Joshi 2006; Kurien 2007; Lawrence 2004; Min 2010)

Figure 1.2 illustrates the religious identities of Asian Americans by generation. Asian Americans are primarily responsible for the religious diversity that we see in contemporary immigration. Among East Asians, nearly one-half are not Christian, and among Central and South Asians, 86% are not Christian. Among the second generation, a slightly smaller proportion of the second generation identifies with non-Christian religions than the first generation does. Interestingly, there are slightly more in the second generation who identify as Buddhist than in the first generation. The most dramatic finding is the drop in the second generation of those who identify as religious "nones": 29% of immigrants claim no religion, whereas only 19% of the second generation claim no religion. This drop seems to indicate that some type of religious affiliation becomes more important as Asian Americans acculturate.

Figure 1.3 illustrates the religions of the Latino population by generation. Latinos today constitute one-third of the American Catholic Church, and with the continuing flow of Latino immigration and Latinos' higher-than-average birthrate, they will become an increasing proportion of the Church (Pew Hispanic Center 2007). Just as Irish Catholics transformed American Catholicism during their mass immigration over 100 years ago, so too are Latinos having a significant influence today. For example, Latinos are generally more supportive of a more charismatic practice of Catholicism (ibid.). Over half of Latinos identify as charismatic Catholics, compared to only one-eighth of non-Latino Catholics. Moreover, Latinos are maintaining the ethnic nature of their Catholicism. Native-born and English-speaking Latinos are not joining white Catholic parishes but rather are continuing to worship in ethnic congregations. Thus, both the Asian American and the Latino presence in Protestant and Catholic congregations mark a significant de-Europeanization of the American church.

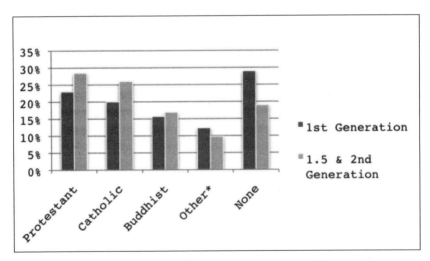

Figure 1.2. Pilot National Asian American Politics Survey (PNAAPS), 2001
* The largest groups in Other are Muslims and Hindus. The sample of second generation Hindu and Muslim respondents is too small to confidently report the results of each religion separately.

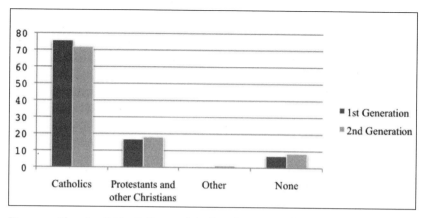

Figure 1.3. Changing Faiths: Latinos and the Transformation of American Religion Survey, 2007

While America's religious diversity increases, the significance of American religious institutions has been on the wane. According to Kosmin et al. (2009), the number of those who do not affiliate with any religion, the religious "nones," has doubled in the past two decades to 34 million. Of all the racial groups, Asian Americans have the highest rates of religious nones, at 29%. Latinos have seen the fastest increase among all racial groups in the number of religious nones, tripling to 13% in the past 20 years.

Those who are young adults, from 21 through 45 years old, are even more likely to be spiritual but not religious than are those who are older. According to one study, only 19% of young adults say that their religion or spirituality is influenced by Christian teachings and practices. In contrast, 48% say their spirituality is shaped by other influences, such as music and art (Wuthnow 2010). Two-thirds have opted to use personal experience as the best means to understand God, while only a quarter have opted for church doctrines (ibid.).

In the 1950s, Herberg described Protestantism, Catholicism, and Judaism as America's three religious communities, "something in which one is born, lives, and dies, something that identifies and defines one's position in American society" (1955, 87). Today, however, these institutional arrangements no longer apply, and Asian Americans and Latinos are developing religious identities in a very different context. The chapters in this volume by R. Stephen Warner et al., Peché, and Jeung illustrate how both the Latino and Asian American members of the second generation have ambivalent relationships with institutional religion. Given this mistrust of established traditions, they are not attending local congregations but are continuing their own personal spiritual practices and values. With the decline of religious institutions, the new second generation is thus able to establish spiritualities that are more fluid, hybridized, and eclectic. Indeed, the spiritualities of these individuals may be more representative of the "American Way of Life" than are those who embrace more orthodox Protestant, Catholic, or Jewish beliefs today.

These three contextual factors—changing demographics, new racialized multicultural discourses, and shifting religious values—intersect such that, as described earlier, we have identified four main trajectories for the new second generation. This book is organized into four parts to reflect these trajectories.

Religious Primacy

The cases discussed in part 1 conform most closely to Herberg's model, in which religion transcends and trumps racial and ethnic categorization/identification. In these chapters, individuals identify more strongly with religion than with ethnicity or race. Interestingly, we see this pattern, or perhaps the potential for this outcome, among only certain religions and not others—namely, evangelical Protestantism, Islam, and Judaism—religions that, in comparison to other religious traditions from Asia, are congregationally based and, with the exception of Judaism, tend to have a proselytizing bent. Evangelical Protestantism, Islam, and Judaism, we argue, have strong group boundaries that differentiate people within from those without. Furthermore, evangelical Protestantism and Islam, with a substantial proportion of their population as converts, tend to emphasize the universality of their tradition and cultural/ethnic particularism as counterproductive to collective unity. Their absolutist claims call for allegiance beyond nation, ethnicity, or even family. Even still, race and ethnicity play important roles in how these individuals negotiate religion in the United States and their religious experiences. Herberg's theory continues to apply to some of the new Latino and Asian American second generation, however, in revised and racially inflected new ways.

Chapter 2, by Gerardo Marti, perhaps best illustrates how religion transcends race and ethnicity for the new second generation. At Mosaic, a multiracial evangelical church in Southern California, Latinos have chosen to leave their ethnic churches and worship in a multiracial community with whites, blacks, and Asians. Because of the church's emphasis on evangelism and its vision to be diverse, Mosaic members downplay their ethnicity. The "ethnic transcendent Latino" at Mosaic prioritizes his or her evangelical Christian faith and identity over his or her racial and ethnic identities and commitments. As Herberg would predict, the Latinos at Mosaic are second- and third-generation individuals who, according to Marti, "have largely lost a meaningful connection to their own ancestral heritage." Still, as a result of the racialized multicultural discourse, race and ethnicity do not fade away completely for these Latino evangelicals. Marti argues that ethnicity is contingent and fluid, at times emphasized and other times downplayed, depending on the context.

Chapter 3, by R. Stephen Warner, Elise Martel, and Rhonda E. Dugan compares attitudes toward religion and ethnicity among South Asian Muslim women and Latino Catholic women. The authors find that the Muslim women separate religion from culture and identify more strongly and affirmatively with Islam than with their ethnic culture. The Latino Catholic women, on the other hand, see their Catholicism as inextricably connected to their Latino heritage and express a great deal of ambivalence toward Catholicism.

Although the Muslim case appears to conform to Herberg's theory, there are important differences that distinguish the new second generation from the descendants of white ethnics. Ethnicity does not naturally fade away for Muslim women. In fact, ethnicity is imposed on them by both society and their parents. These South Asian women are physically marked as "ethnic" by society because of the color of their skin. In this context, Islam is a way for these women to assert their independence from the inherited culture of their parents and, we conjecture, a way for them to assert their independence from the racialization of dominant society. In other words, a Muslim identity is a way for these women to self-identify over against the marginalization they experience.

For the Latino Catholic women, religion is so bound up in ethnicity that the two cannot be separated. To be Latino is to be Catholic. And the Catholicism of these women is not the "mainstream American" Catholicism that Herberg predicts but a Catholicism that is explicitly and unapologetically Latino. Nothing flies in the face of Herberg's theory of religious primacy more directly than the persistence of Latino Catholicism several generations out. The inextricability of religion and ethnicity/culture is a characteristic we see also in later chapters among Vietnamese American Buddhists and Catholics, Indian Hindus, and secular Chinese Americans.

Chapter 4, by Helen K. Kim and Noah Leavitt, touches on a subject that Herberg hardly saw possible: the phenomenon of racial and religious intermarriage between Asian Americans and Jews. The ways that these families negotiate ethnicity and religion suggests the primacy of religion. It is far easier for these couples to pass on Jewish traditions and identities to their offspring than to pass on Asian traditions and ethnic identities. To be sure,

Kim and Leavitt's sample is unusual in that the respondents with children are nonreligious Asian American men who are married to Jewish women. Since women are the traditional bearers of culture in the family, the results could reflect this bias. But the data also show that Jewish traditions and identity are easier to pass on to children because they are institutionalized in Judaism, as Herberg predicted. This points to the significance that religion and religious institutions are accorded in organizing identity and community, over and above ethnicity, in the United States.

Race and Class

The chapters in part 2 highlight how the intersecting processes of racialization and economic restructuring impede the new second generation from simply adopting the triple melting-pot identities of Protestant, Catholic, or Jew. As mentioned earlier, while changes in immigration legislation opened up new geographical sources of immigration, the nature of the American economy changed as well. Opportunities to climb from low- or semiskilled labor to mid- or high-skilled labor shrank, thus creating a segmented pattern of low mobility. Thus, unlike in Herberg's time, new immigrants in poverty or in the working class can no longer be confident that they or their children will ascend to middle-class status. This reality bears heavily on how religious ministry functions for these immigrants and their children compared to the immigrant middle class and their children.

Along with the process of racialization described earlier, institutional racism promotes religious segregation (Deyoung et al. 2003; Emerson and Smith 2001). Both historical racism and contemporary, color-blind racism forge racial inequalities. Historical racism included the Orientalization of Asians as pagans, patriarchal relationships between white-denomination missions and organizations and Latinos and Asians, and the establishment of segregated ethnic congregations (Chang 2010; Iwamura 2011). Entering this religious landscape, new immigrants have patterned their own congregations after the ethnic institutions of late-19th- and early-20th-century Mexicans, Chinese, and Japanese. This emulation of religious institutional form, coupled with the principle of religious homophily that Kim and Kim discuss in this volume, have perpetuated separate ethnic congregations (Dimaggio and Powell 1983).

Contemporary, color-blind racism remains founded on historical racism. Concrete indicators of such racial inequalities include income gaps, underclass ethnic enclaves, health disparities, and consequently, segregation of congregations (Bonilla-Silva 2003; Hirschman 2004). The two chapters in this part explicitly address racialization and these racisms in their case studies.

Chapter 5, by Milagros Peña and Edwin I. Hernández, profiles several Latino congregations and faith-based organizations that demonstrate this trend toward panethnic religious mobilization. Arguing that diverse Hispanic groups such as Puerto Ricans, Mexicans, and Dominicans have similar experiences, socioeconomic backgrounds, and national issues, they show how race relations in the United States construct a different American religious experience for Latinos today than for white immigrants during Herberg's time. Echoing political scientist Catherine Wilson's thesis, they suggest that both the content of Latinos' theology and beliefs and their context intertwine to shape their religious identities. In particular, a sense of community—drawn by space, generation, and common struggle—pull these panethnic groups together.

In chapter 6, Edward Flores asserts that the corrections system in California targets black and brown men of color, such that one in six Latinos will be incarcerated at some time in his life. The perpetuation of such inequality stymies the religious mainstreaming of Catholic and even Protestant Latinos into a triple melting pot and ultimately results in the development of uniquely Chicano faith-based organizations.

Ethnoreligious Hybridity

Whereas part 2 highlights racial dynamics of the new second generation and its religions, part 3 critically explores the intersecting relationship of ethnicity and religion. Roberto Trevino argues in his history *The Church in the Barrio: Mexican American Ethno-Catholicism in Houston* (2006) that the intertwining of Catholicism and Mexican heritage provided Mexican Americans a singular identity to address their minority status in that city. This concept of ethnoreligious community, in which a group's identity combines both cultural tradition and religious affiliation, may be accepted by the immigrant generation but is problematic for the second (Hammond and Warner 1993). Indeed, the intersection of these two major sources of identity complicates how the new second generation will develop religiously. Herberg noted in passing that immigrants face marginalization if they continue in their national, cultural, or ethnic mores. For many Asian American religious communities, retaining ethnic mores does not appear to intensify marginalization but instead can reinforce religious group commitment. In the three chapters in this part, ethnic attachment coupled with religion appears to bolster religious commitment. In other words, these chapters exemplify a kind of ethnic-bonding social capital in which religious group commitment is enhanced by shared ethnic ties.

Jerry Z. Park, in chapter 7, documents how Korean American Protestant students at elite universities are more likely than any other ethnic group to maintain ethnic solidarity and group identity because of hybridized ethnoreligion. He first highlights the racialized university environment, where Korean Americans are lumped with other Asian Americans in programs and studies. In choosing which campus fellowships to attend, Korean American students have organizational options already based on ethnicity. Korean American university students then accept these racialized and ethnic identities as "the way things are." Park's findings from the National Longitudinal Study of Freshmen reveal that not only are Korean Americans more Protestant and religiously observant than their fellow Asian Americans are, but their churches are also more likely to be racially insular compared to other minorities. This insularity is not necessarily due to Korean Americans' feelings that there is racial prejudice against them but instead to a worldview that couples Korean and Protestant identities. This merging of ethnic and religious identities is a process of hybridization that takes on uniquely American characteristics.

Chapter 8, by Joaquin Jay Gonzalez III, illustrates how Filipino Americans "filipinize" their Catholic religiosity through choosing particular types of ministry and charity, especially the practice of sending balikbayan boxes of goods back to relatives in the Philippines. At the same time, the church helps to reinforce and pass on Filipino values, such as utang na loob, a debt of gratitude, and bayanhihan, mutual cooperation for the common good. Even the second generation continues the practice of remitting balikbayan, with 40% of them sending goods back to their parents' homeland. In addition, institutions such as Catholic universities, parachurch organizations, and student groups provide the infrastructure and space to develop Filipinized Catholicism. In these ways, religious institutions and structures merge with ethnic values and transnational connections to further ethnoreligion.

Along with providing the institutional space to establish ethnoreligion, Korean American Protestant congregations also host entrepreneurial leaders who actively hybridize ethnic traditions with contemporary religious sensibilities. In chapter 9, Sharon Kim and Rebecca Y. Kim describe how second-generation Korean American ministers make use of both Korean American spirituality, such as an intense prayer style, and contemporary evangelical worship styles and organizational structures. Their chapter and Gonzalez's point to the fact that these new, hybrid congregations may reconfigure what is considered a minority or mainstream church in today's multicultural America.

Minority Religions

The chapters in part 4 look at religious minorities in the United States—dus, Buddhists, and Chinese popular religionists—who do not assimilate Herberg's tripartite religious world of Protestant, Catholic, and Jew. Among the groups in these chapters, the lines between religion, ethnicity, and family are closely blurred. Many of the respondents in these chapters, like other young Americans, no longer identify with their religious tradition, and others have never identified with a religious tradition in the first place (Greeley and Hout 2006; Smith and Denton 2005; Wuthnow 2010). Yet they all maintain some aspect of their parents' religious/spiritual practices and traditions, which they understand as being closely tied to family and/or ethnicity. The common thread among the Hindus, Buddhists, Catholics, and "seculars" in this section, for whom religion and ethnicity are one and the same, is a strong practice of religion as a home and family tradition rather than as a congregational and public faith (Ammerman 2006).

In all these cases, religion does the opposite of what Herberg predicts: rather than universalizing the boundaries of membership and transcending parochial affinities, religion reinforces the particularistic ties of family especially but also of ethnicity (Min 2010). Furthermore, religion, in and of itself, does not seem to offer a strong sense of identity, as it does for Muslims, evangelical Christians, and Jews. For the second-generation members of minority religions, the meaning and practice of religion and spirituality are highly personal and eclectic, each innovating according to his or her individual needs and sense of family. In fact, the cases of new immigrant religion in this volume do not necessarily take American religious congregational forms, as hypothesized by Yang and Ebaugh (2001).

The family is the center of religiosity and spirituality in chapter 10, Russell Jeung's study of second-generation Chinese Americans. Jeung illustrates the dissonance between Western definitions of religion as a public institutionalized phenomenon and Asian practices of religion that are noninstitutionalized and centered around the family. These Chinese Americans identify as nonreligious; however, they still make use of religious repertoires of Chinese popular religion. The second generation engages in what Jeung calls "Chinese American familism," practices and rituals of family sacrifice and filial piety. Similar to the Vietnamese Americans in Peché's chapter, the family is the object of worship, sacrifice, and moral obligation. The lines between ethnicity and religion are blurred in Chinese American familism. But the Chinese Americans in Jeung's sample do not interpret their practices as religion, because Western discourse defines religion as a matter of belief and truth. Instead, Chinese Americans interpret their practices of Chinese American familism as ethnic and family traditions. Contrary to Herberg's theory, these Chinese Americans do not need a religious identity to belong in the United States. Instead, the collective identity and solidarity of the family seems to be enough.

Family takes center stage as the site for religion and spirituality in Linda Ho Peché's study of Vietnamese Americans in chapter 11. Home shrines play an important role in the religious and spiritual practice of both Catholic and Buddhist second-generation Vietnamese Americas. People in Peché's sample are interested in continuing these personal and individualized religious practices at home, even though some no longer identify with an institutionalized religion. And with considerable leeway and freedom to imbue these rituals with their own meanings apart from the institutionalized religions, these Vietnamese Americans have innovated, creating their own symbols and rituals to represent their own relationships to faith and family. Contrary to Herberg's theory, the highly personal faith practices of second-generation Vietnamese Americans do not draw them to identify with other coreligionists; rather, they are rituals that strengthen the solidarity and identification with family.

In chapter 12, Khyati Y. Joshi highlights how Hinduism's status as a religious minority in the United States shapes the ethnic and religious development of second-generation Indian American Hindus. Joshi points out that the experiences of Indian American Hindus are not monolithic but vary by both life stage and the time of their parents' immigration, which she divides into Generations A and B. To Indian American Hindus, Hinduism and Indianness are interconnected. Importantly, Indian American Hindus explore and negotiate the meanings of being Indian American Hindus as racial and religious outsiders in a white and Christian America. In fact, the persistence of ethnicity among Indian American Hindus seems to be tied to both the racial and religious unassimilability of Hindus in the United States. In examining Indian American Hindus, Joshi shows the limits of an approach that only recognizes religion when it is linked to an identity, an institution, or formalized practices. Joshi's approach to second-generation Indian American Hinduism as a lived religion underlines the persistence of Hinduism in the second generation even when it is not officially professed or formally practiced.

Conclusion

Much in American society has changed since Will Herberg argued that new Americans can affiliate themselves as Protestant, Catholic, or Jew. Racial minorities have emerged and constitute the largest share of Americans under 18 and of the children of immigrants, the new second generation. American cultural discourse has shifted from the religious triple melting pot to one that celebrates ethnic, religious, and racial identities. The members of this new and emerging diverse population, particularly the second generation, are positioned to combine their backgrounds in ways that their parents and earlier generations were not permitted to, lest they risk marginalization from mainstream public life.

The studies in this volume illustrate how these religious innovations have served members of the second generation, affirmed their ties to their parents and families, and reconfigured their social life through the beliefs and practices of faith in its manifold forms. The four trajectories described in this introduction are not typologies exclusive of one another; the groups display a range in their combinations of religious, racial, and ethnic identities.

While we argue that the sociohistorical context of how religion is lived in America has changed much since Herberg's day, we do agree with his conclusions about the continued salience of religion in America's public life and of the secularization of American religion in Americans' private lives. Herberg summarized, "Religion has not disappeared; it is probably more pervasive today, and in many ways more influential than it has been for generations" (1955, 265).

Likewise, religion has been front and center in the political lives of members of the new second generation, who have come of age since the events of 9/11 and the wars in Iraq and Afghanistan. Despite the government's insistence that the United States is not at war against Islam, many Americans feel just the opposite—that they are. Religion also holds sway in several other key public debates, including abortion, the federal budget, same-sex marriage, and even the environment. Similarly, American religious institutions factor in the social construction of racial and ethnic identities. Through the funding of faith-based initiatives and the establishment of ethnic- and racial-specific ministries, these institutions have consciously promoted Asian American and Latino constituencies. Indeed, the fact that members of the Asian American second generation are more likely to affiliate with a religion than their parents are demonstrates the continued significance of religious identity in becoming American.

Paradoxically, while institutionalized religion continues to have an influential public role in American public life, its significance to the new second generation's private life has declined. Herberg coined this social process the "secularization of religion," in which particular creedal beliefs and practices are no longer adhered to or followed. Instead, members of the new second generation, like other young Americans, value an individualistic, therapeutic spirituality that mistrusts religious authority and instead embraces authenticity in being and relationships.

This value for authenticity now frames the questions "Who am I?" and "Where do I belong?" for the new second generation of Asian Americans and Latinos. Their racialized status as outsiders, foreigners, and "probationary Americans" challenges their claim to be truly American (Park and Park 2005). At the same time, racialized multiculturalism and religious pluralism afford them discourses and institutional sites to resist this marginalization and to claim identity in America. By making use of religious, racial, and ethnic resources, the new second generation is staking its claim in America and perhaps forging a new "American Way of Life."

REFERENCES

Alba, Richard, and Victor Nee. 2005. *Remaking the American Mainstream: Assimilation and Contemporary Immigration*. Cambridge: Harvard University Press.

Ammerman, Nancy. 2006. *Everyday Religion: Observing Modern Religious Lives*. New York: Oxford University Press.

Bonilla-Silva, Eduardo. 2003. *Racism without Racists: Color-Blind Racism and the Persistence of Racial Inequality in America*. Lanham, MD: Rowman and Littlefield.

Chang, Derek. 2010. *Citizens of a Christian Nation: Evangelical Missions and the Problem of Race in the Nineteenth Century*. Philadelphia: University of Pennsylvania Press.

Chen, Carolyn. 2008. *Getting Saved in America: Taiwanese Immigration and Religious Experience*. Princeton: Princeton University Press.

Darder, Antonia, and Rodolfo Torres. 2004. *After Race: Racism after Multiculturalism*. New York: NYU Press.

Deyoung, Curtis, Michael Emerson, George Yancey, and Karen Chai Kim. 2003. *United by Faith: The Multiracial Congregation as the Answer to the Problem of Race*. New York: Oxford University Press.

Dimaggio, Paul J., and Walter W. Powell. 1983. "The Iron Cage Revisited: Institutional Isomorphism and Collective Rationality in Organizational Fields." *American Sociological Review* 48 (2): 147–160.

Dixon, David. 2006. "The Second Generation in the United States." Migration Policy Institute. http://www.migrationinformation.org/usfocus/display.cfm?ID=446 (accessed October 21, 2010).

Eck, Diana. 2002. *A New Religious America: How a "Christian Country" Has Become the World's Most Religiously Diverse Nation*. New York: HarperOne.

Emerson, Michael, and Christian Smith. 2001. *Divided by Faith: Evangelical Religion and the Problem of Race in America*. New York: Oxford University Press.

Espinosa, Gastón, Virgilio Elizondo, and Jesse Miranda, eds. 2005. *Latino Religions and Civic Activism in the United States*. New York: Oxford University Press.

Foley, Michael, and Dean Hoge. 2007. *Religion and the New Immigrants: How Faith Communities Form Our Newest Citizens*. New York: Oxford University Press.

Fry, Richard. 2008. *Latinos Account for Half of U.S. Population Growth since 2000*. Pew Hispanic Center report. http://pewresearch.org/pubs/1002/latino-population-growth (accessed October 21, 2010).

Greeley, Andrew, and Michael Hout. 2006. *The Truth about Conservative Christians: What They Think and What They Believe*. Chicago: University of Chicago Press.

Hammond, Philip, and Kee Warner. 1993. "Religion and Ethnicity in Late-Twentieth-Century America." *Annals of the American Academy of Political and Social Sciences* 527:55–60.

Herberg, Will. 1955. *Protestant, Catholic, Jew*. Garden City, New York: Doubleday.

Hirschman, Charles. 2004. "The Role of Religion in the Origins and Adaptation of Immigrant Groups in the United States." *International Migration Review* 38:1206–1233.

Hollinger, David A. 1995. *Postethnic America: Beyond Multiculturalism*. New York: Basic Books.

Iwamura, Jane. 2011. *Virtual Orientalism: Asian Religions and American Popular Culture*. New York: Oxford University Press.

Jeung, Russell. 2005. *Faithful Generations: Race and New Asian American Churches*. New Brunswick: Rutgers University Press.

Joshi, Khyati. 2006. *New Roots in America's Sacred Ground: Religion, Race, and Ethnicity in Indian America*. New Brunswick: Rutgers University Press.

Kasinitz, Philip, John H. Mollenkopf, Mary Waters, and Jennifer Holdaway. 2008. *Inheriting the City: The Children of Immigrants Come of Age*. New York: Russell Sage Foundation.

Kim, Claire Jean. 2003. *Bitter Fruit: The Politics of Black-Korean Conflict in New York City*. New Haven: Yale University Press.

Kosmin, Barry A., and Ariela Keysar, with Ryan Cragun and Juhem Navarro-Rivera. 2009. *American Nones: The Profile of the No Religion Population*. Hartford, CT: Institute for the Study of Secularism in Society and Culture.

Kurien, Prema. 2007. *A Place at the Multicultural Table: The Development of an American Hinduism*. New Brunswick: Rutgers University Press.

Lawrence, Bruce. 2004. *New Faiths, Old Fears: Muslims and Other Asian Immigrants in American Religious Life*. New York: Columbia University Press.

Lee, Taeku, S. Karthick Ramakrishnan, and Ricardo Ramirez, eds. 2007. *Transforming Politics, Transforming America: The Civic and Political Incorporation of Immigrants in the United States*. Charlottesville: University of Virginia Press.

Light, Ivan, and Edna Bonacich. 1991. *Immigrant Entrepreneurs: Koreans in Los Angeles, 1965–1982*. Berkeley: University of California Press.

Lorentzen, Lois, Joaquin Gonzalez, Kevin Chun, Hien Do, and Cymene Howe, eds. 2009. *Religion at the Corner of Nirvana and Bliss: Politics, Faith, and Identity in New Migrant Communities*. Durham: Duke University Press.

Min, Pyong Gap. 2010. *Preserving Ethnicity through Religion in America: Korean Protestants and Indian Hindus across Generations*. New York: NYU Press.

Omi, Michael, and Howard Winant. 1994. *Racial Formation in the United States: From the 1960s to the 1990s*. New York: Routledge.

Park, Jerry. 2008. "Second-Generation Asian American Pan-ethnic Identity: Pluralized Meanings of a Racial Label." *Sociological Perspectives* 51 (3): 541–561.

Park, John, and Edward Park. 2005. *Probationary Americans: Contemporary Immigration Policies and the Shaping of Asian American Communities*. New York: Routledge.

Pew Hispanic Center and Pew Forum on Religion and Public Life. 2007. *Changing Faiths: Latinos and the Transformation of American Religion*. Washington, DC: Pew Research Center.

Raboteau, Albert, Josh DeWind, and Richard Alba. 2008. *Immigration and Religion in America: Historical and Comparative Perspectives*. New York: NYU Press.

Rumbaut, Rubén, and Alejandro Portes. 2001. *Ethnicities: Children of Immigrants in America*. Berkeley: University of California Press.

———. 2006. *Immigrant America: A Portrait*. Berkeley: University of California Press.

Smith, Christian, and Melina Denton. 2005. *Soul Searching: The Religious Spiritual Lives of American Teenagers*. New York: Oxford University Press.

Taylor, Charles, 1992. *Sources of the Self: The Making of the Modern Identity*. Cambridge: Harvard University Press.

Trevino, Roberto. 2006. *The Church in the Barrio: Mexican American Ethno-Catholicism in Houston*. Chapel Hill: University of North Carolina Press.

Waters, Mary. 1990. *Ethnic Options*. Berkeley: University of California Press.

Wuthnow, Robert. 2010. *After the Baby Boomers: How Twenty-Somethings and Thirty-Somethings Are Shaping the Future of American Religion*. Princeton: Princeton University Press.

Yang, Fenggang, and Helen Rose Ebaugh. 2001. "Religion and Ethnicity Among New Immigrants: The Impact of Majority/Minority Status in Home and Host Countries," *Journal for the Scientific Study of Religion* 40 (September): 367–378.

Zhou, Min. 2009. *Contemporary Chinese America: Immigration, Ethnicity, and Community Transformation*. Philadelphia: Temple University Press.

PART I

Religious Primacy

CHAPTER 2

The Diversity-Affirming Latino

Ethnic Options and the Ethnic Transcendent Expression of American Latino Religious Identity

GERARDO MARTI

I was surprised how Jose, a 36-year-old third-generation Mexican American, described his background before coming to Mosaic, a multiracial church in Los Angeles. I had known Jose for several years as a faithful husband and gentle father, but the smiling man talking to me suddenly seemed unrecognizable from the person he revealed himself to be before arriving at Mosaic. "I grew up in El Monte," he told me. "And I grew up racist, La Raza." The area of El Monte is heavily Hispanic and one of several sources of gang violence in Los Angeles. Jose's radical identification with his Mexican heritage through "La Raza" (an ethnic movement among descendants of Mexico who rally under the Spanish term for "The Race") was not in itself unusual. What was unusual is that by joining Mosaic this "racist" Latino who had worked for the civil rights of his "people" left behind the distinctively ethnic interests of his Latino ancestral heritage to join one of the largest multiethnic Protestant churches in America.

Jose described his first experience with the diversity of Mosaic's church service. "I came into the church, and right away I noticed people were here from every color. . . . But when I came, it actually attracted me. Something about seeing that every color was here, that attracted me." Then Jose added, "My first Asian friend was here." He was surprised with his embrace of diversity given his deeply "racist" background. When he first visited Mosaic, Jose was having difficulty in his marriage to his Mexican American wife and with their children. Although he spoke little Spanish and was more connected with the East Los Angeles region than to his ancestry from Mexico, Jose still recognized himself as Mexican American and initially connected more closely to a Latino pastor at Mosaic than to the Caucasian pastors also available on staff. He said, "Only God, only God could change my life. That's what my wife would say, and that's what I say." Jose and his wife joined Mosaic and expanded their relational networks to other Latinos through the congregation in the coming years, but more importantly they also began to have more regular, and more intimate, relationships with Caucasians, Asians, and African Americans also attending the congregation. They soon took responsibility for a weekly small group gathering at their home and as a couple became known as being among the most loyal, most supportive members of this ambitious congregation whose goals are rooted in reaching all the people of Los Angeles and the rest of the world with the saving gospel message of Jesus Christ.

When Jose joined Mosaic, his once-central ethnic identity waned, and his religious identity as a "dedicated follower of Jesus Christ" became more important. Jose is one of hundreds of Latinos I knew, observed, and interviewed during my time at Mosaic who said, "My life changed here."[1] "I believe that the way I've changed in these past couple of years since we've been to Mosaic is because of God." Latinos in this integrated congregation identify themselves as broadly "Hispanic," yet by embracing the religious imperatives of this Protestant congregation they come to understand their religious identities in nonethnic ways.[2] Latinos at Mosaic, such as Jose, contribute to cultivating a successfully multiethnic congregation by taking an overarching group identification as "Christians" that transcends racial and ethnic differences. I call these Latinos "ethnic transcendent Latinos."[3] Whether interacting with Asians, Caucasians, African Americans, Middle Easterners, or members of other ancestral backgrounds, these ethnic transcendent Latinos participate in congregations that encourage them to acknowledge their own ethnic-specific Latino heritage or panethnic Hispanic identity while simultaneously interacting with other ethnic/racial groups in a common religious setting.

In this chapter, I describe the origins of Mosaic in East Los Angeles, present the two dominant religious options for identity among Latinos in the

United States, and then suggest a new, third option for Latino religious identity, which I label the "Ethnic Transcendent Latino Identity."

Examining Race, Ethnicity, and Religious Identity among Latinos

An ethnographic, "lived religion" approach to the study of religion pays close attention to history and context and provides an opportunity to see the variety of ways race, ethnicity, and identity commingle among Latino ethnic groups.[4] It is tempting among researchers to cluster all Latinos together as a single category, to assume they remain among themselves, and to isolate sets of dominant characteristics about them.[5] However, Manuel Vasquez points out that "the label 'Hispanic' is a term imposed by U.S. bureaucracies that, as it has made its way into the civil society, has accumulated all sorts of pejorative connotations."[6] "Hispanic" is therefore more of a bureaucratic than a descriptive term. Nevertheless, despite the inherent diversity among Hispanics, the stigma and segregation that often accompanies the label "Hispanic" for the broad Hispanic population in Los Angeles results in many Latinos isolating themselves as Latinos and maintaining Latino exclusive religious and relational networks. Hispanics constitute 48% of the Los Angeles County population (2010 Census), so it is quite possible for Jose and other Latinos at Mosaic to ethnically isolate themselves and associate with each other as Latinos. Yet because they do not, the experience of Latinos at Mosaic has the potential to add nuance to our understanding of alternative dynamics between identity, ethnicity, and religious community among Latinos.

To recover the complexity of ethnic options operating among Latinos in U.S. congregations, I conducted ethnographic fieldwork between 2001 and 2002 at Mosaic, a large, Southern Baptist, multiethnic church in Los Angeles founded by White midwesterners and southerners in 1943. Mosaic became a Latino-majority congregation in the mid-1970s, located in what became known as the "barrios of East L.A."[7] East Los Angeles is famous for the relative isolation, oppression, and impoverishment of Latinos, and the congregation itself was located a few hundred yards away from Garfield High School, the site of Jaime Escalante's famous struggle to provide exceptional educational opportunities to Latino students.[8] In the mid-1990s, the church further transitioned from being a Latino-White congregation to becoming an equally mixed Latino, White, and Asian congregation, with a smaller proportion of Middle Eastern and African American attendees. Even with this diversification, the congregation remained "Latino-centric" in its atmosphere and leadership until the early 2000s. This chapter therefore gives special attention to the life of the Latinos who attend there.

Becoming a Mosaic in East L.A.

Although the First Southern Baptist Church of East Los Angeles was established in 1943 by White southerners and midwesterners, the ethnic composition of the congregation changed dramatically during the pastoral tenure of
Philip Bowers.[9] As a "White man" held in suspicion by less-trusting Latinos,
he painstakingly built trust, one on one, with the local Mexican American
population after he became lead pastor in 1971. As the church moved into the
1980s, the church became majority Hispanic, making the church around 60%
Hispanic and 40% White, with a handful of Asian and African American
members. In building the church, Brother Phil hired a Mexican American
associate pastor and mobilized Hispanic lay leaders for the ministry. At the
same time, he used extensive denominational ties to recruit younger Whites
into serving the church by networking among Southern Baptist groups and
appealing to ministry and missionary-minded students. "The nations come
to Los Angeles," he preached. Dozens of students resonated with the message
and relocated from places like Texas and Oklahoma ("They were all from
Oklahoma," said several Hispanic members) and moved into the neighborhood, taking the role of church interns.

These pious, missionary-minded midwesterners came eager and ready to
work. "The thing that struck me," said one Latino member, Chuy, "is they
were so ready to just assume leadership and to do whatever God wanted
them to do." Expecting to be in Los Angeles for a few weeks or months, these
young singles brought a zealous energy and enthusiasm to use every available moment do whatever was asked. A Latino church leader who deeply
desired more lay responsibility in the church under Brother Phil said, "Really
honestly, a lot of the Mexican people who were here felt like, 'How am I supposed to compete?'" Thus, a significant tension resulted between midwesterners who were aggressively taking direction and exerting leadership and
local Latinos who were not as available—or as eager—to exert the same kind
of intensity and enthusiasm.

In the midst of these White-Latino tensions, the church stressed a core
virtue of hospitality. An attitude of "welcoming the stranger" was continually
nurtured by Brother Phil. Another Latino member, Francisco, gave a glimpse
of this, saying, "Brother Phil went out of his way to deal with it along the way
and appeal to the higher issue of God's love being universal and not directly
to any ethnic group. God's love was for everybody. So Brother Phil rose
above any ethnic pride or ethnic issues on both sides, and challenged people to do that." Integrating Whites and Latinos despite cultural differences
under Brother Phil's leadership paved the way for integrating the differences

of other racial and ethnic groups in the following decade. As Brother Phil stated,

> In the early stages there was definitely a White/Latino thing. But it was beautiful to see that any issues can all be overcome in genuine love and just made irrelevant. From this experience it became easy for us to accept people from other groups. The core of the church had already experienced that you could completely overlook and overcome any kind of ethnic differences, even admire them and enjoy them. . . . So it became an agreeable kind of environment, a pleasant environment to be. You're comfortable being different from the other person.

An attitude of hospitality, welcoming difference, and appreciating other people became characteristic of the congregation. Margie is among many East L.A. Latinos at Mosaic who connected the hospitality of the congregation with the ability of members to accept differences among ethnic groups. She told me how she came to be involved in the church despite early hesitations and several misgivings. "There was so much caring, and I'd never experienced that. I think people who are alike are more for themselves, and I found that being in a group that was multiethnic made us all more giving [to each other]."

In the early 1990s, Brother Phil recruited a Latino minister originally from El Salvador, Erwin McManus, to become the next lead pastor. His hire was intended both to appeal to and to appease the Latino base of the congregation. Yet Pastor Erwin continued Brother Phil's momentum of adding diversity and resisted making the church Latino-centric. Some Hispanics left the congregation, believing that the distinctive affirmation of local East L.A. culture and concerns of the neighborhood were being ignored; at the same time, other local-area Latinos found the congregation, and a greater number of Latinos came through networks of friends who commuted to services and events.

Under Pastor Erwin's leadership, the church moved its main services to a more freeway-accessible building one mile west of the original campus, initiated a new church service in downtown L.A., expanded small group and event offerings around the region, and renamed the church "Mosaic." The percentage of Asian Americans (a population that was growing dramatically in Los Angeles) in the church grew from 5% to over 30%. The social-class backgrounds of attendees expanded to include more working class members (often among the Latinos who lived closer to the original church building), but the growth of the congregation primarily came from middle-class and aspiring professional-class young adults from all backgrounds who valued diversity and creativity. The lay leadership of the congregation gained a greater percentage of Hispanics and Asians, which brought a greater balance to the largely White leadership. And more Middle Easterners and a few more African Americans began making their way into volunteer roles as well.

Latinos who attended Mosaic combined a mix of working- and middle-class workers who were more "assimilated" third-generation and later Mexican Americans, in addition to a mix of acculturated children from Central America. Most of them identify as "Mexican American" (and less often as "Chicano"), yet other Hispanics identify with their particular Latin American background, whether Brazilian, Peruvian, or Salvadoran. Nearly all the Latinos at Mosaic had immersive experiences with Roman Catholicism but had become largely nonreligious before converting to the evangelical Christianity of the church. And those who had been Catholic before coming to Mosaic found that leaving their Catholic faith meant breaking ties with their family tradition rather than leaving their ethnic heritage.

Latinos and Religious Identity Options in America

In describing the Latino religious identity at Mosaic, it is important to keep in mind the diversity of Latinos in the United States. Latinos in the United States come from dozens of countries for various reasons and speaking various dialects.[10] Some Latinos speak a new hybrid Spanglish, and many indigenous peoples from Latin America do not speak Spanish at all. Yet, because of their country of origin, they are all still labeled "Latino" or "Hispanic." Labeling all these groups together is highly problematic. Allowing Latinos to define themselves only adds to the confusion, as they variously define themselves as Hispanic, Latino, Chicano, mestizo, generically "American," or by their country of origin. Among Latin American countries, there are large regional and cultural differences. This becomes more complicated for people who are multiracial or multicultural, such as Afro-Caribbeans or Chinese Peruvians, who are mixed Black and Hispanic or mixed Asian and Hispanic. Add religion to that mixture, and the complexity and confusion multiplies.

In describing Latinos, it is tempting to simplify their dynamics by making broad statements to generalize their religious orientation. Acknowledging Hispanics in the Southwest as affiliating with Protestantism is a fairly recent phenomenon. Roman Catholicism has a much longer history among American Hispanics. While Catholic parishes provide geographic parameters for bringing together local Hispanics, the outward homogeneity of parish life masks the differentiation in their service to different Latin American constituencies.[11] Protestants are even more diverse; there are at least 7,000 Latino Protestant congregations in the United States—twice as many as there are Catholic Masses in the Spanish language.[12] Not only is the internal diversity obscured, but the greater Catholic-Protestant distinctions in religious orientation are also blurred among researchers. For example, Anthony M. Stevens-Arroyo compares Catholicism's influence over Latino religious practices to Protestantism's influence, but the tone of his work constitutes an attempt to generalize "the patterns of Latino religion."[13] Other researchers accentuate differences between Protestants and Catholics in the Hispanic religious experience, but the most specific classifications consist of "Hispanic Protestants" versus "Hispanic Catholics" or, more often, "Hispanic Catholics" versus "Hispanic Pentecostals."[14] Furthermore, terms such as "popular religious expressions and ideas" and "popular religious notions" found in some of the literature perpetuate further generalities on Latino religion.[15] Larry Hunt acknowledges the problem of categorization for understanding Latino religion, saying in a journal article, "The term Hispanic is used throughout this study primarily for convenience. It is important to recognize any simplification captured by this term is also potential distortion . . . and may not be an identifying term meaningful to some segments of the diverse population to which it is applied."[16]

Social scientists desperately want to use the label "Latino immigrant congregations," but with so much diversity, it is impossible to identify a single "Hispanic culture," it is problematic for Hispanics to identify themselves as a single group, and it is misleading to characterize all Latino-based congregations as the same. We must continually be reminded that Hispanics are not a homogeneous group; they differ immensely in origin, race, customs, education, religion, and even language. Instead, it is more important—particularly in the case of Latinos in the United States—to look closely at the context of religion "on the ground" and to pay attention to the concrete dynamics played out in particular congregations. In considering this challenge, I suggest that we approach Latino religious identity around the various ways ethnic identity interacts with religious involvement. Specifically, I suggest we approach ethnic particularities either as taking priority in religious interactions or as being transcended in favor of cross-ethnic religious affinities.[17] The resulting interactions translate into several "ethnic options" operating among Latino-based congregations in actualizing the contemporary American religious Latino identity.

Placing my understanding of the Hispanics at Mosaic in the context of the literature on immigrant congregations with an eye toward isolating the religious ethnic identity options available to American Latinos, I see three general options. First, there are ethnic-specific Latinos who participate in congregations that emphasize their particularistic, nationalistic identities. Latino churches freely adapt to their members' needs in the United States, and congregations respond to Latino immigrants' needs in very different ways, such that congregations continuously adapt their religious institutions to fit ethnic-specific constituencies. These congregations cultivate an ethnic-specific Latino identity based in an ethnic group or a country of origin (Salvadorian, Peruvian, etc.). On the other hand, there are panethnic Latinos who participate in congregations that absorb their national affiliations into a broader "Latino" identity. These pan-Latino congregations encourage members to adopt a panethnic Latino identity that encompasses all Latin American origins. Rather than accommodating to particular groups, these congregations promote a broader and more inclusive Hispanic identity.

In contrast to both of these and based on the 12 months I studied Mosaic, I see a third option: a religiously based ethnic transcendent Latino identity. I found ethnic transcendent Latinos who regularly live out their religious commitments in constant, intimate interaction with church members who are not Latino. This implies that there are congregations that encourage members to put forward a broader religious identity as more important than any particularistic or pan-Latino identity. These congregations foster an accommodation of different ethnic groups within the congregation.

To describe all three ethnic options available to Latinos in the United States, I draw on case studies of congregations by Manuel Vasquez alongside my own case study of Mosaic.[18] All three congregations illustrate the importance of close, contextual, and congregationally specific study of Latino race, religion, and identity. The religious diversity of American Latinos therefore lies not only in the variety of differences in national background (Salvadorian, Mexican, Cuban, etc.) but also in the extent to which ethnic-specific, panethnic, or ethnic transcendent Latino identity is encouraged and embraced. In the life of Latino-centric congregations, these ethnic specific, panethnic, and ethnic transcendent options are encouraged and sustained over time as part of their religious identities.

Ethnic-Specific and Panethnic Latino Identity

At La Iglesia De Apostoles Y Profetas, a Pentecostal congregation studied by Manuel Vasquez in the U.S. Northeast, church members accentuate their individual Salvadoran culture. Instead of their main referent being the larger Hispanic community of the United States, these Salvadorans remain rooted in the churches and small towns back in El Salvador and retain a regionally specific ethnic identity through an active, mutual exchange that occurs across nations, between these two Salvadoran communities. In contrast to Will Herberg's vision of ethnic groups dissolving their unique ethnic heritage by ridding themselves of their national identity to more easily become accepted in the American society, the Salvadorans of La Iglesia De Apostoles Y Profetas feel a "perceived exclusion from the dominant Anglo world" and therefore accentuate their particular Salvadoran ethnicity.[19] The church "tends to take a sectarian approach vis-à-vis the outside world, . . . which it sees as utterly sinful."[20] Overall, Vasquez believes the congregation's particularistic religio-ethnic orientation empowers its working-class constituents for living in the world as Latino immigrants.[21] Maintaining ties to their homeland, members also exert an "evangelistic thrust towards El Salvador" rather than to the larger American Hispanic community.[22]

The Salvadorans at La Iglesia De Apostoles Y Profetas accentuate an ethnic-specific Latino identity, one that is difficult to generalize to all Latinos yet remains powerful and sustainable for this particular community. By implication, there are Latino churches in America that rally around an ethnic-specific Latino identity. The development of the congregation and the sources of its continuation are rooted in cultural specifics, as indicated by profound transnational ties to the home country, in addition to clear ethnic boundaries that separate members from the non-Latino world around them.

In contrast to Latino churches such as La Iglesia De Apostoles Y Profetas that emphasize an ethnic-specific Latino identity, other congregations take on a broader, panethnic Latino identity that intentionally blurs the lines between national boundaries and cultural distinctiveness. Among the Peruvians at La Gran Comision, another Pentecostal church studied by Vasquez, Peruvian members view their national identity as associated with Catholicism. They believe that the "deeply ingrained Catholicism that informs traditional Peruvian national identity (peruanidad or Peruvianness) is 'pagan and idolatrous.'"[23] Because they believe that "God is going to bring people of all ethnic groups" to the church, they do not believe their Peruvian nationality matters. Therefore, they "define their collective identity as membership in a 'multinational' community of the saved,'" an identity that is intentionally constructed as a pan-Latino identity.[24] As a result, the church is composed of individuals from diverse Latin American countries.

In congregations that emphasize a panethnic identity, such as La Gran Comision, ethnic specificity is viewed as both spiritually problematic and socially disruptive. Members of La Gran Comision believe that if they remain separated along national lines, they can never achieve proper representation in the rest of American society, but together, they can "erase the negative stereotypes that follow Hispanics" and embrace their "Hispanic roots." They seek to rise above their particular national identities in favor of a larger group identity, to "defend their rights as citizens against racism." By ridding themselves of national identity divisions, they are able to use their new religion to better, and more easily, assimilate into broader American society. In short, we can see from the Latinos at La Gran Comision that some Hispanics adopt a panethnic Latino identity and form religious communities to build camaraderie among all Latino groups, regardless of their regional differences.[25]

New Option: Ethnic Transcendent Latino Identity

In contrast to the ethnic specificity of Salvadorans at La Iglesia De Apostoles Y Profetas and to the panethnic solidarity promoted by Peruvians at La Gran Comision, the Mexican and Central Americans at Mosaic straddle between the "ethno-racial" specificity of their family and friends and their church's expansive inclusivity. Los Angeles has many Latino congregations that are monoethnic and intended to be "a refuge from an alien culture" that surrounds them by providing an "alternative community."[26] But Mosaic provides a haven for second- and third-generation ethnics escaping from monoethnic orientations that exclude regular interaction with people from other ethnic heritages. Within the congregation, Latino members "transcend" their ethnic identifications to promote an identity rooted in "religion" rather than "race."

At Mosaic, members consistently describe the experience of church services and church events as places where people are welcomed, build friendships, and quickly integrate into the ongoing ministries of the church. They build relationships based on affinities and shared interests, and ethnic description based on one's appearance or ethnic performance is not an issue. Members are acknowledged as having racial and ethnic ancestries but are not expected to fulfill expectations for loyally performing that ancestry.

Within the broadly Americanized culture of Mosaic, second- and later-generation ethnics find refuge for "being" ethnic without having to "act" ethnic. Overall, the Latinos at Mosaic understand themselves to be "Latino" and actively maintain family, work, and school relationships that are mostly with other Hispanics. As open and accommodating as the Latinos of Mosaic are, members from other ethnic backgrounds still would think of Mosaic as a Latino-based congregation (at least until the congregation sold its East Los Angeles property in 2003). At the same time, Latinos at Mosaic understand themselves to live in the "broader world" of American culture, are much less likely to be connected to the Chicano cultural scene of East Los Angeles, and view interactions with people from other ethnic backgrounds as a normal part of everyday, urban life.

Eric, an associate pastor on the staff, told me about the Hispanic high school students who come to Mosaic's youth group. While students come and stay, their parents do not. According to Eric, parents often are not fluent English speakers, and they do not bother even to visit Mosaic services. While parents and grandparents of the youth are often part of monoethnic, immigrant Latino churches, the ethnic transcendent Latino youth who attend Mosaic tell me they do not "fit" into those contexts. They chafe against the demand to be representative of their ancestral culture. They do not intentionally leave their churches for the goal of being upwardly mobile. They seek contexts that mesh with their ethnic experiences throughout their everyday lives. Mosaic's current lead pastor, Erwin McManus, explains, "They work cross-culturally, they tend to be more global in their orientation anyway, but their church life is homogeneous." Children leave their parents' homogeneous churches to pursue religious communities that manifest the diversity they already experience in the rest of their everyday lives.

Churches have historically served as an ethnic haven for recent immigrants,[27] but Mosaic provides a different kind of ethnic haven for the children of Latino immigrants. Mosaic provides a haven for Latinos who want to step out of their monocultural networks. The movement away from homogeneous networks occurs not only among youth but among ethnic transcendent Latino adults as well. Margie, a longtime resident of East L.A., said, "I liked the fact that it was multiethnic. I always tell people I'm from back east [laughs]; I'm from East L.A. You know, it's 99.9% Hispanic here. I'm very happy with that, but I loved it that it was multiethnic." For Margie and other older second- and third-generation Latinos, Mosaic is prized because the congregation provides opportunities for religiously based, cross-ethnic relationships.

In the context of the congregation, members' ethnic specificity no longer matters. They are free to form relationships with others on the basis of religious convictions rather than the particular neighborhood they come from (where street addresses and school affiliations become important in the barrios of East Los Angeles), the region of Latin America their family came from (where not only countries but particular provinces become important among many ethnically committed Hispanics), or the particular dialect of Spanish spoken (where differences in emphasis, pronunciation, and accentuation become important for determining insider/outsider status among Hispanics). Instead, individual members freely associate with a variety of particular Latino identities; Jack can be Columbian, Maria can be Dominican, and Pablo can be Guatemalan without having to prove, hide, or in any other way enact their Latino heritage.

The distinction between "being" ethnic and "acting" ethnic becomes especially important in forming interethnic marriages. Miguel is a Mexican American who grew up in Los Angels and met and married Sandy, a Caucasian woman at Mosaic originally from Texas. They came to know each other at social events and then served together in the ministry of the church before dating. Both described how their parents were more committed to being Mexican or southern than they were themselves. Similar stories of other Latinos in the congregation reveal a consistent pattern. Members such as Miguel and Sandy ground their interactions less on ethnic or racial differences than on similarity of religious interests as expressed in this congregation.[28]

In Mosaic's promotion of an ethnic transcendent Latino identity, religious commitments there are not formed by leaving one's home culture or by reappropriating one's grandparents' heritage but rather by adopting a mission-driven, evangelical Christian religious orientation. As members struggle with issues of family and work as well as prejudice and discrimination, they look to the resources provided in religious solidarity with other believers in the congregation. The multiethnic/multiracial experience of committing to an ethnically diverse congregation does not conflict with their sense of self; rather, their continual experience of the diversity of the congregation strengthens their religious devotion as the visible evidence of diversity affirms among them that the power of their religion extends to all people.

Actualizing Ethnic Transcendent Latino Identity

Mosaic's ministry practices accentuate a shared religious identity over particularistic ethnic identity, such that being involved in the congregation through services, small groups, and ministry teams initiates contacts between ethnic groups, which encourages mutuality rather than exclusion. The resulting cross-ethnic relationships are admirable. By participating in common projects that accentuate religious over ethnic identity, many people at Mosaic routinely cross ethnic boundaries to find commonality and, often, friendship.

Chuck, who is White, told me about one of his earliest experiences at the church, when it was largely Hispanic. On a ministry trip to Mexico,

a Hispanic sister and I worked together with children and youth and the drama productions, but I could sense that there was something not comfortable between us. I didn't know if it was a man/woman thing or a college-graduate/high-school-graduate thing. I just knew there was some-thing there. We were on a missions experience together in Mexicali, and I volunteered to work with the children. We were working shoulder to shoulder two nights and three days in Mexicali together. When we came back from that trip, she said to me, "Brother Chuck, I need to talk to you." And I'm thinking, what did I do to offend her now? With tears in her eyes, she tells me, "You know, Brother Chuck, I just wanted to let you know that I love you." And I said, "I love you too, Maria." And she said, "I just wanted to let you know that I saw Jesus in you these last few days, working with the kids. I know how smart you are, and I know how skilled you are, and I know that you could have done a lot of different things, but it meant a lot to me that you chose to work with the kids and that you told them stories about Jesus and God. I just want to let you know that I thought you were one of those stuck-up, smart, White guys that wouldn't like somebody like me. And I'm wrong." From that day on, our relationship—it was a water-shed moment. Here we are pursuing the Great Commission, which was her heart language, and it meant a lot to her.

The ministry at Mosaic tends to be broken into different "projects," shorter-term commitments that accommodate well to the sporadic employ-ment patterns increasingly evident in late capitalism. Community is built by those who may not have a mutual natural affinity but are willing to work together toward common religious goals. In Mosaic's project orientation to ministry, commitment to the goal takes over ethnic affinity. Francisco, an older Mexican American, also describes the experience of Hispanics in the congregation. "Many of us never were exposed to White people. So it was a learning experience together to meet someone who had shared the same faith and the same motives, genuine motives, and then they were from a different place and culture on top of it. It was good, enjoyable." In sum, Mosaic builds connections between ethnic groups on a religious basis largely through volunteer involvement in ministry.

The project-driven nature of ministries at Mosaic affirms an impor-tant principle in cross-racial relations according to Intergroup Contact Theory.[29] Thomas Pettigrew theoretically formalized the conditions nec-essary for intergroup contact to reduce prejudice.[30] Pettigrew agreed with Gordon Allport that mere contact between races is not enough to reduce prejudice. Instead, ethno-racial integration exists when two races are equal status, with access to equal resources, and working for a com-mon goal.[31] Pettigrew further suggests four interrelated processes that operate through contact and mediate attitude change: learning about the out-group, changing behavior, generating affective ties, and in-group reappraisal.[32] The thrust of Pettigrew's research is that when contact meets these conditions, then conflict and prejudice between ethnic groups will cease. Moreover, "in religious institutions, integration allows the members of many groups to work together toward common goals rather than compete against each other. Such integration may also enable individuals within religious institutions to develop primary relationships rather than secondary relationships with members of different racial groups."[33] George Yancey applied these insights to the study of diverse congregations and found that White members of integrated churches are significantly less likely to have negative stereotyping of African Americans and exhibit lower levels of social distance.[34]

The moral base of unity at Mosaic is not a shared ethnic heritage but rather a religious one. After several years of involvement at Mosaic, Lazaro, a 51-year-old Hispanic business owner, is like many who tried to come to terms with how to describe and explain the diversity so evident in the congregation:

> The cultural mixing is not what stands out the most to me at Mosaic. It's the strength for following God's Word that stands out to me. It's based purely on the Bible. And because of that, you get a lot of people that really live it; you get a lot of integrity there. People live what they believe. That would be, I think, the strength of Mosaic. In any other—I don't know a lot of churches, but the Christians I have met before didn't really have that. To live what they believe—that, I think, is one of Mosaic's strengths.

Lazaro reflected on his own involvement, saying, "It's a place where the opportunities there are just endless. There is so much opportunity there to meet people, to learn, to really open your eyes to what God has really created, to really fulfill your optimal, your dreams, beyond your dreams, because that's where God is." For Lazaro and others, the priority of the congregation is not to sustain a particular cultural heritage but to see opportunity for others to pursue personal development through a distinctively religious medium. The ethnic diversity of the church only affirms that

> wherever God is, so many things can happen. You see the talent in the church; it's unbelievable. You see the intellectuals, the everything, the technology, everything. It's great. I love it. I see life. They are using God's talent. I'm amazed at some of the stuff you see there. At different times, it's different people. And you see they're using their talent. I want to do that. I want

my kids to enjoy that. And I want to help other people to get there, and just unleash them.

Being connected as Christians to God in this particular fellowship is more important than coming from a particular ethnic or racial background. As Lazaro told me, "I see a lot of people who love God. That's what we all have in common."

At Mosaic, the ethos described is a distinctively religious imperative that revolves around evangelism and spiritual growth. While the Christianity found at Mosaic has a distinct flavor of American Christianity, it is not simply a mainstreaming of an ethnic religion to fit a mainstream civic culture.[35] It is more dynamic in alternatively accentuating and obscuring ethnic affiliations. It is seeking neither to gain or to lose one's ethnicity absolutely; ethnicity is rather a variable aspect of the self that becomes oriented around the demands of a religious devotion.

Ethnic Transcendent Latino Identity in a Multiethnic Church

In negotiating the relationship between ethnic identity and religious involvement, the second- and third-generation Latinos at Mosaic take on a range of identities and vary their identifications in ways that encourage cross-ethnic interactions. Latino identity is not simply ignored; rather, members use subtle and sophisticated forms of ethnic signaling to "stretch" Latino connections, making them more able to connect with those who are "other Hispanic" or "non-Hispanic." At times Latino identity is accentuated, and at other times it is ignored. Still, at Mosaic, immensely subtle patterns of speech and posture as well as the symbolic use of certain words or gestures essentially "give away" one's Latino specificity. Latino identity is therefore fluid yet still marked. Last names are a quick, although unreliable, indication. References to Spanish words and phrases are another. Food consumption is another important signal that includes restaurant preferences, what is ordered on the menu regardless of cuisine, and how a person's food is seasoned at the table (such as using Tabasco sauce). Other ethnic indicators I observed include attention to clothing labels, vacation plans, and musical listening choices.

While Whites and Asians are largely unaware of such signals, Latinos at Mosaic are more aware of the differences that point to how close one is in the generational succession from a home country and the extent to which certain markers of Latin American identity indicate rootedness in a specific ethnic community. Leaders at Mosaic are particularly adept at strategically selecting their level of ethnic abstraction when talking with members of the church and building an appeal to ethnic affinity. For example, one of Mosaic's elders, Francisco, varies his ethnic connections so that sometimes he is "Mexican American," other times he is just "White," and other times he is just "Hispanic," all depending on which will give the best connection to a person he is trying to establish affinity with. And other times he is simply a "Christian" (broadly) or a "member of Mosaic" (narrowly) in order to accentuate the religious aspect of his identity over his ethnic one. Thus, the ethnic transcendent Latino identity at Mosaic is contingent and shifting.

The opposite of such identity malleability I observed among some of the members of Mosaic is what Sheldon Stryker describes as "identity commitment," defined as "the degree to which the individual's relationships to specified sets of other persons depends on his or her being a particular kind of person."[36] By this usage, one is committed to the role of "husband" to the degree that the extensiveness and intensiveness of one's social relationships require that role. With regard to ethnicity, those at Mosaic who insist on remaining tied to a specific ethnic identity do not remain in the congregation for very long. One Mexican American member was particularly concerned with issues among Chicanos and attempted to stimulate initiatives directed toward Chicanos in the region. Eventually, he left and joined a more Mexican American–oriented neighborhood church. He and others whose cultural resources are centered in a particularistic ethnicity find themselves limited in their ability to connect deeply with others.

In the religious context of Mosaic, the ambitious imperative of evangelism and church outreach encourages members to downplay ethnic particularism, which is a hindrance to inviting and welcoming strangers. The congregation encourages the cultivation of a diversity-affirming community in order to affirm radical solidarity based on evangelical Christian faith and practice.[37] In other words, while the great majority of Latinos at Mosaic are second- and third-generation (sometimes fourth- and fifth-generation) Mexican American, members who did not fall into such designations did not automatically assign them to the periphery of the church community, as long as they were committed Christians.

This is why an ethnic designation such as "Hispanic" operates in a complex manner at Mosaic. From the 1970s through the early 2000s, the promotion of a religious identity for Mosaic members as "dedicated followers of Jesus Christ" sought to overcome the potentially marginalizing effect of not belonging to the majority Latino group. While there was some benefit on the part of some members to label themselves specifically Mexican American or Salvadoran or other particularistic identities as a source of self-orientation, they used the fluidity available through such designations to bridge relationships with others from similar ancestral heritages. At the same time, most showed themselves willing to subsume their Latino specificity into a shared solidarity with non-Latinos in their pursuit of a religiously motivated corporate mission. The willingness—and enthusiasm—of ethnically committed Latinos for stretching and even losing the criterion of being appropriately "Hispanic" for building personal relationships allowed a space for second- and third-generation Latinos who have largely lost a meaningful connection to their own ancestral heritage.

Conclusion

By comparing ethnographic studies of other Latino congregations with the experience of Latino members at Mosaic, this chapter underscores the nuanced and diverse ways that religion intertwines with race and ethnicity. I offer a heuristic framework for exploring the contemporary alternatives available for American Latino religious identity: ethnic-specific, panethnic, and ethnic transcendent. I suggest there exists a largely unacknowledged population of ethnic transcendent Latinos who live out their congregational involvements in a manner that is more informed by their religion than their ethnicity, in contrast to both ethnic-specific and panethnic Latinos. They place less value on the continuous enactment of an ethnic identity but rather allow variability and context to assess when and if a form of Latino specificity is appropriate or beneficial. The fluidity of their ethnic identity allows relationships not only between members of various Latino groups but also with members of other ethnic and racial groups. Indeed, ethnic transcendent Latinos appreciate interethnic relationships and come to value diversity as a base for accentuating their religious commitment as well as affirming the strength of their religious orientation.

Religion may not always "trump" ethnic identity, yet religion provides both a motivation and a resource for alternately accentuating or obscuring one's ethnicity. Multiple identities inevitably pose different sets of dilemmas and negotiations. Craig Prentiss reminds us that race and ethnicity are social constructs and argues that racial and ethnic categories "do not spring from a divine cookie cutter but rather from the complex interplay of human consciousness."[38] By conceptualizing "race" as a construct of the imagination rather than a property intrinsic to the person, Prentiss frees us to consider the manner of identity formation. We are forced to take seriously that these categories are "social and political realities" that both come from and "produce real effects on the world."[39] So it seems that, though "race" and "ethnicity" are invented categories, they are constantly evolving. The goal for enlightened students of society is to challenge normative definitions of race and ethnicity amid fluctuating mythic reinterpretations and variable reconstructions of racial and ethnic categories, so as to regain the ability to discover new configurations of identity as they are mutually affected by both religious and ethno-racial dynamics.[40]

NOTES

1. See Marti 2005.
2. In this chapter, the terms "Hispanic" and "Latino" are used interchangeably to denote the broad category of persons typically categorized in the United States as either (or both), although this is not intended to ignore the complexity of either term. See Oboler 1995.
3. On the notion of "ethnic transcendence," see Marti 2008, 2009a, 2010a, 2010b.
4. For examples of such ethnographic, "lived religion" research that includes Latinos, see Vasquez 1999; Juffer 2008; Marti 2005; Ramirez 1999.
5. The category "Hispanic" first appeared on the census in 1980; however, it is different from other racial categories because being Hispanic is not really based on being a specific race. There are White Hispanics, Black Hispanics, and Asian Hispanics. Before 1970, the census attempted to measure "Hispanic" by discerning the origin of a person's last name or country of birth. But defining "Hispanic" by country of origin becomes a difficult criterion in part because many people immigrated from Mexico, Spain, or other parts of Latin America over a century ago. And the Hispanic origins among families in Los Angeles date from its founding as El Pueblo de Nuestra Señora la Reina de los Ángeles de la Porciúncula in 1781.
6. Vasquez 1999, 625.
7. Marti 2005. See also Marti 2009b.
8. The story of Jaime Escalante is the subject of a book entitled *Jaime Escalante: The Best Teacher in America* (Mathews 1989) and a film titled *Stand and Deliver* (Warner Bros., 1988), starring Edward James Olmos.
9. For a more comprehensive profile of the history and ministry of Mosaic, see Marti 2009b.
10. For a recent overview, see Portes and Rumbaut 2001.
11. Badillo 2006.
12. Yang and Ebaugh 2001. For a survey of Hispanics among Mainline Protestants, see Maldonado 1999.
13. Stevens-Arroyo 1998, 174.
14. For example, see Crane 2003; McIntosh 2006, which also contains an introduction by José E. Limón; Sánchez Walsh 2003.
15. Deck 1990.
16. Hunt 2001, 158.
17. My approach to the relationship between ethnic identity and religious identity can be found in Marti 2008, 2009a, 2010a, and 2010b.
18. For case studies by Manuel Vasquez, see Vasquez 1999. For more on the case study of Mosaic, see Marti 2005.
19. Vasquez 1999, 628.

20. Vasquez 1999, 627.
21. A Salvadorian identity was also noted in Menjívar's (1999) study contrasting a Salvadoran evangelical church with a larger Roman Catholic congregation.
22. Vasquez 1999, 627.
23. Vasquez 1999, 623.
24. Vasquez 1999, 624.
25. Other research describing pan-Latino congregational identity is found in Ruiz Baía 2001; Marquardt 2005; and Menjívar 1999.
26. Holifield 1994, 40. See also Warner 1994, 47–58.
27. Burns 1994; Papaioannou 1994; Shaw 1991.
28. See Marti 2005, 2008, 2009a, and 2010a.
29. Pettigrew 1971, 1975, 1997a, 1997b, and 1998.
30. Pettigrew 1975. See also Pettigrew 1971, 1975, 1997a, and 1997b.
31. Allport 1954.
32. Pettigrew 1998.
33. Pettigrew 1998, 83.
34. Yancey 1999.
35. Herberg 1983.
36. Stryker 1981, 24.
37. See Marti 2005, chap. 7.
38. Prentiss 2003, 3.
39. Prentiss 2003, 2–3.
40. See Marti 2008.

REFERENCES

Allport, Gordon W. 1954. *The Nature of Prejudice*. Reading, MA: Addison-Wesley.
Badillo, David A. 2006. *Latinos and the New Immigrant Church*. Baltimore: Johns Hopkins University Press.
Burns, Jeffrey M. 1994. "¿Qué Es Esto? The Transformation of St. Peter's Parish, San Francisco, 1913–1990." *American Congregations*, vol. 1, edited by James P. Wind and James W. Lewis, 396–462. Chicago: University of Chicago Press.
Crane, Ken R. 2003. *Latino Churches: Faith, Family, and Ethnicity in the Second Generation*. El Paso, TX: LFB.
Deck, Allan Figueroa. 1990. "The Spirituality of United States Hispanics: An Introductory Essay." In "Hispanic Catholics: Historical Explorations and Cultural Analysis," special issue, *U.S. Catholic Historian* 9, nos. 1–2: 137–146.
Herberg, Will. 1983. *Protestant-Catholic-Jew: An Essay in American Religious Sociology*. Rev. ed. Garden City, NY: Doubleday.
Holifield, E. B. 1994. "Toward a History of American Congregations." In *American Congregations*, vol. 2, edited by James P. Wind and James W. Lewis, 23–53. Chicago: University of Chicago Press.
Hunt, Larry L. 2001. "Religion, Gender, and the Hispanic Experience in the United States: Catholic/Protestant Differences in Religious Involvement, Social Status, and Gender-Role Attitudes." *Review of Religious Research* 43, no. 2: 139–160.
Juffer, Jane. 2008. "Hybrid Faiths: Latino Protestants Find a Home among the Dutch Reformed in Iowa." *Latino Studies* 6:290–312.

Limón, José E. 2006. Introduction to *The Latino Religious Experience*, edited by Kenneth R. McIntosh. Broomall, PA: Macon Crest.

Maldonado, David. 1999. *Protestantes/Protestants: Hispanic Christianity within Mainline Traditions*. Nashville, TN: Abingdon.

Marquardt, Marie Friedmann. 2005. "Structural and Cultural Hybrids: Religious Congregational Life and Public Participation of Mexicans in the New South." In *Immigrant Faiths: Transforming Religious Life in America*, edited by Karen I. Leonard, Alex Stepick, Manuel A. Vasquez, and Jennifer Holdaway, 189–217. Lanham, MD: AltaMira.

Marti, Gerardo. 2005. *A Mosaic of Believers: Diversity and Innovation in a Multiethnic Church*. Bloomington: Indiana University Press.

———. 2008. "Fluid Ethnicity and Ethnic Transcendence." *Journal for the Scientific Study of Religion* 47:11–16.

———. 2009a. "Affinity, Identity, and Transcendence: The Experience of Religious Racial Integration in Multiracial Churches." *Journal for the Scientific Study of Religion* 48:53–68.

———. 2009b. Preface to *A Mosaic of Believers: Diversity and Innovation in a Los Angeles Church*. Updated ed. Bloomington: Indiana University Press.

———. 2010a. "The Religious Racial Integration of African Americans into Diverse Churches." *Journal for the Scientific Study of Religion* 49:201–271.

———. 2010b. "When Does Religious Racial Integration 'Count'? A Caution about Seeking Ideal Ethnographic Cases." *Journal for the Scientific Study of Religion* 49:291–298.

Mathews, Jay. 1989. *Jaime Escalante: The Best Teacher in America*. New York: Holt.

McIntosh, Kenneth R. 2006. *The Latino Religious Experience*. Broomall, PA: Macon Crest.

Menjívar, Cecilia. 1999. "Religious Institutions and Transnationalism: A Case Study of Catholic and Evangelical Salvadoran Immigrants." *International Journal of Politics, Culture, and Society* 12, no. 4: 589–612.

Oboler, Suzanne. 1995. *Ethnic Labels, Latino Lives: Identity and the Politics of (Re)Presentation in the United States*. Minneapolis: University of Minnesota Press.

Papaioannou, George. 1994. "The History of the Greek Orthodox Cathedral of the Annunciation." In *American Congregations*, vol. 1, edited by James P. Wind and James W. Lewis, 520–571. Chicago: University of Chicago Press.

Pettigrew, Thomas F. 1971. *Racially Separate or Together?* New York: McGraw-Hill.

———. 1975. "The Racial Integration of the Schools." In *Racial Discrimination in the United States*, edited by Thomas F. Pettigrew, 224–239. New York: Harper and Row.

———. 1997a. "The Affective Component of Prejudice: Empirical Support for the New View." In *Racial Attitudes in the 1990s: Continuity and Change*, edited by Steven A. Tuch and Jack K. Martin, 76–90. Westport, CT: Praeger.

———. 1997b. "Generalized Intergroup Contact Effects on Prejudice." *Personality and Social Psychology Bulletin* 23:173–185.

———. 1998. "Intergroup Contact Theory." *Annual Review of Sociology* 7:65–85.

Portes, Alejandro, and Rubén G. Rumbaut. 2001. *Legacies: The Story of the Immigrant Second Generation*. Berkeley: University of California Press.

Prentiss, Craig R. 2003. Introduction to *Religion and the Creation of Race and Ethnicity: An Introduction*, edited by Craig R. Prentiss, 1–12. New York: NYU Press.

Ramirez, Daniel. 1999. "Borderlands Praxis: The Immigrant Experience in Latino Pentecostal Churches." *Journal of the American Academy of Religion* 67, no. 3: 573–596.

Ruiz Baía, Larissa. 2001. "Rethinking Transnationalism: National Identities among Peruvian Catholics in New Jersey." In *Christianity, Social Change, and Globalization in the Americas,* edited by Anna L. Peterson, Manuel A. Vasquez, and Philip J. Williams. New Brunswick: Rutgers University Press.

Sánchez Walsh, Arlene. 2003. *Latino Pentecostal Identity.* New York: Columbia University Press.

Shaw, Stephen J. 1991. *The Catholic Parish as a Way-Station of Ethnicity and Americanization: Chicago's Germans and Italians, 1903–1939.* Brooklyn, NY: Carlson.

Stevens-Arroyo, Anthony M. 1998. "Americans and Religions in the Twenty-First Century: The Latino Religious Resurgence." *Annals of the American Academy of Political and Social Science* 558:163–177.

Stryker, Sheldon. 1981. "Symbolic Interactionism: Themes and Variations." In *Social Psychology: Sociological Perspectives,* edited by Morris Rosenberg and Ralph H. Turner, 3–29. New York: Basic Books.

Vasquez, Manuel. 1999. "Pentecostalism, Collective Identity, and Transnationalism among Salvadorans and Peruvians in the U.S." *Journal of the American Academy of Religion* 67, no. 3: 617–636.

Warner, R. S. 1994. "The Place of the Congregation in Contemporary Religious Configuration." In *American Congregations,* vol. 2, edited by James P. Wind and James W. Lewis, 54–99. Chicago: University of Chicago Press.

Yancey, George. 1999. "An Examination of the Effects of Residential and Church Integration on Racial Attitudes of Whites." *Sociological Perspectives* 42:279–305.

Yang, Fenggang, and Helen Rose Ebaugh. 2001. "Transformations in New Immigrant Religions and Their Global Implications." *American Sociological Review* 66, no. 2: 269–288.

CHAPTER 3

Islam Is to Catholicism as Teflon Is to Velcro

Religion and Culture among Muslims and Latinas

R. STEPHEN WARNER, ELISE MARTEL, AND RHONDA E. DUGAN

My family—they really put culture more into our lives than religion. . . . But as we grew up, we started to look and search [for religious meaning] on our own. . . . There are some cultures that do arrange marriages, but that's not an Islamic thing. I think that's cultural. If my parents said, "Marry this person," there's no way in Islam they can force me.
—Nusrat, Indo-Pakistani Muslim student

It is like synonymous with Catholicism. A lot of [Mexican] traditions are viewed as Catholic. . . . I don't agree with the ideology, but I agree with the traditions. I want to instill in [my son] . . . those traditions.
—Ana, Mexican Catholic student

Early on in our research for a project on youth and religion, we stumbled on some intriguing empirical findings that we eventually made productive theoretical sense of.[1] The serendipitous findings concern patterns of identification with religion and ethnic culture expressed in focus groups conducted in 1997 with two groups of college women, Muslim and Latina, all but one of whom were American-born or American-raised children of immigrants. The Muslim women distinguish emphatically between their religion and their culture and embrace the former while distancing themselves from the latter. The mostly Catholic Latinas express deep ambivalence about their religious identity but find it nearly impossible to disentangle it from their more valued cultural identity. The theories that we employ in this chapter to account for these contrasting patterns are Neil J. Smelser's postulate of ambivalence and Fenggang Yang and Helen Rose Ebaugh's discussion of immigrant religion. We believe that the results will be of interest to students of gender, youth, ethnic identity, and religious social psychology, as well as to religious and educational leaders.

The chapter begins with a brief account of the Youth and Religion Project's (YRP) research agenda, before zeroing in on the two focus groups. Before theorizing the focus group data, we argue that the participants express discourses that are widespread in their respective communities. Then we show how two theoretical statements, Smelser on ambivalence (1998) and Yang and Ebaugh on immigrant religion (2001a, 2001b), help make sense of the two discourses. We conclude with a summary of our theoretical retrodictions and thoughts on some implications and limitations of our analysis.

The YRP Focus Groups

The research reported here is part of a larger project concerning the ways in which religious participation and identification affect the development of youth in the United States, especially ethnic and religious minorities. Our research began with students at the University of Illinois at Chicago (UIC) and then moved outward into religious institutions and families in the communities that send students to UIC, one of the most diverse student bodies in the United States. One of our first tasks was to learn what we could about the "cultural stories" (Peterman 1996) that are told in the various religio-ethnic communities that we intended to study. To find windows on these communities, we were particularly interested in learning about the way that students in two of the most visible and active student populations on campus—Latino/as and Muslims—would talk about the place of religion in their lives. Toward that end, we conducted focus groups, identified by gender, race, ethnicity, and religious background.[2] A professional focus group leader served as moderator and assisted in designing the discussion guide. The group discussions, all conducted in English, were tape-recorded and transcribed for later analysis. Generating lively discussions, they ran for 60 to 90 minutes.

Participants were asked about the role of religion in their family life while growing up, including involvement in worship, youth groups, choir, camps, and other religious activities; the current role of religion in their lives, especially their religious participation, if any, while in college; how they perceive religion as affecting attitudes, personal relationships, and the development of skills; and a global assessment of positive and negative aspects of religion in their lives. Participants were steered away from disputing each other's religious commitments and encouraged instead to discuss their personal experiences with their respective religions. It is to their stories that we now turn.

The Focus Group Data

The group of Latinas was relatively homogeneous, with seven of eight participants saying they had been "raised Catholic" and having self-identified Mexican origins. (The other was a Puerto Rican Protestant.) The Muslim women were also relatively homogeneous, with six of the eight Muslim women stemming from Indo-Pakistani immigrant families, while another was Palestinian. Despite a theological dispute within the Muslim group between these seven second-generation Sunni Muslims and the lone African American Muslim, who was a disciple of Louis Farrakhan's Nation of Islam, both groups of women shared a great deal of personal experience on the issues that concerned us, manifesting much agreement, no doubt as much consensus as we could have attained had we recruited on narrower criteria.

Muslim Women

Let us begin with the Muslim women. After the moderator went through the ground rules—including the encouragement that "everyone here is the world's leading expert on themselves"—and asked the participants to identify themselves and their ethnic or national backgrounds, she asked the students, "Tell me a little bit about the role of religion in the way you grew up, the kinds of things you did as a family, centered around religion."

The first person to volunteer, Nusrat,[3] identified herself as the daughter of immigrants from India and sounded a theme that informed the rest of the hour-long discussion. "For me, I know that when we grew up, my family—they really put *culture* more into our lives than religion" (italics added). The recording soon becomes unintelligible as other second-generation Indo-Pakistani women jumped into the discussion, but it is clear that Nusrat's distinction between religion and culture had sounded a responsive chord. Soon, Layla, the self-identified Palestinian woman, also the daughter of immigrants, spoke of her experience in nearly identical terms. "Like them [referring to the Indo-Pakistani women who had already chimed in], when I was growing up, everything was culture more so than religion. I knew I was a Muslim, but we didn't really do much. Nobody in my house prayed or anything like that." She knew she was different from her suburban neighbors by reason of being an Arab as well as a Muslim and felt deprived that her family did not celebrate Christmas.

Nusrat and Layla agreed on another aspect of this distinction that wound up carrying the day, the idea that in the nexus of religion and culture, religion represented the youths' striving for self-determination. Nusrat, immediately after characterizing her upbringing as more cultural than religious, said of herself and her sister, "But as we grew up, we started to look and search on our own," and they came to identify more with the religion. Layla, who was sent to an Islamic school beginning in the sixth grade, said she found religion on her own. "Religion didn't come into my home until I started accepting the religion and started learning. Then my parents started practicing and my brothers and sisters kind of too." Only when the family began to observe religious practices did she realize that as Muslims they had their own special holidays and did not need Christmas; this recognition freed her from envying the neighbors and gave her an experience of autonomy.

Noticing that four of these women wore a head covering—the hijab—and the others did not, the moderator asked the women how they felt about this matter, and they spoke about it in terms of the same theme of adult autonomy. Layla, the Palestinian, said that the decision to wear hijab was hers alone; her mother's generation did not cover. "When I did start wearing it, everyone in my family discouraged it, because I was very young and stubborn. So I kept it on. I believed in it. I had learned about the religion. My parents didn't really teach me 'you have to cover, you have to do that,' so when I learned about it, I accepted it. As I got older, I got to understand it more." Another of the Indian women spoke in similar terms: "It wasn't really taught to me. My mom doesn't wear it, my grandma doesn't wear it. No one wears it. But I found out. I researched, I talked to people. Just one day it hit me, and I decided to wear it." She added that the hijab prevents her "from being taken as an object" and allows her "to be taken for what's inside, not what's on the outside." Even those who were not covered tended to agree with these rationales, saying that hijab represents a principle of self-control and modesty of demeanor that directs attention to what is essential and away from what is superficial; yet some of them felt they were not yet ready for the "responsibility" that wearing hijab entails, given that it identifies the wearer as a representative of the Muslim community.

Throughout this discussion, "culture" was said to be the way one lived as a dependent child and coded as inferior, whereas "religion" and religious practice were things one chooses, a domain of autonomous determination, and superior. In the immigrant families these women were raised in, they could appeal to "religion" to trump parental demands that they saw as narrowly "cultural," for example, the attempt to arrange a marriage without the consent of the bride. Acknowledging an Islamic prohibition on "dating" (construed as premarital heterosexual physical contact), these women nonetheless maintained an Islamic right to choose their husbands. As Layla put it, "There are some cultures that do arrange marriages, but that's not an Islamic thing. I think that's cultural. . . . I don't plan on being arranged with anyone. I will choose my spouse." And Nusrat agreed: "In Islam, the woman has—if my parents came to me and said, 'Marry this person,' if I said no, there's no way in Islam they—they can't force me to marry that person. The woman's consent is ultimate in that."

As we had planned, the moderator explicitly tried to turn the discussion toward what might possibly be negative about the role of religion in these women's lives, but the responses remained in the same vein. Any negatives attributed to Islam were due to ignorance on the part of the observer, not to the essence of the religion. As we analyzed the transcript, a whole series of such oppositions emerged. "Religion" pertains to what is cosmopolitan, enlightened, and conducive to autonomy. Whatever is parochial, benighted, or driven by obsequiousness to public opinion is attributed to "culture." Even when critical observations were made about the local Muslim Student Association—for example, an incident in which a woman's attempt to question the (male) presenter of the khutbah (sermon) was actively discouraged by her sisters at prayer—they were attributed to the ignorance, immaturity, or recent immigration of the malfeasants, not to Islam, the Qur'an, or the Prophet, all of which were said to embody perfection. In this story line, not all cultures were said to be alike. In particular, Layla addressed the matter of respect for education, which she said was greater in the Indian cultures of the other participants than in her own Arab culture. "In Arab culture, it [education] is more important for guys than for girls just because of the culture. The culture is like that. The culture is messed up." In the sense that nothing negative adhered to Islam for these women, we say it has the advantages of an ideological Teflon.

Only one of the Muslim women demurred from this interpretive line: Deena, whose family came from Pakistan. Early in the discussion, she noted that "Islam purports itself as not being a religion but as being a lifestyle. . . . It invaded every area of life." Later, she reiterated the point. "I guess you can't break apart the religion and culture," and she upheld both her religion and her culture as a "value system" or "lifestyle" in contrast to "American culture," which she said is "in a horrible state of degradation in various ways." For Deena, insofar as religion and culture are both group phenomena—and she spoke of Muslim student groups at UIC as "cliquish"—they promote conformist thinking and narrow-mindedness. For herself, Deena said, "I'm more into the spiritual part than the religious part. I think spirituality is the essence of the religion." She said she needed no reminder that she represents the Muslim community. "I have a system of ethics that I believe in, and I have to follow that." Nonetheless, Deena said she felt a bond with the other women, a bond that she affirmed is a religious one, that of Islam.

Latinas

We now turn to the Latina focus group. As we have reported, seven of the eight participants in the Latina group self-identified during the round of introductions as "raised Catholic." These seven also had Mexican origins, including the five who simply said "I'm Mexican" as they introduced themselves.[4] Another, as reported, identified herself as Puerto Rican; introducing herself after all but one of the Mexican women, she said she was "raised Lutheran." The first author, stationed behind the one-way mirror, was not surprised to hear these women say that, having heard many UIC sociology of religion students so identify themselves over the years. But our moderator naively asked the Latinas what they meant by having been "raised Catholic," and that expression turned out for most of them to represent both an ambivalent attitude toward their parents' religion and an awareness of their identities.

Olga, for example, responded to the moderator's question by saying, "My mom's really Catholic. I went to a Catholic elementary and high school. . . . I was a practicing Catholic, but now I just don't [practice]." Later, she elaborated:

> I didn't question [my religion] until I came to the States because in Mexico all my classmates—everybody was Catholic. People didn't ask you, "What is your religion?" Because everybody just assumes that you're just Catholic. But when I came to the States, I encountered so many different racial backgrounds and religious backgrounds, and . . . that's when I became aware of my ethnicity and my religious background.

Some of the Latinas had grown up in the United States, but the rootedness of their Catholicism with their Mexican origins was most evident to those who had immigrated. For example, Lena said, "I was raised Catholic. First of all, I was born in Mexico. I was raised very Catholic. . . . We were in church on a daily basis. Or every other day. For sure on Sundays." Milly agreed: "I lived in Mexico most of my childhood, so if you live in Mexico, you don't have much of a choice. . . . Plus I lived in a very small town. . . . You have no choice but to be raised Catholic. So you end up going to church and end up in the Catholic school, . . . all that stuff."

From the outset, these women voiced a flood of complaints against the Catholic religious tradition within which they were raised. Olga rejected the notion that the Roman Catholic Church is the only true religion. Yolanda was turned off by the church's rituals and wished it had more of a place for young people. Ana took issue with the church's "ideology," especially as represented in the Inquisition. Lena spoke of the "domination" of male priests. And all this was before the moderator came to the point in the discussion guide where she was to ask the participants to give her a list of the negative as well as the positive aspects of their religious upbringing. At that point, more came out on the negative side: the pope, confessions, exclusivity, submissive roles for women, rules and punishments. The church was accused of hypocrisy about sex and money, upholding a double standard of machismo for men and virginity for women, and always appealing for donations, seemingly oblivious of its history of exploitation of indigenous Americans. We doubt this indictment would surprise anyone in the field of Latin American studies, but it surely represents a different attitude toward religion than that articulated by the Muslim women.

Yet these Latinas had positive things to say about their religion when the moderator turned to that side of the ledger. Good things also adhere to religion for them. Olga, who had earlier said that she had stopped practicing her mother's religion, liked the fact that religion promotes psychological security. Judy, who had earlier likened herself to Olga in having "no religious preference," thought it was good to have theological answers to life's questions. Ana sought out the spirituality she encountered in church. Judy and Lena especially spoke of the importance of having tradition, and they mentioned the festival of the Virgin of Guadalupe and the house-to-house ritual of the posada that closely follows it in December. The rub is that the good and the bad seem to be inextricable, both being aspects of a religion that is bound up with the Mexican identity that most of these women affirm.[5] For these Latinas, Catholicism has the qualities of Velcro: everything sticks to it.

Earlier in the discussion, the value of religious tradition had come up when the women discussed dating and marriage. Two of them were in fact married with young children and thus had faced the problem of passing on their heritage. Here is Lena's paradoxical statement:

> For me it's kind of funny, when I started questioning the Catholic Church. When I got married, where was I going to get married? My husband was Catholic. And how was I going to raise my child? . . . I can't really get married in the Catholic Church because I'd be a hypocrite, because I disagree with most of the things. I haven't gone to church in like years. Only once

in a big while. Finally, I ended up getting married in the Catholic Church because that's what I grew up with. I baptized my son into the Catholic Church, although I don't agree completely with the Catholic Church. But that's all I know.

Olga, who had likewise stopped practicing, looked ahead hypothetically to marriage and motherhood and came to the same conclusion. "I'll do the same thing my dad did, because my dad doesn't believe in the Catholic Church. . . . So I told my mom, I'll raise my kids Catholic, but when they grow older [they'll be free to make up their own minds]."

Ana, the other young wife and mother, linked her return to the church most explicitly to Mexican culture. "It's like synonymous with Catholicism. A lot of the traditions are viewed as Catholic. . . . So I want my child to grow up with those traditions. They're synonymous with the Catholic religion. . . . I don't agree with the ideology, but I agree with the tradition. I want to instill in him those morals, those values, those traditions." When another participant asked if the traditions Ana valued included the Day of the Dead, she responded, "Yes. It has Catholicism in it, but it also has indigenous meaning to it. That's very important to us in our tradition and our culture." Lena summed it up late in the discussion when she said, "We're mixed, you know."[6]

For all the maturity and wisdom in these thoughts—and they strike us as remarkably perceptive and articulate—they do not seem to offer much leverage for the person who would like to employ religion to change her life or to confront a father or a husband with demands for just treatment. So enculturated is the Mexican Catholicism these women know that for most of them religion appears more of a fetter than a force for personal change.

One of the participants, Milly, had left Catholicism to escape these contradictions—especially what she called the "idolatrous" mixtures of indigenous and Spanish elements and the paradox of her Mexican grandmother watching her novelas on television and praying the rosary during commercials. Milly decided to convert to evangelical Protestantism.[7] But in so doing, she has regrets centering on the thought that she would be turning her back on her heritage: "Like when I told my mom I wasn't going to be Catholic anymore. . . . It was hard at first because I realized how many traditions are associated with [the Catholic Church], around Easter, around Christmas. I didn't believe in them [and thought], 'Why are we doing that?' But then I kind of missed it. Dang, everybody's doing it." Yolanda was also partly drawn to Protestantism, especially for its offering a direct relationship between the believer and God. (She said she does not believe in the saints or in saying confession to a priest.) But her mother told her that if she left Catholicism, she would be renouncing her ethnicity as well, which is something she is not ready to do. ("I find myself more compatible with Hispanic guys.") So she says, "I can still consider myself Catholic and kind of not." For her, disengagement from Catholicism would not be worth the consequent deracination. Nevertheless, Protestantism may allow for some Latinas like Milly and Yolanda the qualities of Teflon that we see for the Muslim women's attitudes toward Islam.

Catholics may well wonder if these women were aware of liberation theology, but there is nothing in the transcript to suggest that they were. (It is quite possible that the college courses some mentioned, in which they learned of the atrocities perpetrated by the church in colonial times, had been informed by the writings of liberation theologians.) For example, in the focus group discussion with Latino men, one man referred to liberation theology as one way the church, as an inherently political institution, can position itself, but his lone comment was the end of that thread in the discussion. What seems more likely as a lever for change as experienced by both the Latinas and the Latinos is education. Education became a topic in the men's group and was a presupposition for several of the women, for whom the consciousness of having been "raised Catholic" came as soon as they got out of high school. For most of these Latinas, their religion is neither something that they experience as a force for their advancement nor something they can (or wish to) escape. The contrast with the Muslim women is stark.

Religion and Culture beyond the UIC Campus

The themes expressed by the young women in our groups are not anomalous. Indeed, the ways our students speak about religion is echoed in the literatures on Muslims and Latino religion. Harvard religionist Diana Eck, in her portrayal of American Muslims, quotes the leaders of the influential Islamic Center of Southern California addressing the parents of the second generation in terms of a distinction between (absolute) religion and (contingent) culture: "Parents who are still torn apart between two cultures, the old and the new, should bear in mind that their children are the fruit of only one culture, the American. This does not mean that Islam is to be compromised or changed. But parents should not confuse ethnic habits and Islamic religion" (2001, 268). Asma Gull Hassan, an American-born Muslim child of Pakistani immigrant parents and self-described "Muslim feminist cowgirl" (2000, 3), sees the Prophet Muhammad as "one of the world's first feminists" (124) and similarly distinguishes religion and culture:

To some extent, it is true that Muslim women living in Islamic countries have the short end of the stick. Literacy is appallingly low, birth control is hard to come by, and patriarchy often reigns in Islamic countries. However, none of these facts has any direct connection to Islam or the Qur'an. . . . Patriarchal culture that existed in these countries before Islam has become ingrained with the interpretation of some Qur'anic passages. . . . We must distinguish between what is culture and what is religion. (127, 132)

A post-9/11 New York Times article on East Coast campus Muslims quotes a Wellesley woman making the same point: "We have more freedom being American Muslims because we don't have the cultural baggage from the countries our parents are coming from" (Goldstein 2001; see also Williams and Vashi 2007). Studies of Muslims in Britain cite them making similar distinctions (Dwyer 1999; Jacobson 1997). For example, a British Pakistani Muslim woman reported, "Culture is a way of living in society. Religion is living on your own" (Jacobson 1997, 242).

Those who write about religion among Latino/as report a quite contrasting consciousness similar to that expressed by the focus group women. For decades, the U.S. Catholic Church relegated its Latino constituents in general to second-class status, and Chicana feminists in particular are said to regard the Catholic Church as an oppressive force (Blea 1992; Cadena and Medina 1996). Yet "cultural embeddedness is an important facet of Latina religious practice" (Peña and Frehill 1998, 621), and many Latinas who want to part company with the Catholic Church recognize that they remain "culturally Catholic" (Medina 1998, 190). Moreover, for many, the Protestant alternative is perceived, rightly or wrongly, as "an action of cultural abandonment and denial of the Ibero American religious tradition" (Hernández 1998; see also Armendariz 1999, 251; and Hurtig 2000, 46–54). Díaz-Stevens and Stevens-Arroyo summarize the paradoxical result:

Considering past slights, insults, and attacks directed at Latino tradition, language, and religious practices, it is truly remarkable that 63 percent of young Latino Catholics responded in a recent survey that "they could not imagine any circumstances under which they would leave the Catholic church," whereas less than one-half of their Euro-American counterparts were that thoroughly committed to Catholicism. (1998, 216)

The point is that what we heard among Muslim women and Latinas at UIC is heard among their coreligionists and coethnics all over the country.[8] We are convinced that in these two focus groups, we have tapped into two "cultural stories" (Peterman 1996), discourses about the place of religion and ethnic identity that are widespread among the daughters of Muslim and Mexican immigrants. One group of women distinguishes religion and culture in order to speak glowingly about their Islamic identity even as they attribute norms and values inimical to their aspirations (norms and values that some people would attribute to Islam itself) to their parents' cultures. The other group attributes analogously negative features to their religious background, but instead of disavowing that religious identity, they agree that it is bound up with a cultural (or ethnic) identity that is indelibly part of who they are. The following discussion is motivated by the premise that the 16 women whose viewpoints we first heard in 1997 speak for legions more than themselves.

Theoretical Discussion

It is clear to us that the way the moderator posed our questions to the students could hardly have been better designed to elicit expressions of what we eventually had to recognize as ambivalence, defined by Neil Smelser as "the simultaneous existence of attraction and repulsion, of love and hate," toward the same object (1998, 5). Although the presence of ambivalence is clearest for the Latinas, who are so clearly both alienated from and drawn back into the Catholic tradition, it is the case also for the Muslim women, who remember their culturally saturated childhoods with mixed feelings and who—as in the instance of women silencing a sister at the Muslim Student Association prayer or in Hassan's (2000) grappling with anti-Muslim stereotypes—have to contend with mixed impressions others have of their religious identity.

Smelser (1998) argues that intrapsychic ambivalence—the simultaneous existence of attraction and repulsion, of love and hate—is an emotional state the existence of which (1) can be expected under certain circumstances and (2) in such circumstances vitiates the assumption of actors' rationality. To that extent and in such circumstances, theorists need to entertain the postulate of ambivalence as an alternative to that of rational choice. Following Freud, Smelser thinks that the circumstances that generate ambivalence are especially found in relationships that are inescapable, those on which the actor is dependent, those from which he or she is not free to depart. Smelser's "general proposition is that dependent situations breed ambivalence, and correspondingly, models of behavior based on the postulate of ambivalence are the most applicable" in situations of dependence (ibid., 8). Parent-child relationships are relationships of dependence and the locus classicus of ambivalence (8–9). Another prime setting for ambivalence is found in "those groups, organizations, and social movements that demand commitment, adherence and faithfulness from their members" (6). This category includes "churches, ethnic and racial identity groups" (9). Typically, religion is not experienced by dependent minors—at least those who grow up in religiously affiliated families—as a realm of their own free choice. Many of the youthful informants in other phases of YRP, indeed, recall that they were "forced" to go to church and Sunday school. Whatever the attitude of grown-ups toward their religion, young people for the most part do not experience it as something they are free to leave. As both Layla, the Palestinian, and Olga, the Mexican, said, at first religion is just something that is given to you.

If dependent relationships breed ambivalence, those relationships from which individuals are free to withdraw or those in which they know that they will live only temporarily are settings wherein individuals can, with psychological impunity, indulge impulses toward emotional involvement. Such situations are therefore "typically lived and remembered with unalloyed sentimentality and nostalgia" (Smelser 1998, 9). Calling them "odyssey" situations, Smelser includes within the category ocean voyages, summer camps, the college years, and scholars' temporary residence at his own Center for Advanced Study in the Behavioral Sciences (Smelser 2009). In such settings, we should expect to find less ambivalence generated; indeed, about them we should expect to find expressed an exhilarating experience of freedom.

Here it is important to point to a contrast between the two religions we are observing. Whereas the obligatory day of Catholic worship is Sunday, the corresponding day for Muslims (although not a sabbath) is Friday. Given that UIC students often commute to school from home, Muslims' communal prayer occurs at school on a school day. Indeed, the Muslim Student Association is the most populous religious group on campus. Insofar as the primary religious venues for our Muslim women are the MSA or the MWA (Muslim Women's Association) rather than the mosques they may have attended with their parents or the Islamic schools they were sent to as dependent minors, religious involvement for the Muslim women at UIC may partake of the freely chosen "odyssey" experience, something associated with the college years, not their families. By contrast, the Latina women, most living with family members and no doubt subject to Sunday-morning pressure, speak of their religion as practiced (or not practiced) not on campus—they seem oblivious to the existence of the campus Newman Center—but only in the contexts of their parents' parishes, whether in Chicago or Mexico.

More generally, groups credited with making choice possible are the recipient of positive affect, whereas "negative emotion weakens ties to those blamed for constraining choice" (Smelser 1998, 9). Here Smelser, citing the research of Edward Lawler, might as well be talking about our Latinas, who seem to resent the (Catholic) church not only as a barrier to their aspirations but also for its inescapability. (One of our focus group participants said she feels "closed in" at church; another agreed: "Like you're trapped kind of.") For all these reasons, we can expect that the ambivalence built into the Latinas' religious situation will be greater than that of the Muslim women.

To speak of variations in ambivalence brings up another contribution of Smelser's paper. Having essayed an explanation of the generation of ambivalence, he also, although less systematically, considers the various expressions of ambivalence, the ways it is manifested, taking a lead once again from Freud. Being a "powerful, persistent, unresolvable, volatile, generalizable, and anxiety-provoking feature of the human condition," ambivalence is something we try to avoid experiencing, and its expression is correspondingly convoluted (Smelser 1998, 6). Originating in one relationship, ambivalence may find expression in another, as mixed feelings about one's father are projected onto one's analyst or one's God. Ambivalence may be repressed, reversed (where the negative emotion is given a positive expression, as in "love thine enemy"), displaced, or split. An example of "splitting ambivalence" is when the positive side of the ambivalence is transferred into "an unqualified love of one person or object and the negative side into an unqualified hatred of another" (ibid., 6). Using less extreme emotional language, what the Muslim women say about religion and culture is an excellent example of such splitting, with religion receiving unqualified endorsement from them and culture seen as, at best, a mixed blessing. Another common example of splitting that Smelser cites is the expression of in-group solidarity and out-group hostility, so that actors in the actually complex world of social relations are viewed "dichotomously—as friends or enemies, believers or non-believers, good or evil" (10).

The research of Yang and Ebaugh helps us specify what kinds of ambivalence are to be expected under what kinds of circumstances. In their comprehensive look at "transformations in new immigrant religions," Yang and Ebaugh (2001b) note that in the process of settling in a new country, immigrant religious communities often, but not always, see themselves as returning to their theological foundations. One impetus for such foundationalism[9] is that immigrant coreligionists in the United States today often come from many different home countries, where "diverse subtraditions" of the religion are practiced. The presence of such "internal pluralism" in the religious group "compels people to go through a process of . . . attempting to identify the essentials in their religion" (ibid., 279). The search for religious foundations, in turn, contributes to "the process of attempting to separate religion from culture" (280). "When Muslim immigrants come together, . . . they begin to realize that Islam has been adapted to various cultures in various parts of the world and what they have been doing religiously may not have a scriptural basis" (280). "Muslim leaders in the community frequently make this plea: We must learn to separate what is cultural Islam and what is the real Islam" (280). Yang and Ebaugh's leaders speak the same way as the Muslim women at UIC.

In another paper based primarily on the study of two Chinese congregations in Houston, one Christian and one Buddhist, Yang and Ebaugh (2001a) further argue that a religion that enjoys traditional legitimacy or mainstream status[10] in the home country of an immigrant group and has become a minority faith in the host country is induced by market opportunities to slough off elements of the home country culture, to accommodate to the culture of the host country, and to reach out to non-coethnics, as does Chinese Buddhism in the United States. By contrast, a religious institution with minority or marginal status in the home country but majority status in the host country is constrained by market forces to express the home country culture in the host country, a situation that Chinese Christian churches in the United States find themselves in.

As a traditional religion in the Middle East and South Asia and a perceivedly marginal religion in the United States, Islam fits the profile of Yang and Ebaugh's case of Chinese Buddhism. Although Indo-Pakistanis predominate in the MSA and MWA at UIC, these religious groups foster an environment in which Muslims from other cultures perceive that the community encompasses a diversity of racial and cultural groups whose common bond is their religion, Islam. An African American Muslim focus group participant reported that his experience at UIC differed from his high school and his freshman-year college experience at another institution. "When I go to the [student union] where most of the Muslims hang out at, it's really a comforting experience, because I can see Muslims of different nationalities getting together, without any national conflict." A Bosnian Muslim man spoke similarly of the MSA at UIC: "We have diversity at its best. We have people who are from India, from Pakistan, from Arab countries, people who converted, people from the [public housing] projects who converted, from everywhere." And a Pakistani Muslim, aware that he is in the majority group of Muslims at UIC's MSA, was similarly exhilarated by the MSA's diversity. Speaking of the Friday prayer, he said,

It's like regardless of your race or background, everybody comes. You see— well, there's not too many whites, [but] you know, we had that Bosnian guy, he came. And we have some African American, we have a whole lot of Arabs and people from the Indian subcontinent. We have an Indonesian guy who comes. . . . It's just everybody comes together. We come and pray together, and its just awesome. . . . It's—we're all equal, all standing in line together, we're all praying to the same Lord, and we're all listening to the same speaker. It's unreal.

Following Yang and Ebaugh's reasoning, it is clear how the Muslim women, viewing this diversity from their position behind the men at prayer, are likely to have at hand an approved channel for the splitting of their ambivalence between the religion that unites and inspires them and the cultures that they feel divide and impede them. Moreover, insofar as they are members of a religiously diverse subgroup, as are Indo-Pakistani Muslims on the UIC campus, where Hindus and Asian Christians are also highly visible, religion will seem less inevitable, less inescapable to them.

Let us look at the situation of the Mexican-origin women using this logic. Clearly in neither home nor host country is their religion a "minority" one: Catholicism is nearly hegemonic in Mexico and is not only mainstream in America but, at least in its dominantly Irish American incarnation, the majority faith in Chicago. For our focus group participants, the Catholic Church is felt to be inescapable. Adding to the ambivalence about their religion that this situation must (by Smelser's hypothesis) generate is the perceived marginal status of the most feasible religious alternative, Protestantism, not only in the home country but in the host country as well. Thus, one avenue of escape is narrowed if not cut off altogether. It must then be unusual among Mexican Americans in Chicago to experience adherence to Catholicism as an exercise of choice.

Furthermore, the structure of the community, including the residential concentration to which Latinos in Chicago are subject and the geographic parish system of the church to which Mexican Americans seem to adhere (Ebaugh and Chafetz 2000; Hurtig 2000), is not conducive to the internal pluralism that might bring on the reflection on theological foundations, and consequent opportunity to distinguish between religion and culture, that Yang and Ebaugh see among immigrant Buddhists and Muslims. Moreover, if an Anglo (or non-Mexican American) in Chicago wishes to explore Catholicism, he or she has many opportunities to do so other than attending a Mexican parish. Thus, Mexican Americans in Chicago are most likely to attend culturally homogeneous parishes or masses.

It is understandable why those who grow up in such circumstances will, like the Palestinian Layla before she went off to college or like most of the

Mexican American focus group participants even after they come to college, tend to experience their religion as more or less the set of prejudices reigning in their homes and neighborhoods. Such a traditionalist rationale for religion may work in Mexico, but once its adherents go to public school and on to college in the United States, they will want better answers to their religious questions. "In a pluralist environment, the authority of a religion that is based simply on tradition (i.e., we must follow the religion that our ancestors believed) loses its power, especially for young people in public schools and colleges" (Yang and Ebaugh 2001b, 280–281).

To this point our theorizing helps us understand why the Latinas, unlike the Muslim women, seem both to feel deeply ambivalent about their religion and to have less occasion to try to separate their religion from their culture. But, again unlike the Muslims, the Latinas also are not offered such a distinction by their religious leaders. Quite the contrary. Latin American Catholicism is in fact one of the prime exemplars of the Roman Catholic theology of "inculturation" (Schreiter 1985), which proposes that the culture of local communities is properly valorized by the church. In this view, such icons as the Virgen de Guadalupe and such practices as posada and All Saints/All Souls masses in observance of Dia de los Muertos proudly and properly celebrate indigenous culture (Elizondo 1983), as our UIC Latinas seem aware. Although an immigrant religion that is part of the mainstream in both the home and host country that does not attempt to overcome cultural barriers in the interest of reaching out to new constituencies may seem contrary to Yang and Ebaugh's theorizing, it is possible to use their reasoning to understand it.

First, the immigrant group is itself of such a size in Chicago (where hundreds of thousands of persons of Mexican origin now reside), as well as in many other cities, that religious suppliers, in this case the Catholic Church, already have such a large potential market that they do not need to seek out non-coethnics. If non-coethnics, in turn, are Catholic, they can practice Catholicism in many other parishes; if they are not Catholic and desire "authentic otherness" in their religion, they would likely seek out something with more otherness than Catholicism (cf. Yang and Ebaugh 2001a, 375–376). The internal ethnic constituency is huge, and the potential external constituency has many religious options. From this point of view, there is little reason for Latino Catholic parishes to reach out to non-Latinos.

In fact, the theology of inculturation may be read as an expression of the opposite need, one that Yang and Ebaugh articulate, namely, the imperative that faces a religious institution of contested legitimacy to ensure that its immigrant constituents can express an authentic identity through its offerings. Beginning with the U.S. conquest of northern Mexico in the war of 1846–1848, the U.S. Catholic Church imposed on its new Mexican constituents a form of Catholicism that was profoundly alien to the newly conquered people. The church compounded the insult by a long unwillingness to accept Mexican Americans into its leadership structure (Diaz-Stevens and Stevens-Arroyo 1998; Matovina and Riebe-Estrella 2002). Only in the past 30 years has the church tried to speak to its rapidly growing Mexican American constituency in terms that they could understand (Davis, Martinez, and Warner 2010), welcoming cultural practices such as Day of the Dead altars and quinceañeras into the parish. Concerned that the Catholicism of the church was experienced by Mexican Americans as Anglo-Irish imperialism, the church is newly constrained to show Mexican immigrants that the culture they brought with them (or the culture they remember having left behind in Mexico) can be found in the neighborhood church. With respect to the Catholic Church's Mexican immigrant constituents, it is thus in a position analogous to the Chinese Christian churches of which Yang and Ebaugh speak (2001a, 373, 375–376); it was guilty of bad faith until proven innocent.

The attentive reader will have recognized that the logic we apply to the situation of the Catholic Church is a rational one, at least a soft version of rational choice, whereas we have argued that nonrational ambivalence probably influences the viewpoint of the individual women in our focus groups. We are untroubled by our use of two different logics to account for the actions of organizations and individuals. (See table 3.1.) Although both rational choice and ambivalence can be usefully employed as postulates or presuppositions of theorizing (which we do when we assume that children who inherit their religion from their parents will be ambivalent about it and when we assume that religious leaders will respond to what they see as the needs of their constituents), neither rational choice nor ambivalence is (or ought to be) an ideology that demands consistency. Moreover, we have also treated ambivalence (and could treat rationality) as an explanandum, a dependent variable, specifically a mind-set whose variable intensity can be explained (see also Warner 2005 for a summary of the argument).

Implications and Limitations of the Analysis

The Youth and Religion Project began with focus groups in order to become sensitized to the way that groups of college women (and men) who share some salient ascriptive status (gender, ethnicity, race, religion) would speak to outsiders about the place of religion in their lives, and we made a point to elicit negative as well as positive accounts. Not all the groups focused so

Table 3.1. Retrodictions of the Theory

	for Muslims	for Latinas
Individual logics explaining prevalence of ambivalence		
Religious identity is ascriptive, i.e., originally given by parents, and is therefore conducive to ambivalence (Smelser 1998, p. 8)	Yes	Yes
Religious activity in college years approximates "odyssey" situations, therefore reducing ambivalence by giving youth an experience of freedom (Smelser 1998, p. 9)	Yes	No
Religion is experienced by youth as inescapable, therefore conducing to greater ambivalence on their part (Smelser 1998, pp. 6, 9)	No	Yes
Authority of religion is perceived to rest primarily on tradition, which diminishes its power and invokes ambivalence (Y&E 2001a, pp. 280-281; Smelser 1998, p. 9)	No	Yes
Individual logic explaining direction of ambivalence		
Relative cultural and religious heterogeneity of youth peers promotes their splitting ambivalence between religion and culture (Smelser 1998, p. 9 ; Y&E 2001a, pp. 279-280)	Yes	No
Organizational logic explaining direction of ambivalence		
To gain legitimacy and broaden constituencies, religious leaders perceive and act on the need to differentiate between religion and culture as opposed to melding them (Y&E 2001a, p. 280; 2001b, pp. 375-376)	Yes	No

intensely on matters of group identity, let alone the specific factors of religion and culture, as did the Muslim and Latina women. The Muslim women/Latina Catholic findings are serendipitous. Nonetheless, they do illustrate two very different modes in which young women speak (in common) about the place of religion in their lives.

One mode, that of the Muslim women, claims religion as a liberating force. In Nusrat's words, speaking about the practice of arranged marriage in Indo-Pakistani culture, "There's no way in Islam" that parents can force a marriage without their daughter's consent. The other mode, that of the Mexican Catholic women, sees religion as mostly inimical to their ideals and aspirations but something so bound up with their identities as to be inescapable. As Lena said (her position so ambivalent that her words are arranged by us in a different order for clarity), "Although . . . I disagree with most of the things [taught by] the Catholic Church, . . . I ended up getting married in the Catholic Church, [and] I baptized my son into the Catholic Church . . . because that's what I grew up with, . . . that's all I know." These thoughts make Lena feel like "a hypocrite." By contrast, Layla, the Palestinian—who said, "Religion didn't come into my home until I started accepting the religion and started learning. Then my parents started practicing"—enjoys a sense of autonomy in her religion. To judge from the way Muslims like Layla talk, they expect that they may be able to draw on religion as a resource in future gender struggles. As these Muslim women speak of religion, it is a source of "cultural power," cooperatively constructed in the context of an immigrant second generation (Williams and Demerath 1998, 367). For Mexican women like Lena, by contrast, their Catholic religion does not seem to offer a comparable resource. For such women, "the ambivalence from the clash of voices results in mental and emotional states of perplexity. Internal strife results in insecurity and indecisiveness" (Anzaldúa 1999, 100).

Although the contrast between the two modes is stark, the story of religion and culture is only begun in these accounts. From the transcripts alone, we cannot tell what role religion will in fact play in these women's futures. After all, the UIC women are by definition students under 25 years of age, and as the children of immigrants, they are pioneers in new social circumstances, who can look forward to long lifetimes of uncharted experience. We do not know whether the Muslim women will succeed in invoking Islam to neutralize "cultural" barriers to their aspirations thrown up by the men (and gendered social forces) in their future. They are young women, at a stage of life when they are arguably at the peak of their social power (Neitz 1985). Perhaps they are deluding themselves about the years ahead of them. Perhaps the religion/culture distinction they favor may turn out to be too facile a conceptual tool to serve as a survival strategy in their "frontline" experiences (Lopez and Hasso 1998). We also do not know that the years to come will prove Lena and Ana to be ill advised in their reluctant but unshakable determination to maintain their ties to the Catholic Church. Perhaps the ambivalence they seem perplexed by will in time resolve into a clearer path toward an emancipatory appropriation of their heritage.

Canadian scholar Shanaz Khan (1998) pointedly warns North American Muslim women against embracing religion as enthusiastically as do the participants in our focus groups. Recognizing the "structured ambivalence" that Muslim women face in America, Khan suggests that they may have reason to regret aligning themselves with what she calls the Islamist project of exerting "social and sexual control" on women (469, 489). Khan thinks such women may need to live with their ambivalence, affirming both their religious and ethnic affiliations and being ready play one off against another.

As for the Latinas, a growing literature ponders their ambivalent religious consciousness, especially that of Mexican American women or Chicanas (e.g., Anzaldúa 1999; Blea 1992; Lopez and Hasso 1998; Medina 1998). Latina interviewees, focus group participants, literary theorists, and reflective essayists express alienation toward the Catholic Church at the same time that they find aspects of popular Catholic culture of deep value, essential to their identity.

Most promising for the UIC Mexican American women, in our view, is the strategy by which Catholic traditions are understood as the work of the people, not of the hierarchy or the organized church, a reading of popular Catholicism that is given warrant by the Vatican II concept of the church as the people of God (Greeley 1990) and passionately articulated by theorists and theologians of Latino (Goizueta 1995) and specifically Mexican American (Elizondo 1983; Matovina 2000) Catholicism. Yolanda, one of the participants in our Latina focus group, spoke this way when she asked in irritation about the hierarchy, "Who are they to say what the rules are for Catholicism?" In this construction, ambivalence about Catholicism is split not between religion and culture but between the organized church as the (contingent) property of colonizing Anglos and the church of the (Mexican or mestizo) pueblo as an incarnation of the true people of God (Elizondo 1983).

Latina feminists have taken this tack in viewing such icons as La Virgen de Guadalupe as a "supportive," "accepting," "nurturing," and "mothering" source of strength, a "coping mechanism for those who have no other resources" (Rodriguez 1994, 129; see also Trujillo 1998; Medina 1998; Peña and Frehill 1998). Maybe this is what Lena had in mind by insisting that she and her sisters were "mixed, you know." But if such populist readings of Mexican Catholic symbols play a muted role in our focus group transcript, they may become more prevalent in the participants' lives as they grow older and more experienced.[11]

Just as our theorizing of the focus group findings concluded with a brief mention of organizational logics, it is fitting to conclude the chapter with a recognition that the foregoing speculations about possible resolutions of ambivalence in the minds of Latinas and Muslim women have organizational implications. If young American Muslim women look to their religion as a source of support for their aspirations, their expectations should be borne in mind by those whose efforts shape the emerging Islamic institutions. Similarly, if Mexican American women find it impossible to shed the Catholicism with which they carry on a love-hate relationship, those who would nurture their aspirations, whether they work in the church or the university, may be well advised to help them contend with their stubborn religious identity rather than denying it or wishing it would go away.

NOTES

1. The research reported in this chapter was made possible by a grant to the University of Illinois at Chicago from the Lilly Endowment, whose support is gratefully acknowledged. We are also indebted to Rhys Williams, coprincipal investigator of the Youth and Religion Project, and to Sharon Feldman, who served as moderator of the Y&RP focus groups described herein. Our greatest debt is to the participants in those groups, the young women who so frankly shared with us their convictions and perceptions about the place of religion in their lives. Although we do not use their real names in this chapter, we remember all of them with gratitude.
2. Recruits for focus group discussions were classified by YRP researchers to yield groups of six to eight, corresponding to the most active self-identified ethnic and religious student populations on the UIC campus. Thus, the identities analyzed in this chapter—Latina and Muslim—are not parallel, the one being ethnic and the other religious. Details of focus group administration are available from the first author.
3. All names of participants are pseudonyms.
4. None called herself a "Chicana" or used any cognate expression during the hour-long discussion.
5. Juanita, the Puerto Rican Protestant, said, "I think it's neat what you guys said about how Catholic religion is tied really closely into Mexican culture."
6. Lena said this twice, as if to suggest that she had in mind the concept of *mestizaje*, as articulated, among others, by Elizondo (1983).
7. She did not use the word "Protestant" but said she had "converted to Christian." Despite the frequency of the usage of "Christian" among Latina/os at UIC, we do not wish to endorse this exclusivist use of the term and, unless in direct quotation, refer to "Protestant."
8. In our review of the literature, however, our specific *comparison* of these two groups' discourses on identity is approximated only by Lopez and Hasso (1998), whose specific comparison is between Latinas and Arab American women, not Muslims per se. The intriguingly titled paper by Zolberg and Woon (1999) deals more with national policies toward immigrants than the identities of immigrants.
9. Due to the often liberalizing effects of the attempt to return to theological "foundations," Yang and Ebaugh distinguish it from traditionalist "fundamentalism" (2001b, 281).
10. Yang and Ebaugh (2001a) direct their attention explicitly to the "minority" or "majority" status of the religion in the home and host countries. But close reading of their

reasoning and their examples makes clear that a religion need not enjoy actual majority status in the home country to be above suspicion but only that it be perceived to
be legitimate, "indigenous," "traditional," or "mainstream" in the home country (cited
material from Yang and Ebaugh 2001a, 368, 369, 373, 376).

11. It is worthy of mention in this context that the women interviewed by Rodriguez
(1994) and the focus group participants gathered by Peña and Frehill (1998) were
significantly older, with more experience of both motherhood and paid employment,
than the UIC focus group women.

REFERENCES

Anzaldúa, Gloria. 1999. *Borderlands/La Frontera*. 2nd ed. San Francisco: Aunt Lute Books.

Armendariz, Rueben P. 1999. "The Protestant Hispanic Congregation: Identity." Pp. 239–254 in
Protestantes/Protestants: Hispanic Christianity within Mainline Traditions, edited by David
Maldonado, Jr. Nashville, Tenn.: Abingdon.

Blea, Irene. 1992. *La Chicana and the Intersection of Race, Class, and Gender*. New York: Praeger.

Cadena, Gilbert R., and Lara Medina. 1996. "Liberation Theology and Social Change: Chicanas
and Chicanos in the Catholic Church." Pp. 99–111 in *Chicanas and Chicanos in Contemporary Society*, edited by Roberto M. DeAnda. Boston: Allyn and Bacon.

Davis, Stephen P., Juan R. Martinez, and R. Stephen Warner. 2010. "The Role of the Catholic
Church in the Chicago Immigrant Mobilization." Pp. 79–96 in *¡Marcha! Latino Chicago
and the Immigrant Rights Movement*, edited by Amalia Pallares and Nilda Flores-González.
Urbana: University of Illinois Press.

Díaz-Stevens, Ana María, and Anthony M. Stevens-Arroyo. 1998. *Recognizing the Latino Religious Resurgence in U.S. Religion: The Emmaus Paradigm*. Boulder, Colo.: Westview.

Dwyer, Claire. 1999. "Veiled Meanings: Young British Muslim Women and the Negotiation of
Differences." *Gender, Place, and Culture* 6 (1): 5–26.

Ebaugh, Helen Rose, and Janet Saltzman Chafetz. 2000. *Religion and the New Immigrants*.
Lanham, Md.: AltaMira.

Eck, Diana L. 2001. *A New Religious America: How a "Christian Country" Has Now Become the
World's Most Religiously Diverse Nation*. New York: HarperSanFrancisco.

Elizondo, Virgilio. 1983. *Galilean Journey: The Mexican American Promise*. Maryknoll, N.Y.:
Orbis Books.

Goizueta, Roberto S. 1995. *Caminemos con Jesús: Toward a Hispanic/Latino Theology of Accom-
paniment*. Maryknoll, N.Y.: Orbis Books.

Goldstein, Laurie. 2001. "Muslims Nurture Sense of Self on Campus." *New York Times*, November 3.

Greeley, Andrew M. 1990. *The Catholic Myth: The Behavior and Beliefs of American Catholics*.
New York: Scribner.

Hassan, Asma Gull. 2000. *American Muslims: The New Generation*. New York: Continuum.

Hernández, Edwin I. 1998. "Moving from the Cathedral to Storefront Churches: Understand-
ing Religious Growth and Decline among Latino Protestants." Pp. 216–235 in *Protestantes/
Protestants: Hispanic Christianity Within Mainline Traditions*, edited by David Maldonado,
Jr. Nashville, Tenn.: Abingdon.

Hurtig, Janise. 2000. "Hispanic Immigrant Churches and the Construction of Ethnicity." Pp.
28–55 in *Public Religion and Urban Transformation*, edited by Lowell W. Livezey. New
York: NYU Press.

Jacobson, Jessica. 1997. "Religion and Ethnicity: Dual and Alternative Sources of Identity among Young British Pakistanis." *Ethnic and Racial Studies* 20 (2): 238–256.

Khan, Shahnaz. 1998. "Muslim Women: Negotiations in the Third Space." *Signs* 23 (2): 463–494.

Lopez, Laura M. and Frances S. Hasso. 1998. "Frontlines and Borders: Identity Thresholds for Latinas and Arab American Women." Pp. 253–280 in *Everyday Inequalities: Critical Inquiries*, edited by Jodi O'Brien and Judith A. Howard. Malden, Mass.: Blackwell.

Matovina, Timothy, ed. 2000. *Beyond Borders: Writings of Virgilio Elizondo and Friends.* Maryknoll, N.Y.: Orbis Books.

Matovina, Timothy, and Gary Riebe-Estrella. 2002. *Horizons of the Sacred: Mexican Traditions in U.S. Catholicism.* Ithaca: Cornell University Press.

Medina, Lara. 1998. "Los Espiritus Siguen Hablando: Chicana Spiritualities." Pp. 189–213 in *Living Chicana Theory*, edited by Carla Trujillo. Berkeley, CA: Third Woman.

Neitz, Mary Jo. 1985. "Resistances to Feminist Analysis." *Teaching Sociology* 12 (April): 339–353.

Peña, Milagros, and Lisa M. Frehill. 1998. "Latina Religious Practice: Analyzing Cultural Dimensions in Measures of Religiosity." *Journal for the Scientific Study of Religion* 37 (December): 620–635.

Peterman, Jean P. 1996. *Telling Their Stories: Puerto Rican Women and Abortion.* Boulder, Colo.: Westview.

Rodriguez, Jeanette. 1994. *Our Lady of Guadalupe: Faith and Empowerment among Mexican-American Women.* Austin: University of Texas Press.

Schreiter, Robert J. 1985. *Constructing Local Theologies.* Maryknoll, N.Y.: Orbis.

Smelser, Neil J. 1998. "The Rational and the Ambivalent in the Social Sciences." *American Sociological Review* 63 (February): 1–15.

———. 2009. *The Odyssey Experience: Physical, Social, Psychological, and Spiritual Journeys.* Berkeley: University of California Press.

Trujillo, Carla. 1998. "La Virgen de Guadalupe and Her Reconstruction in Chicana Lesbian Desire." Pp. 214–231 in *Living Chicana Theory*, edited by Carla Trujillo. Berkeley, CA: Third Woman.

Warner, R. Stephen. 2005. "Enlisting Smelser's Theory of Ambivalence to Maintain Progress in Sociology of Religion's New Paradigm." Pp. 105–122 in *A Church of Our Own: Disestablishment and Diversity in American Religion.* New Brunswick: Rutgers University Press.

Williams, Rhys H., and N. J. Demerath III. 1998. "Cultural Power: How Underdog Religious and Nonreligious Movements Triumph against Structural Odds." Pp. 364–377 in *Sacred Companies: Organizational Aspects of Religion and Religious Aspects of Organizations*, edited by N. J. Demerath III, Peter Dobkin Hall, Terry Schmitt, and Rhys H. Williams. New York: Oxford University Press.

Williams, Rhys H., and Gira Vashi. 2007. "Hijab and American Muslim Women: Creating the Space for Autonomous Selves." *Sociology of Religion* 68 (Fall): 269–287.

Yang, Fenggang, and Helen Rose Ebaugh. 2001a. "Religion and Ethnicity among New Immigrants: The Impact of Majority/Minority Status in Home and Host Countries." *Journal for the Scientific Study of Religion* 40 (September): 367–378.

———. 2001b. "Transformations in New Immigrant Religions and Their Global Implications." *American Sociological Review* 66 (April): 269–288.

Zolberg, Aristide R., and Long Litt Woon. 1999. "Why Islam Is Like Spanish: Cultural Incorporation in Europe and the United States." *Politics and Society* 27 (March): 5–38.

CHAPTER 4

Second-Generation Asian Americans and Judaism

HELEN K. KIM AND NOAH LEAVITT

Q: When Asian Americans become the "new Jews," what happens
to the Jews?[1]
A: Sometimes they decide to marry the "new Jews."

With the passage of the Immigration and Nationality Act of 1965, the United
States began and continues to experience profound transformations in its
racial, ethnic, cultural, and religious landscape. While immigration during
the pre-1965 era was primarily marked by individuals and families of White,
European, and Judeo-Christian backgrounds, the post-1965 era ushered
in a vast expansion of America's diversity and heterogeneity. Now it is not
uncommon, especially in urban areas, to find Mexican churches, Taiwanese Buddhist temples, Islamic mosques, and Russian-speaking synagogues
within a few blocks of one another.

This sea change in America's demographic composition raises a multitude
of sociological questions pertaining not only to diverse immigrant populations
but also to their children. For members of the second generation, born and
raised in a country whose social and political dynamics are often quite different from those of their parents' countries of origin, issues regarding institutional incorporation, group boundaries, and belonging loom large, illuminat-
ing how various markers of identity within the United States operate.

In this chapter, we address some of these questions, which reflect inter-actions among race, ethnicity, and religion, for a particular subset of the second-generation population: Asian Americans who are partnered with Jewish Americans. While intermarriage for members of the second gen-eration is certainly not limited to those with Jewish Americans, there is reason to believe that these partnerships will become increasingly common among second and subsequent generations of Asian Americans. For exam-ple, Fong and Yung (2000) note a tendency among their Chinese and Japa-nese American subjects to date and marry Jews, with a surprisingly high 18 percent of their interview sample married to Jewish partners. The authors suggest that romantic relationships among members of these groups may be connected to economic compatibility in terms of socioeconomic back-ground and socialization within similar professional circles, and they argue that future research in the area of interracial marriage should further explore these factors.

This chapter picks up where Fong and Yung leave off by examining the following question: how do religion, race, and ethnicity interact in the daily lives of Asian Americans who are partnered with Jewish Americans? To address this question, we draw from analysis of in-depth interviews con-ducted during 2009 with fourteen second-generation Asian Americans residing in the San Francisco, Los Angeles/Orange County, New York, and Philadelphia metropolitan areas.[2]

To frame our discussion, we draw from the literature on intermarriage, focusing specifically on its implications for these two groups. More than 40 years after *Loving v. Virginia*, the landmark U.S. Supreme Court deci-sion abolishing race-based restrictions on marriage, interracial unions have become more common, raising significant questions about identity, bound-aries, and acceptance. For marriages between Asian Americans and Jewish Americans, in particular, these questions incorporate not only racial differ-ences but also ethnic and religious differences.

More broadly, we revisit Will Herberg's *Protestant, Catholic, Jew* (1960), his seminal work on immigration and religion that theorized the salience of religious, ethnic, and cultural ties for immigrants to the United States and their descendants. Over half a century after its initial publication, Herberg's work continues to call into question the importance and mean-ing of religion for first and subsequent generations of immigrants to the United States as well as those components that may or may not constitute a "common faith" and "American way of life" for members of the new second generation.

Intermarriage: Asian Americans

Especially following the passage of the Immigration and Nationality Act of 1965, studies of interracial marriage have increasingly focused on Asian-White marriages[3] (Lee and Yamanaka 1990; Aguirre, Saenz, and Hwang 1995; Jacobs and Labov 2002) primarily because of the rapid growth of these relationships, particularly between White men and Asian women. According to statistics from the 2000 U.S. Census, intermarriage rates between White men and Asian women far exceed intermarriages between White men and women of any other racial or mixed-race background.[4] Similarly, the number of marriages between Asian men and White women significantly exceed the number of those between Asian men and women of any other racial or mixed-race background.[5]

Various frameworks have been utilized to understand the reasons for these patterns. In addition to the assimilation perspective, which sees intermarriage as the final stage in the assimilation process for immigrants, the theory of hypergamy (Davis 1941; Merton 1941) posits that racial minorities such as Asians exchange material resources for racial status when marrying Whites, who are racially dominant within U.S. society. More recent research posits that as most married couples have similar levels of education, interracial couples would also be expected to have relatively equal levels of educational attainment. During the post-1965 era, Asian Americans attend college at rates on par or sometimes exceeding rates among Whites. Thus, one might expect high levels of intermarriages between Asians and Whites with similar levels of education, as these are indicators of similarities in background, social status, and values (Qian 2005, 35).

Intermarriage: Jewish Americans

In contrast to the literature on intermarriage and Asian Americans, which is predominantly concerned with racial and ethnic differences between partners, the scholarship on intermarriage for Jewish Americans has almost exclusively focused on interfaith unions, namely, those in which one partner is Jewish and the other partner is Christian. While Herberg's (1960) notion of the "triple melting pot" is based on midcentury data collected by R. J. R. Kennedy (1944) indicating very high rates of endogamy among Jewish Americans, the picture of intermarriage for this population has changed substantially during the later part of the 20th and early part of the 21st centuries. Due to constitutional restrictions on the mixing of religion and government, the U.S. Census does not ask questions about religious identification. However, some quantitative efforts to track rates of intermarriage among the U.S. Jewish population do exist, such as the National Jewish Population Survey (NJPS), sponsored by United Jewish Communities and the Jewish Federation system (United Jewish Communities 2003).[6] Data from the 2000–2001 NJPS report a 31 percent overall intermarriage rate for Jewish Americans currently in their first marriage. The few qualitative studies on intermarriage among Jewish Americans are primarily concerned with how couples and families who are mixed along religious lines negotiate religious practice within the home and how, in turn, these decisions impact questions pertaining to identity. Sylvia Fishman (2004), in her investigation of Jewish-Christian marriages and households, argues that the growing rate of interfaith marriages has steered American society's bias away from endogamous marriages toward acceptance of partnerships that are exogamous.

The literature on intermarriage among Jewish Americans, at its core, raises a fundamental question pertaining to religious, racial, and ethnic identity: what does it mean to be Jewish?[7] While many Jewish Americans would make the distinction between identifying as Jewish culturally versus religiously, we take the position that these two identities are not extractable from each other. Rather, Judaism as a religion has necessarily informed the secular and cultural components of self-identifying as Jewish and belonging to a Jewish people. Thus, we agree with Pyong Gap Min, who states, "Jewish Americans have been successful in retaining their cultural traditions mainly because their religious values and rituals are inseparably linked to their ethnic cultural traditions" (2002, 18).

Overall, these bodies of literature on intermarriage exhibit several significant gaps. First, while studies on intermarriage appropriately focus on racially or religiously exogamous partnerships, we find no research that incorporates variation in religious background among racially and/or ethnically intermarried couples. For example, Maria Root (2001) conducts an extensive qualitative study of approximately 175 interracial families yet pays almost no attention to the role of religion.[8] More specifically, the literature on intermarriage for Asian Americans does not account for religious difference at the same time that the literature on intermarriage for Jewish Americans does not consider racial difference. Furthermore, these various bodies of literature lack meaningful qualitative investigations of how individuals think about their racial, ethnic, and/or religious identities in light of being intermarried.

Will Herberg: Religion as the Primary Source
of Ethnicity for the Second Generation

In *Protestant, Catholic, Jew*, Will Herberg argued that the children of immigrants to the United States would maintain the religion of their parents while shedding their parents' particular ethnic and cultural ties. Focusing on the wave of immigration that primarily included White Europeans, Herberg emphasized the blending of first-generation national origin identities (e.g., Italian, Polish, Irish) with religious affiliation in subsequent generations. According to Herberg's model, intermarriage along national origin lines for the descendants of immigrants would produce a weakening of ethnic and cultural ties. However, such partnerships would not necessarily result in a diminished connection to one's religious background. In fact, maintaining the religion of one's ancestors would allow descendants of immigrants to sustain a connection to the homeland of the first generation while carving out a place in American society as defined by one's faith. Thus, "becoming American" for Herberg, while requiring changes in nationality, language, and culture, does not demand a change in one's religion (1960, 22). Drawing from Kennedy's (1944) investigation of intermarriage in New Haven from 1870 to 1940, Herberg concluded, "America is indeed, in Mrs. Kennedy's terminology, the land of the 'triple melting pot,' for it is within these three religious communities that the process of ethnic and cultural integration so characteristic of American life takes place" (1960, 37).

Related to the idea of the "triple melting pot" and central to Herberg's thesis on immigration and religion are those core components that define what Americans believe as key tenets of their "faith." He noted that while approximately 95 percent of Americans claimed a belief in God and 75 percent affiliated with a church, only 39 percent indicated that religious beliefs had any effect on their ideas of politics or business (1960, 72, 73). To understand this discrepancy between religious identification and its relationship to other arenas of social life, Herberg argued that religious affiliation provided Americans a sense of meaning and a way to understand what it meant to be American—he called that outlook the "American Way of Life."

Various scholars have recently revisited, and questioned, Herberg's work. For example, building off of Alejandro Portes and Rubén Rumbaut (1996), Russell Jeung (2005) contends that the notion of a triple melting pot no longer applies. Rather, immigrants and their descendants are folded into a "multicultural America that establishes racial, ethnic, and gendered categories for groups to align with, resist or rearticulate" (Jeung 2005, 6).[9] In a different critique, Joel Schwarz (2004) argues that while Herberg's depiction of American religion at midcentury has some application to the present day, his position is less plausible considering the shifts in the demographic composition of immigrants in a post-1965 era. Schwarz also points to vastly different rates of intermarriage and conversion at the end of the 20th century to challenge Herberg's depiction of the "triple melting pot" as involving very little migration between and among the three major American religions.

Methodology

A quick tour through the Internet reveals many comments about romantic attachments between Asian Americans and Jews, ranging from the serious to the silly.[10] One of the most famous of these was a series of discussions about whether Asian American women were among the most frequent visitors to Jewish dating websites, such as JDate.com.[11] No matter what their tone or perspective, though, all of these stories demonstrate the strong emotional reactions that such couples evoke.

Despite this attention, however, a variety of challenges exist when trying to understand Asian-Jewish couples, from U.S. Census restrictions on asking about religion to the range of ways that people define being Jewish to stereotypical media images of Asian-Jewish couples. Simply put, there is not any way to know exactly how many Asian-Jewish couples live in the United States or any easy way to find them.

To address these challenges, we decided to partner with Be'Chol Lashon, an arm of the Institute for Jewish and Community Research (IJCR).[12] As a first step toward identifying potential candidates for interviews, an online screening survey was created in order to obtain a snapshot of the ethnic, racial, and religious views, and religious practice, of potential couples. IJCR distributed the survey through its extensive national database of Jewish organizations, synagogues, rabbinical associations, and social service organizations, in addition to its monthly newsletter, which reaches members of its organization as well as numerous other organizations addressing diversity and American Judaism. We also sent personal e-mails to Jewish organizations, as well as to multiracial and interfaith networks and newspapers, requesting assistance with our project. Thus, a significant number of the surveys were completed by individuals or couples connected to Jewish organizations, networks, listservs, and congregations. We acknowledge that other ways to recruit couples exist and that our recruitment choices limit the generalizability of our results. For example, recruitment could take place through contact with Asian American–specific organizations and outlets. However, we chose not to pursue these avenues because our pre-existing relationship with IJCR allowed for greater and more convenient recruitment opportunities.

We particularly targeted the San Francisco Bay Area, the Los Angeles/ Orange County Area, New York City, and Philadelphia, four major metropolitan regions in the United States that are home to high proportions of Asian Americans and Jewish Americans relative to the total population. We also chose to focus on these locations because of the high numbers of responses from intermarried couples residing in these regions.

The several hundred survey responses we received demonstrated a surprisingly broad range of couples who fit this demographic. To take just one example, the aforementioned census data show high rates of intermarriage between Asian American women and White men. Yet we saw the exact opposite trend: most of the survey respondents (and most of the couples eventually interviewed for this investigation) were actually Asian American men partnered with Jewish women. Similarly, there was surprisingly wide variation according to religious identification and involvement (for both the Jewish spouse/partner and the other person's religion, if any), ethnic background, sexual orientation, gender pairings, presence or absence of children, urban or suburban residence, as well as previous states of residence. When we saw this broad range of responses, we decided to select couples to interview whom we determined would capture the widest variation along all these demographic variables.

To date, a total of 37 couples living in one of the aforementioned metropolitan areas have been interviewed. Interviewees range in age from late 20s to early 70s, and all participants have received at least a college degree. All interviews took place in person, most frequently in couples' homes and also in local coffee shops and synagogues. Open-ended questions were asked about respondents' upbringing, family, school, dating history, relationship with current spouse/partner, children (if any), and ethnic, racial, and religious practices in the home. Interviews typically lasted between an hour and a half to two hours and were audiotaped and transcribed with the permission of the interviewee. The data we rely on for this chapter incorporate only the interviews with 14 second-generation Asian Americans. Again, our small sample size and recruitment methods present limitations to the generalizability of our results. However, the data point to some interesting trends that may be worth expanding on in future research consisting of a larger and more representative sample.

Data

Asian American respondents described religion, race, and ethnicity interacting in complex ways in their daily lives. This interaction is particularly visible in their recognition that the value systems in which they were raised often work alongside their partners' Judaism to reduce obstacles in their intimate relationships. Respondents also described how all of these markers of identity interact when they face decisions about how to instill the backgrounds and value systems of both parents in the children.

In general, respondents were ambivalent about organized religion and, in particular, about the religion they grew up with. Some did not even recall whether their families of origin practiced a religion in the home. When they did remember a religion in the home, many respondents abandoned the religion they were raised with. For some, this means they do not presently claim any formal religious affiliation. For others, it means they have adopted a completely different religion, which more often than not is Judaism. Only a few still have religious views similar to those with which they were raised.

These characteristics are consistent with broader trends of non-Jews—primarily White Christians—who marry Jews. In Keren McGinity's qualitative study of 43 Jewish women who intermarried, the author found that "most Jewish women . . . married non-Jewish men who no longer perceived themselves as connected to a Christian denomination, were atheists, or had renounced their birth religion" (2009, 169), leading to a degree of ease in marrying outside their tradition. Similarly, some of our respondents voiced comments that are consistent with broader trends of non-Jews—again, primarily White Christians—who marry Jews because of a degree of family instability in their backgrounds. For instance, Fishman's (2004) national study of interfaith households reveals that non-Jews who married Jews disproportionately came from homes that experienced religious or geographical mobility, divorce, or another type of situation that produced instability. Fishman argues that these types of changes may lead non-Jews to be attracted to what they regard as caring and stable Jewish home life.

One difference, though, as we explain in the following pages, is that some of our respondents also thought that Judaism was consistent with a set of values that they grew up with, which might or might not have been explicitly religious.

Values

While some respondents were not enthusiastic about affiliating with any organized religion, they spoke about how much of their ethnic and religious identities are connected to and are demonstrated through upholding a system of values, often instilled in them in their childhoods. Those values often obviated the need for a formal religious practice or affiliation. Most respondents who spoke about this topic agreed that this value system consists primarily of supporting one's family, striving for as much education as possible, and working hard. The religious backgrounds of these respondents include atheist, agnostic, Jewish (converted or in the process of converting), and Buddhist. Thus, differences in religious background do not appear to play a role in participants' very similar discussions of values.

Some respondents recalled this set of values being specifically linked to their ethnic background. For example, Chen remembered a strong sense of family loyalty instilled during his upbringing. His family followed what he defined as the Buddhist practice of "do unto one as you would like to be done unto." Moreover, such practices were specifically linked to his ethnic background: Chen recalls his parents often telling him, "This is how we do it as Chinese." In this sense, Chen and others appear to reinforce Jeung's notion of Chinese American familism, whereby second-generation Chinese Americans maintain a strong sense of identity by utilizing the repertoires of Chinese popular religion to emphasize narratives of strong family values and filial piety, all the while rejecting Chinese popular religious practice (see Jeung, "Family Sacrifices," chap. 10 in this volume).

Respondents who grew up and/or attended school with Jews spoke about their general connection with Jews in large part because of these values. Amy, who was raised in a Chinese family in a community with a relatively high percentage of Jews, noted, "We were never religious, very cultural though. So Chinese upbringing. Similar values to a lot of my Jewish friends. Education was important. Family, food." Other interviewees commented that this "reverence for education" aligns Judaism with a variety of Asian beliefs and values.

Regarding their partnerships, interviewees frequently noted similarities between the value systems they were brought up with and the values of their Jewish partners. Moreover, they discussed these similarities as supporting their relationship with their partners. Chen noted, "I feel the Jewish culture and the Chinese culture are very family oriented. . . . It has to do a lot with family. I feel that both of them are very similar to that. When I came into Rebecca's family, it was . . . comforting—it seemed very similar in that respect."

In addition to the similarities, respondents who adhere to or follow another religious or spiritual practice did not see their partner's Judaism as a source of conflict. Chen, who self-identified as Buddhist, noted, "As we went along [in our dating], after going to two, three of her family events, bar and bat mitzvahs, slowly but surely realizing if we did go this way, it's going to be Jewish. I was looking at things, and it wasn't that bad. I wasn't concerned with not being able to do Buddhism or Zenism."

Similarities between these value systems were discussed as eliminating obstacles for long-term partnerships. Interviewees who grew up around a lot of Jews recognized this opportunity for their relationship early on. From the beginning of Sam's relationship with his future wife he thought that these resemblances could be helpful in sustaining his relationship. "In terms of value system[s], I felt very similar." Kelly, who grew up with friends of many different religions, including Judaism, views Judaism more as a value system and less as a belief system: "I felt very comfortable with Judaism as a culture more than a religion," thereby easing the challenges of being with a Jewish partner.

This awareness of possible connections also held true for interviewees who did not know any Jews before becoming involved with their Jewish partner. For example, Chen did not know any Jews in his youth, did not know anything about Jews or Judaism, and did not know that his wife-to-be was Jewish until some time into their relationship. As a result, he was not aware of and never thought about any similarities in values when he first started dating Rebecca. However, when he saw the relationship taking a more serious turn, and as he learned more about Rebecca and her family ("I'm not sure exactly when I started to realize when she was Jewish. Somewhere along the line. I just knew she did a lot with her family."), he imagined that those shared priorities would help them be able to build a family together. "I think at the very beginning of the stages, at least for us, it had nothing to do with the family values. But as we got closer, as we figured out if one another would be good life partners, I think that [did] come into play." Over time, he came to realize that the value systems were similar enough and, therefore, unproblematic.

While those couples who believed in similarities between Jewish and Asian ethnic values did not explicitly mention race in their discussions, we interpret these comments within larger group and societal contexts in which race possibly plays a significant role in understanding why couples would link themselves to each other along these lines. In *Racism without Racists*, Eduardo Bonilla-Silva (2003) indicates a continued lack of support for and acceptance of interracial marriages in a society that largely purports to be without racists. Interviews with Whites who claim to be nonracist and desire to live a multiracial and multicultural lifestyle but who are largely surrounded by White neighborhoods, have White friends, and marry Whites reveal continued disapproval of interracial unions. One of Bonilla-Silva's informants stated, "I don't have a problem with it [interracial marriage] at all, [but] there's gonna be problems. White and Chinese, White and even Italian, there's gonna be problems. . . . And they're not gonna be accepted" (120). That many of our interviewees indicated a similarity between Jewish and Asian cultures rather than focused on what makes them different appears to take into consideration mainstream society's assumption that interracial and intercultural marriages are still unsafe from criticism and lack of acceptance. The following quotation from Lisa, an elementary school teacher, illustrates this tension and how couples have negotiated these assumptions:

> I just think because we bring so many things to the table that [long pause] . . . It's so neat that we can celebrate two different cultures. We both love each other's culture. I mean, the more I've been learning about Jewish culture, like with Passover, . . . there are so many similarities, like the importance of food, right? And all the foods have different symbols. Things like that that, I mean, wow, I feel like I've grown as a person, or I've become more worldly because I'm learning about this one other culture. So I think it just really helps enrich our lives that we're sharing these things. . . . We're even better people, because not only do we know ourselves, but we're getting to know something else as well. And I feel like this helps me relate to some of my students. Because on an outward appearance—"Oh, you're Asian." And you may think I know nothing about matzoh ball soup or challah, but I can share some stories with my students. So sometimes I can find connections.

The Next Generation

Respondents with children talked at great length about various struggles and opportunities posed by questions of racial, ethnic, and religious identity when contemplating how to raise a family. Overall, children of these intermarriages are being raised as Jews. Nine of our respondents have children and are all raising them as Jews. Three out of eight respondents are childless but plan to have children and raise them as Jews. One respondent married a man who already had children who were raised as Jews. In numerous ways, the children self-identify, and in many cases are identified by their non-Jewish parents, as Jewish. Such transmission and identification is not the case, however, when it comes to passing on a sense of ethnic/cultural identity from the Asian American parent.

Even when respondents identified a clear sense of their own Asian ethnicity, they supported raising their children with a Jewish home and education.

More specifically, having a Jewish home included home-based practices and rituals such as observance of Jewish holidays, developing a daily Jewish "table practice" including blessings and giving thanks, celebrating the Sabbath, cooking and eating Jewish foods, or studying Hebrew. While one's intention in creating a Jewish home does not have to be exclusively religious and can be cultural, these types of practices have their basis in Judaism as a religion. Sam, who grew up in a household with numerous markers and practices of Chinese culture, viewed his support as coming out of what he sees, again, as two similar value systems. "I think my personal experience is that both Jewish and Chinese value systems are very compatible. I wasn't really ever concerned about how we wanted to raise our kids and teaching them right and wrong—learn to respect others. . . . Just from growing up and my peers, I was pretty confident that wouldn't be an area of conflict."

Most participants who did not self-identify as Jewish commented that raising children in a Jewish household is a priority for their Jewish spouses. Often, they knew early on in their relationships of their partner's opinions regarding instilling Judaism in their children. While they may not be totally enthusiastic about Judaism itself, they are helping Jewish learning and practice to happen. Chris said, "I'm kind of antireligion. . . . So whether it's Christian, Jewish, whatever, I'm not too keen on organized religion. I'll go [to synagogue] because I want to support what Julie wants for the kids, but I'm not comfortable there."

In contrast to Jewish households, respondents primarily discussed Asian households as upholding specific cultural traditions and symbolic expressions of ethnicity less intricately linked to religious practice. Thus, the instilling of ethnicity and culture through, for example, the consumption of certain foods, the celebration of particular holidays, and the learning of languages was largely divorced from any basis in religion. While Jewish homes may not be incompatible with Asian homes, the distinctions between the two, according to respondents, are worth noting because they highlight different orientations to the melding of religion and culture or ethnicity within one's home.

The men saw their children as being connected to Judaism in numerous ways. Despite what Sam characterized as "ambivalence" about pushing any particular religion on child, he describes his daughter as "Chinese-Jewish." Similarly, Chen said his two children are "happy kids with Jewish backgrounds who happen to be Chinese." He went on to point out, "They're very Jewish right now." Chris acknowledged that his two young children "identify as both [Jewish and Chinese]."

When it comes to passing down ethnicity, men generally saw it as their responsibility to instill a value system or sense of identity in their children.

Yet, at the same time, and despite claiming strong senses of Chinese ethnic identification, the men feared that their children are not developing a sense of an Asian ethnic identity. Sam stated, "I may not practice what I preach" when it comes to instilling a sense of his children's Chinese heritage. Accordingly, he also worries about the dearth of communication to his family on his part regarding an ethnic/cultural heritage:

> Call it hopeful or higher hopes for her generation than my own in some sense. It's maybe a "claw back" [previous benefits of Chinese language which no longer exist] and get a little bit more Chinese. In some sense, I fear, even now, my Chinese fluency has certainly slipped in this household. [My daughter] certainly will have less exposure than I had growing up and picking up a lot of basics. Again, that's probably why this kind of focus on family and family exposure for me is fairly important. I feel like it's a way to give her some exposure that I myself had. . . . In some sense, I don't think we'll be able to provide that same environment for her to learn.

Chris noted, "I think they'll have loss of an identity, because I'm not that instructive about passing things down to them."

This anxiety was also true for those who did not express a strong sense of their ethnic identity. Chris said, "I don't think I've thought too much about identity, and I know that I'm losing mine in a way." Later he pointed out, "When I said I'm losing touch with my ethnicity, that's because a lot of my friends now aren't Asian. I think that after I got out of college I started doing things that weren't, I don't know, seen as traditional." Chris also said his wife sometimes keeps him focused on doing the work to transmit culture to their children: "I don't think she prods me to do things, but she's done things to promote them [cultural traditions]. There was a mooncake festival at the school. So she brought the kids to go to that. They have a Chinese-language program in first grade. It's not Cantonese, it's Mandarin. I mentioned that I wanted them to do that. She supports that." Ironically, Chris grew up speaking Cantonese, so if his children learn Mandarin, it will not necessarily connect them with their father's heritage.

Respondents' discomfort with their children's disconnect from their ethnic or cultural heritage went beyond issues of consistent cultural exposure. Ultimately, they expressed concerns regarding how their children may or currently self-identify. Chen acknowledged, "He [our son] didn't really think of himself as Chinese. I missed the boat there. We were sitting on the couch, [and our son was] asking something about 'what does a Chinese do?' I said,

'Well, honey, you're Chinese too.' He kind of alluded that he wasn't. Then he backtracked and said, 'Oh, yeah, I am.'"

While respondents were concerned that their children do not think they have an Asian identity, they also worried about what it would take to provide exposure to and training in both sets of their children's heritages. They identified a series of costs associated with such transmission. For some, the cost is time:

> I'm very concerned of how [my daughter] has two times the cultural experience and information that she needs to pick up. . . . If she's got all this extracurricular on the Jewish side, extracurricular on the Chinese side, when is she going to have a chance to be a kid? Are we going to turn her off, inundating her with so much information from both sides that she just becomes disinterested? Then later, just extracurricular stuff that she wants to do—dance, sports, whatever—I'm just trying to imagine this type of schedule this child might have, and it's mind-boggling.

For others, the cost is money. Chen, who listed "frugality" as an Asian value he identifies with, quipped:

> They [the kids] went to preschool at the JCC [Jewish Community Center]—which is one of the best preschools around here anyway. . . . From there, after they got out, they have been at the temple. They've kept up ever since preschool, . . . and it's just natural. And I didn't make it a priority to say, "Okay, every week they need to go to a Chinese school." I've never made that a priority. Part of that once again goes back to the Chinese thing and saving money: "But that will cost money. Maybe if we didn't have to pay temple dues, we could to this!"

Yet, in the absence of making these kinds of cultural investments, respondents did not have a vision for how their kids will develop any Asian ethnic identity. One respondent talked about traveling to his parents' home country for the sake of their kids' cultural education. Chen noted, "Ultimately what I want to do is bring them to Taiwan over the summer and spend lots of time there. At that point . . . you're going to be immersed. . . . And I was hoping they will learn the language too." However, this trip has yet to take place. "Putting it off and putting it off and putting it off. We're hoping that this year we'll get to do that [trip]. Not positive, but we're hoping to do that."

Finally, an ambivalence about transmitting an ethnic, racial, and religious identity to one's children emerged from our discussions. For example, Sam talked about wanting all these complex elements in his children to "blend together," adding, "That's the American Dream, right?" On a related note, respondents saw their kids as having options for how they want to self-iden-tify. Chen noted, "I just want them to know [about their Chinese as well as their Jewish heritage]. Once again, so they can pick and choose what they would like to do."

Some participants did not subscribe to the idea that their mixed-back-ground children will necessarily experience differential treatment as a result of their various identities. This implies a perceived acceptance of difference within their racially and ethnically diverse neighborhoods and communi-ties. Chris acknowledged, "I know that they are [mixed race], but I don't have to think about what that means. . . . It may be naive of me, but I don't think they'll be treated differently because of it. . . . Part of it is 'cause they live here. It's pretty diverse." Yet these respondents' perceptions contrasted with an underlying fear of racism and an acknowledgment of the primacy of race and racialization in the United States for some interviewees. Thus, while some participants' experiences with discrimination may be tempered by living in racially and ethnically diverse neighborhoods, the possibility of confronting racism, especially for one's children, did not vanish for every-one. Some did express concern that their children might be stigmatized in the future on the basis of their physical appearance. For example, Sam, who did not experience blatant racial discrimination growing up, said of himself and his daughter,

> Maybe it's a fear. So it's maybe more a fear of Sally, . . . being Asian. . . . I've been fortunate enough to really not have that many experiences [with rac-ism]. . . . That's not to say it's not there in other people or they're thinking it. In some sense, for any child I bring up, I think at least part of the Asian mix will be obvious. . . . Will she experience any type of prejudice or be called out or separated or treated differently because of some physically obvious traits?

Revisiting Herberg: Religion as the Primary Source of Ethnicity for the Second Generation . . . or Not?

Ultimately, Herberg's argument regarding the retention of religion alongside the erosion of ethnicity is a statement about assimilation into American soci-ety. For scholars studying immigration during the first half of the 20th cen-tury, assimilation was largely conceptualized as a process whereby increasing structural, economic, social, and political integration into the host society would take place with each successive generation in a "straight line" path (Park 1950; Gordon 1964). Furthermore, assimilation was a largely uniform concept defined by a core set of values and norms that defined what it meant to "be American." Thus, for Herberg, "becoming American" hinged on one's religious identification with a "common faith" and less so on the retention of ethnically or culturally specific ties.

In the post-1965 era, immigration scholars have questioned the applicability of a "straight line" approach to assimilation, arguing that racialization by the host society plays a considerable role in outcomes for immigrants and their children and does not necessarily contribute to a linear path ending with full integration into American society (Portes and Zhou 1993; Waters 1999; Kibria 2002). Thus, the achievement of an American identity in relation to religion and ethnicity may look different for members of this new second generation. If we consider the intermarriages of our respondents, in which racial, ethnic, and religious differences demographically define their partnerships, it would appear that Herberg's central thesis regarding the retention of one's ancestral religion combined with the erosion of one's ethnic or cultural ties does not apply to our second-generation Asian Americans. They do, though, grudgingly or happily, enable their children to be brought up in households where Judaism plays a major role in shaping their identity. Given that all our respondents have agreed to raise their children as Jews, it appears that being Jewish and American along the lines of Herberg's thesis fits for the current and future offspring of our participants. Simultaneously, ethnicity— conceptualized by our interviewees as a system of values, symbols, language, and/or belonging to a people—does emerge as a primary identity for all our interviewees and as something that they uphold in daily life and/or contemplate passing down to their children.

Yet, while our respondents by and large rejected or discontinued an affiliation with the religion of their first-generation parents, the notion of a "common faith" seems to be prominent in their lives, though not explicitly based in religious affiliation. Most noticeable is the idea expressed by interviewees regarding the value system among Asian ethnicities, which reinforces education, close-knit families, frugality, and hard work, and the resulting ties between Asian Americans and Jewish Americans along similar cultural lines. For example, Kelly, reflecting on her Filipino background, stated, "The only time I could get out of church was when I had school. School work—that really had to be done. Education was always really important, even more so than religion." Suzie, although she did go to church sporadically when she was young, said, "I wasn't really raised with religion. But I was a pretty disciplined kid anyway. Maybe Chinese culture could have been as strict as any religion." As stated previously, respondents characterized this value system as one of common bond with Jews. Thus, the values that constitute a "common faith" and exist on their own at the same time that they form the basis of intimacy with members of a different religious and cultural group are not explicitly attached to religion but, fundamentally, to ethnicity. Moreover, this value system is arguably a manifestation of Herberg's "common faith" in society, which lauds upward social and economic mobility, a pathway that hinges on these cultural traits.

Interestingly, while on the surface this "common faith" for second-generation Asian Americans has its roots in their ethnicities, it may very well be grounded in religion—and in Judaism, specifically. Jonathan Freedman's *Klezmer America*, a sweeping investigation into the ways that Jewish and American cultural production interact, argues that the Jewish experience in America has become the model that has informed the ways subsequent waves of non-Jewish immigrants—Latinos, Asians, even North African and other Muslims—are thought about and even think about themselves in relation to being American. "New itineraries of belonging and their fate in the nation at large will continue to be intertwined with older narratives and the social and imaginative structures they wrought—and as both remain . . . fundamentally connected with Jewish, Judaism and/or Jewishness" (2008, 331–332).

Yet, while Freedman may be correct in arguing that non-Jewish and non-White immigrants to the United States and their children may understand their path toward becoming Americans through a Jewish religious and/or cultural lens, it would be erroneous to say that utilizing this frame of reference equates to complete acceptance by and integration into American society as a whole. While our respondents generally did not think of themselves and their intimate partnerships on a day-to-day basis in racial terms, their identification of a "common faith" between themselves and Jews cannot be understood without reference to a larger racialized cultural narrative that encompasses the "model minority" stereotype. Scholarly analysis of the model minority discourse, arguably a positive marker of the potential for assimilation into American society, has criticized its usage as an instrument for the perpetuation of racist attitudes toward Asian Americans as well as of divisions among racial groups. For example, Gary Okihiro (1994) argues that 19th-century racialized images of Asians as the "yellow peril" work together with contemporary notions of Asians as the "model minority" to reinforce members of this population as perpetual foreigners. As Nazli Kibria notes, "In both the model minority image and that of the yellow peril, Asian achievement takes on an inhuman, even species-different character" (2002, 133). Furthermore, while statistics on Asian American educational and occupational attainment may affirm a picture of mobility that surpasses the rest of the U.S. population, this questionable image further perpetuates a social hierarchy that pits "deserving" against "undeserving" groups on the basis of race.[13]

Implications for Future Research

Extending Herberg's framework, our interviews leave a number of unanswered questions that may prove fruitful for future investigation. First, how does variation in ethnic identification influence negotiations pertaining to religion and ethnicity? While our sample does contain some variation according to ethnic background, a larger sample size that takes into account these differences would yield a more reliable assessment of these relationships.

Second, how does gender factor into how second-generation Asian Americans retain and, in some cases, pass on a connection to their heritage? Chris, for example, spoke about how his wife encourages their kids to go to Chinese-language programs, in the absence of his doing so. In other interviews, women shared similar stories about encouraging a degree of their Asian American husband's ethnic identity to be part of other important family moments, such as weddings. Whereas in one instance a Jewish wife pushed for a greater visibility of her husband's Chinese background, in another, a non-Jewish Asian American wife advocated for a greater visibility of her husband's Jewish background in their wedding ceremony. While women are often recognized as "keepers of the culture" (Billson 1995), what does the maintenance of a spouse's culture, even when it is not one's own, signify? At this point, the respondents discussed in this chapter do not offer firm answers to these questions, especially given that the Asian American females have children who are quite young, while the Asian American males are raising children who are older. Preliminary analysis of subsequent interviews indicates a possible relationship between gender and the transmission of Asian and Jewish identity. More specifically, it appears that Asian American women have or are becoming keepers of both cultures by taking on the necessary time and energy that it takes to learn and ensure the practice of these elements within a household. It may be worth considering that Judaism traditionally follows matrilineal descent, meaning that a child born to a Jewish mother is automatically considered Jewish.[14] Thus, the transmission of Judaism and Jewish identity by an Asian American female spouse may reflect this religiously based gender division.

Third, our sample currently does not include couples who are not raising their children with some element of Judaism. Thus, how would second-generation Asian Americans see themselves if they were partnered with spouses who actively resist including Judaism in their children's upbringing or who choose to raise children with an alternative religion?

Finally, how will the children of our respondents view themselves? Several of our interviewees spoke of their children's often strong and well-articulated attachment to Judaism, adding that the children did not attach themselves so strongly when it came to connecting to their Asian heritage. Most of the children of these families are young (preadolescent), and so it is not known how they will think about their identities as they get older. In the era of President Barack Obama, the child of a father from Kenya and a mother from Kansas and born in Hawaii, the United States appears to be trying to understand what it means to be a child of a mixed racial, ethnic, and religious relationship. A burgeoning literature exists regarding growing up as a child of mixed heritage (Winters and DeBose 2005). Some of these works even explore what it means to be the child of an African American–Jewish union (Azoulay 1997; Walker 2001). However, there is not yet an in-depth picture of growing up Asian-Jewish. The children of our respondents will pave the way.

NOTES

1. This provocative question comes from the title of an article in *Slate* magazine, by Nicholas Lemann, posted June 25, 1996, exploring common trends of assimilation between the two groups.
2. These data are part of a much larger study currently under way to understand how couples in which one partner who is Asian American of any ethnic or religious background and one partner who is Jewish American of any racial or ethnic background negotiate these identities as individuals and within the context of their family life.
3. "Asian" and "White" are referred to as racial categories, not as ethnic categories.
4. U.S. Census Bureau, Census 2000, PHC-T-19, "Hispanic Origin and Race of Coupled Households: 2000," table 1, http://www.census.gov/population/cen2000/phc-t19/tab01.pdf.
5. Ibid.
6. This study, while influential, is not the final word on the subject. Many researchers took issue with the NJPS figures, suggesting they were both inaccurate and low. For example, a 2002 national telephone survey conducted by the Institute for Jewish and Community Research estimates there are over 6 million Jews in the United States, far more than the 5.2 million indicated in the 2000 NJPS (Tobin, Tobin, and Rubin 2005). The authors note that "many American Jews think of themselves in ethnic or cultural terms rather than in religious ones" (21).

7. Historically, Jews were not accepted as racially White because of their inferior economic, ethnic, and religious status. Over time, American Jews as a group have largely economically assimilated into the U.S. mainstream and have thereby been able to gain status as "White." However, continuing anti-Semitism related to their position as religious and ethnic minorities has not resulted in full acceptance by the U.S. mainstream. While many Jews self-identify and are identified as White, many actively resist self-identification as White and choose to solely identify as Jewish (Brodkin 1998).

8. Root acknowledges, "Although I did not set out to study how religious differences influence the integration of family members, it became clear that these differences also made blending more difficult" (2001, 131).

9. This depiction of American society should not be construed to mean that religious identity does not play a role in the construction of individual and group identity.

10. See, for instance, "No More Jewish Husbands," ASKQ, *Asian Week*, posted November 15, 2008, http://www.asianweek.com/2008/11/15/no-more jewish-husbands/; Song Oh, "Asians: The New Shiksas?," *JewishJournal.com*, April 17, 2003, http://www.jewishjournal.com/singles/article/asians_the_new_shiksas_20030418/.

11. See, for instance, ck, "Saucy Asian Adventures on JDate," *Jewlicious* (blog), March 31, 2005, http://www.jewlicious.com/2005/03/saucy-asian-adventures-on-jdate/.

12. IJCR is an independent think tank whose research focuses on demographic trends among the American Jewish population, including intermarriage. See its website: http://jewishresearch.org/.

13. Our usage of the terms "deserving" and "undeserving" should not be construed as agreement with the idea, popularized by public policy and mass media, that sees certain racial groups as truly deserving or undeserving of success on the basis of supposed inherent cultural traits. Rather, we recognize the troubling ways in which these terms have unfairly been used against certain racial groups and have highlighted a problematic model minority discourse as supporting these views.

14. The religion of the child's father is not determinative of religious affiliation.

REFERENCES

Aguirre, Benigno E., Rogelio Saenz, and Sean-Shong Hwang. 1995. "Remarriage and Intermarriage of Asians in the United States of America." *Journal of Comparative Family Studies* 26:207–215.

Azoulay, Katya Gibel. 1997. *Black, Jewish, and Interracial: It's Not the Color of Your Skin, but the Race of Your Kin, and Other Myths of Identity*. Durham: Duke University Press.

Billson, Janet Mancini. 1995. *Keepers of the Culture: The Power of Tradition in Women's Lives*. New York: Lexington Books.

Bonilla-Silva, Eduardo. 2003. *Racism without Racists: Color-Blind Racism and the Persistence of Racial Inequality in the United States*. Lanham, MD: Rowman and Littlefield.

Brodkin, Karen. 1998. *How Jews Became White Folks and What That Says about Race in America*. New Brunswick: Rutgers University Press.

Davis, Kingsley. 1941. "Intermarriage in Caste Society." *American Anthropologist* 43:376–395.

Fishman, Sylvia Barack. 2004. *Double or Nothing? Jewish Families and Mixed Marriages*. Lebanon, NH: University Press of New England.

Fong, Colleen, and Judy Yung. 2000. "In Search of the Right Spouse: Interracial Marriage among Chinese and Japanese Americans." Pp. 589–605 in *Contemporary Asian America: A Multidisciplinary Reader*, edited by Min Zhou and James V. Gatewood. New York: NYU Press.

Freedman, Jonathan. 2008. *Klezmer America: Jewishness, Ethnicity, Modernity*. New York: Columbia University Press.

Gordon, Milton M. 1964. *Assimilation in American Life*. New York: Oxford University Press.

Herberg, Will. 1960. *Protestant, Catholic, Jew: An Essay in American Religious Sociology*. Chicago: University of Chicago Press.

Jacobs, Jerry A., and Teresa Labov. 2002. "Gender Differentials in Intermarriage among Sixteen Racial and Ethnic Groups." *Sociological Forum* 17:621–646.

Jeung, Russell. 2005. *Faithful Generations: Race and New Asian American Churches*. New Brunswick: Rutgers University Press.

Kennedy, R. J. R. 1944. "Single or Triple Melting Pot? Intermarriage Trends in New Haven, 1870–1940." *American Journal of Sociology* 49:331–339.

Kibria, Nazli. 2002. *Becoming Asian American: Second-Generation Chinese and Korean American Identities*. Baltimore: Johns Hopkins University Press.

Lee, Sharon M., and Keiko Yamanaka. 1990. "Patterns of Asian American Intermarriage and Marital Assimilation." *Journal of Comparative Family Studies* 21:287–305.

McGinity, Keren R. 2009. *Still Jewish: A History of Women and Intermarriage in America*. New York: NYU Press.

Merton, Robert M. 1941. "Intermarriage and the Social Structure: Fact and Theory." *Psychiatry* 4:361–374.

Min, Pyong Gap. 2002. "A Literature Review with a Focus on Major Themes." Pp. 15–36 in *Religions in Asian America: Building Faith Communities*, edited by Pyong Gap Min and Jung Ha Kim. Lanham, MD: AltaMira.

Okihiro, Gary. 1994. *Margins and Mainstreams: Asians in American History and Culture*. Seattle: University of Washington Press.

Park, Robert E. 1950. *Race and Culture*. Glencoe, IL: Free Press.

Portes, Alejandro, and Rubén Rumbaut. 1996. *Immigrant America*. Berkeley: University of California Press.

Portes, Alejandro, and Min Zhou. 1993. "The New Second Generation: Segmented Assimilation and Its Variants." *Annals of the American Academy of Political and Social Sciences* 530:74–96.

Qian, Zhenchao. 2005. "Breaking the Last Taboo: Interracial Marriage in America." *Contexts* 4 (4): 33–37.

Root, Maria P. P. 2001. *Love's Revolution—Interracial Marriage*. Philadelphia: Temple University Press.

Schwarz, Joel. 2004. "Protestant, Catholic, Jew . . . ," *Public Interest*, Spring, 106–125.

Tobin, Diane, Gary A. Tobin, and Scott Rubin. 2005. *In Every Tongue: The Racial and Ethnic Diversity of the Jewish People*. San Francisco: Institute for Jewish and Community Research.

United Jewish Communities. 2003. *The National Jewish Population Survey 2000–01: Strength, Challenge and Diversity in the American Jewish Population*. New York: United Jewish

Communities; Storrs, CT: Mandell L. Berman Institute—North American Jewish Data Bank at the University of Connecticut.

Walker, Rebecca. 2001. *Black, White, and Jewish: Autobiography of a Shifting Self.* New York: Riverhead Books.

Waters, Mary. 1999. *Black Identities: West Indian Immigrant Dreams and American Realities.* New York: Russell Sage Foundation; Cambridge: Harvard University Press.

Winters, Loretta I., and Herman L. DeBose, eds. 2005. *New Faces in a Changing America: Multiracial Identity in the 21st Century.* Thousand Oaks, CA: Sage.

PART II

Racialized Religion

CHAPTER 5

Second-Generation Latin@
Faith Institutions and Identity Formations

MILAGROS PEÑA AND EDWIN I. HERNÁNDEZ

My parents were from the island [Puerto Rico]. I was born and
raised here, my first language was Spanish, but my first method of
thinking was English. I grew up speaking Spanish, but I grew up
thinking English. And that is a major challenge for me. But as I
have gone into the ministry I have realized that I am dealing with a
diversity of community that is—I don't think you would find anywhere else in the world. . . . And it's a diversity of a reality that is a
tremendous challenge to try to find the common ground in ministry focus that to me is probably the biggest challenge.
—a Los Angeles pastor and community organizer

The minister quoted in the epigraph, whose parents came from Puerto Rico
after World War II, explains the complexity of being a second-generation
Latino. He straddles two worlds but is also pulled to be deeply engaged in
Hispanic ministries despite the challenges of doing so. The pastor's remark
sheds light on a second generation of Latinos and Latinas who remain drawn
to their cultural heritage, which is also reinforced in a faith expression committed to serve the needs of the community. In fact, this chapter argues that
the place where first and second generations, including cross-ethnic Hispanic groups, converge is in social ministry programs precisely because of
their call to community action. We argue that despite the challenges facing Hispanic ministry programs, Latin@s[1] find common ground in social
issues and the community needs that affect them. The outreach programs
supported by faith-based organizations highlighted in this chapter illustrate
examples of what draws second and third generations to remain identified
within Latin@ faith communities.

Latin@ Identities Inform Faith in Action

As a Latino pastor from New York City described it, his church facilitates faith, but it does more because of its constituency. It has to address social needs that cut across Latin@ generations and ethnicities.

> Here we have an after-school center, we have youth programs, we run our own charter school. We have a gymnasium, body building, we have martial arts, we have high school equivalency, we have ESL, we have SAT preparation. We have a boxing club, we have dance, and we have hip-hop. . . . We have several basketball leagues, football leagues, baseball leagues. We have a welfare-to-work program, we have a computer lab. So pretty much there's a lot we offer.

With this strategy Hispanic pastors throughout New York City and elsewhere in the United States have infused into their faiths and identity formations ways of positioning themselves as second-generation, third-generation, and beyond immigrant Latin@s. A Mexican American Bronx pastor describes why these programs are necessary in his neighborhood:

> We're repeating the Puerto Rican experience here. "La experiencia Mexicana" [the Mexican experience], it's almost the same . . . bilingual issues, kids are not learning in school, the parents don't know how to demand accountability from teachers, they're intimidated by schools. So it's like repeating the Puerto Rican experience all over again because the people are going through the same. The same issues come up in the social ministry demands, particularly for the children.

Consequently, for this pastor and others, faith-based community action ministries serve as pull factors or cultural reinforcement agents not only for immigrants but for their children who have to navigate identities and social realities that cut across generations.

Building on observations and interviews, this chapter focuses on two points. The first highlights how community organizing motivated by faith empowers pan-Latin@ community engagement efforts. The second reveals how these ethnic identity formations activate religious institutions within Latin@ ethnic communities to support particular social ministry programs. They draw in religious leaders who respond inspired by faith articulations made relevant by the needs and demands of their communities. In this chapter, the link between communities' faith and ethnic articulations reveal not a compartmentalized view of faith versus ethnicity but rather a reality in which one reflects on or informs the other.

Faith and Identities Expressed in Action

Political scientist Catherine E. Wilson notes that the "definition of religious identity politics suggests that it is both the context and content of religious beliefs, values, and culture that inform social and political action" (2008, 63). Sharing this view and the view of a number of New York City Latin@ pastors, a Brooklyn district pastor noted that good ministry is "holistic." He added, "By that I mean that it ministers to not only the spiritual needs but the social, economic, political, and cultural needs [of the community]." Therefore, by examining Latin@ activism in faith-based organizations, one is able to see how faith, religion, and ethnic identity come together. It is a dynamic that underscores how peoples informed by their faith articulate their identities by engaging their social locations within the larger society.

Nowhere has this dynamic become more evident than in the ways that second, third, and later generations of Latin@ descendants are engaging the social justice theologies of their faith traditions. A Manhattan youth pastor, whose parents came from Puerto Rico, and friends of his started their own youth ministry organization because they saw needs particular to their generation. "The story of our organization is fairly unique in that a group of us from the projects, who had no money, no staff, no school, no equipment, started a youth center purely on volunteer efforts. Nine and half years later, it still operates and has grown." Despite some people being pushed out by neighborhood gentrification and others leaving as their economic circumstances improve, the pastor noted, "[Our generation comes back because they] still have roots and ties to the neighborhood, and so they come back to the church." This sense of community serves to shed light on faith organizations, most notably Latin@ faith-based organizations (FBOs) and the spaces they provide for ethnic generations to articulate and engage their community and culture. New York City serves as a perfect site to explore these relationships.

The Site

New York City is a place where immigration and migration have defined the Latin@ contexts. Though the observations and discussion in this chapter focus on New York City, the research that informs this discussion is part of a larger study based on ethnographic and in-depth surveys of Latin@-serving community faith-based organizations located in four major metropolitan areas in the United States (Chicago, Los Angeles, Miami, and New York City).[2] The majority of our sample (thirty-six respondents, or 80 percent) expressly included faith or some other religious identification in their self-definitions. Twenty-eight organizations (62 percent) in our study described themselves as faith-related nonprofits, five were religious congregations (four with a 501(c) and one without), and three were agencies officially affiliated with a denomination. All but two of the nine organizations that reported being formally unaffiliated with any religious body had some other connection to religious communities. Three were started in a congregation but have since branched out on their own, three have no formal affiliation but have leaders who self-identify as religious, and another indicated that a Mainline Protestant denomination bears fiduciary responsibility for them.

In trying to identify our sample's religious identifications, several of the leaders we interviewed were reluctant to categorize their organizations as either religious or secular and indicated that even if they do define themselves as faith-based, their chief concern is to serve whoever comes through their doors.[3] The emphasis on inclusiveness was such that one respondent insisted his organization be charted as simply "community based" as he explained his resistance to our categories: "When you're a community-based organization, you are related to your community. . . . So we relate to our community." In fact, the nature of affiliations and relationships with religious institutions varied such within our sample that it became clear that Latin@ FBOs did not position their outreach as Protestant or Catholic. Over a third (36 percent) of our organizations were formally unaffiliated with any agency, administrative body, or congregation of any particular denomination or tradition. One-third (33 percent) were somehow affiliated with the Catholic Church, 22 percent with Evangelical or Pentecostal Protestant denominations or congregations, and 9 percent with Mainline Protestant congregations or institutions. However, what became clear in interviews was the emphasis Latin@ pastors placed on the faith-inspired service mission of their outreach and the larger needs of their communities. Thus, New York City serves as a case for illustrating how the children of immigrants engage their ethnic communities through faith organizations and in doing so affirm their ethnic locations by embedding themselves in the life and leadership of the religious-cultural institutions of their ethnic communities.

New York City is particularly important for this discussion—it is a city defined by old and new immigrants and their descendants. Most ethnic studies have focused on immigrants, and only recently has attention turned to those generations who are not immigrant (Díaz-Stevens 1993; Hernández,

Peña, and Davis 2006; Lopez 2002; Villafañe et al. 1995; Wilson 2008). There is also the recognition that Latin@ communities have diversified to make a New York City that today includes Dominicans, Mexicans, and Central and South Americans (Abu-Lughod 1994a). But at nearly a third (32 percent) of the New York Latin@ population, Puerto Ricans are still the single most represented national origin found among New York Latin@s. Since 1990, when nearly one out of every two Latin@s in New York was Puerto Rican (47 percent according to the 2000 U.S. Census), the increase in persons of Mexican descent has been significant (about 12 percent of Hispanics[4] in New York).

Lived Religion in Context

Many FBOs are in ethnic communities that are receiving streams of new immigration. While much of the immigration scholarship focuses on the immigrants themselves (the first generation), this chapter highlights the communities they move into and how persisting social issues in the community mark second- and third-generation children of immigrants. Through interviews with pastors and lay leaders we saw that Latin@ ministries focused outreach opportunities around engaging their faith communities in community social problems that included but extended beyond immigrant needs. Directly and indirectly, the research allowed us to explore the role of FBOs in community persistence. We extend Pierre Bourdieu's conceptualization of social capital to understand the place of Latin@ social ministries as both community activism and faith in action, in which churches are called to a "lived religion"[5] rather than being mere substitutes for ethnicity. Latin@ social ministries engage social theologies enmeshed in the ethnic social context, identities, politics, and faith articulations of their communities. As Villafañe et al. note, "The brokenness of society, the scriptural missional mandate, and the Spirit's love constrain us to feed the hungry, visit the sick and prisoners, shelter the homeless and poor—to express God's love in social concerns" (1995, 14). As the pastors quoted earlier in this chapter underscore, FBOs become the spaces where faith and ethnicity engage the consciences and identities for second- and third-generation Latin@s.

In illustrating the point, Catherine Wilson (2008) argues that in Latin@ FBOs a new generation of liberationists—second, third, and beyond—are at work. For example, Reverend Ray Rivera, founder of the Latino Pastoral Action Center (LPAC) in New York City, was influenced by Pentecostalism and Orlando Costas's theology of "Misión Integral," which entails community ministry with "a two-pronged approach: (1) preaching the gospel and (2) taking into account the cultural, structural, and institutional context of the times" (Wilson 2008, 79). Similarly, Reverend Luis Cortés, founder of Nueva Esperanza in Philadelphia, was influenced by Robert McAfee Brown's writings, black liberation theologian James Cone, and Costas's teachings when Cortés moved to Philadelphia. In fact, he studied under and served with Costas when he became professor of theology and cofounder of what is known today as Palmer Theological Seminary in Philadelphia (ibid., 81). In other words, FBOs rooted in any number of church traditions are an outgrowth of the second, third, and beyond generations of Latin@ leaders. They mobilize religious institutions to support various social ministries that are rooted in a faith in action deeply embedded in Latin@ ethnic identity and religious values. In engaging their religious institutions in this manner these second, third, and beyond generations are mobilizing significant resources for their ethnic communities.[6] Gastón Espinosa et al., in a national survey they conducted, showed that "4 percent of Latinos want their churches or religious organizations to aid undocumented immigrants even when providing such help is illegal, and 61 percent believe that immigrants who arrive in the United States illegally should be eligible for government assistance such as Medicaid or welfare" (2003, 17). In other words, one's social location informs one's "lived faith" and shapes it for the larger church community. To illustrate the point further, we offer the following community contexts and excerpts from interviews with Latin@ FBO leaders we interviewed in New York City.

"Beyond Bondage": Bridging Capital

Juan Voz,[7] director of the faith-based prison outreach program Beyond Bondage, articulated how he sees the link between his ministry and his engagement in the community in reintegrating Latinos who spent time in prison. "It's our faith that moves us to do the [community] work. . . . Our work is inspired by the Bible." The organization and its mission is "entirely based around the book of Exodus: bondage, wilderness, and Promised Land."

> It is actually working through the wilderness on which the entire model is built, and with that the six-step programs focused on family, vocation, education, substance abuse, addictive personalities, and being holistically fit. . . . We looked at those experiences in Exodus, the Book of Exodus, [based on a people who experienced] bondage, wilderness, and Promised Land. [For our work] bondage means prison, wilderness represents prison thinking. We are promoting thinking "beyond bondage."

Beyond Bondage is in Spanish Harlem, or what is known as "El Barrio." It is situated in Manhattan's District 11. Placing communities by districts in New York City is important because in New York's politics and distribution of resources, districts define the political boundaries of a community and its representation. District representations are also driven by their demographic composition and depend on the capacity of their constituency to mobilize its social capital for the community. The more economically and politically disenfranchised the community, the more challenges it faces in meeting local needs. Spanish Harlem covers an area that extends from about 98th Street to the south up to about 125th Street to the north, where black Harlem begins, and it includes from the East River to the east over to about 5th Avenue to the west. Though Spanish Harlem is experiencing gentrification, with new condo construction for those who can afford them, the area is still mostly blue collar, working to underemployed poor, and predominantly made up Puerto Ricans, who were among the first Hispanics to settle into this area of the city. Most of the area surrounding Beyond Bondage is composed of old poorly maintained brownstones or public section 8 housing known to locals simply as "the projects." The 2000 U.S. Census data presented in table 5.1 show the racial and ethnic composition of Manhattan's District 11 compared to the rest of the city.

Local mom-and-pop businesses are visible throughout the community and show that this area is still a mostly Puerto Rican neighborhood, given the names of the bodegas (grocery stores), with signs of the area increasingly becoming more mixed, including Dominicans and Mexicans, given the names of other local businesses.

Table 5.1

Single Race, Nonhispanic: (by percentage)	Manhattan District 11	All of Manhattan	All of NYC
White	7.3%	45.8%	35.0%
Black / African American	35.7%	15.3%	24.5%
American Indian and Alaska Native	0.2%	0.2%	0.2%
Asian	2.7%	9.3%	9.7%
Native Hawaiian and other Pacific Islander	0%	0%	0.0%
Some other Race	0.3%	0.4%	0.7%
Hispanic Origin (of any race)	52.1%	27.2%	27.0%

Though the Hispanic demographic is changing to include more Hispanic groups, according to the census, signs of the predominance of Puerto Rican residents are still visible in other ways. On one street corner near Beyond Bondage is a plaque that was put there by Hope Community Inc.; it reads, "Rebuilding neighborhoods one block at a time." Near the plaque is a mural highlighting community activities. The mural was painted by James de la Vega and is titled La Calle de Pedro Pietri (Pedro Pietri's street); Pietri is a well-known Puerto Rican New York poet. Other murals dot the neighborhood, celebrating residents greeting each other, playing musical instruments, and playing dominoes. It is here in this environment that Beyond Bondage has opened its doors. Beyond Bondage in fact is an outgrowth of this community and the Pentecostal church that was called to be present to the young people of the community and to address the prison reality facing its congregants and their families. For Beyond Bondage, the goal is to keep young people from ending up in prison or returning to prison if they have fallen to the lure of the streets; getting them to work and to integrate with the community and their family is critical. Beyond Bondage represents the ideals of a second, third, and beyond generation that looks to bridge faith ideals and church presence into an ethnic community's reality that is as much about the church and its teachings as it is about where the church is located and the community it serves. This Pentecostal-inspired ministry focuses on holistic approaches to empowering individuals within the community. However, the approach is not unique to Beyond Bondage. It is a strategy adopted by other Latin@ FBOs because of its emphasis on empowering Latin@ communities.

Latin@ FBOs Offer Cultural and Social Capital

In recent years, a number of scholars, particularly Ram Cnaan and Stephanie Boddie (2002) and Helen Rose Ebaugh and Janet Chafetz (2000), have focused attention on immigrant and ethnic FBOs, the services they provide, the financial value they have for local governments, and their role in the mobilization of social capital in local communities, particularly their potential in the arena of delivering social services. FBOs also offer cultural and social capital that provides opportunities for connecting generations through programs and activities. Bridging across generations can be seen in the birth and work of Generation Xcel. Generation Xcel grew out of a 501(c)(3) nonreligious not-for-profit called Community Solutions, Inc. (CSI), which was formed in 1996 by a group of residents from Manhattan's Lower East Side (a heavily Latin@ area of New York City) who partnered with Rev. Richard Del Rio, senior pastor of Abounding Grace Ministries, and his son Jeremy

Del Rio. At the start, CSI adopted a mission statement, developed an action plan, and established, as its first initiative, a comprehensive youth outreach program called Generation Xcel.

Thirteen young people joined Jeremy Del Rio, then 21 years of age, to design and staff Xcel as volunteers. At the outset, they were instructed to think constructively about neighborhood problems and creatively about solutions. They then harnessed that creativity and were challenged to do something to implement their ideas and strategies. Generation Xcel became their something, their vehicle for community outreach and renewal. (Generation Xcel, "Xcel History," http://www.generationxcel. com/1history.htm; accessed February 25, 2010)

Prior to CSI and Generation Xcel, the Latino Pastoral Action Center (LPAC) in the Bronx borough of New York City, founded in 1992 by Rev. Dr. Raymond Rivera, instituted a series of similar strategies to cut across generations as part of a holistic ministry model that would build on what it identified as the pillars of the community (families, schools, community-based organizations, and churches/houses of worship). Similarly, in a Catholic context, the Asociación Tepeyac de New York, under the leadership of Jesuit Brother Joel Magallan Reyes, SJ, in 1997 focused attention on the growing number of young Mexicans in New York City. One of Asociación Tepeyac's outreach efforts, the Guadalupano Center, follows labor, immigration, and tenant-landlord cases, as well as coordinating monthly reunions and cultural events such as the Festival de la Expresión and La Feria del Sol (Asociación Tepeyac, "Brief History of Asociación Tepeyac de New York," http://www. tepeyac.org/eng/about_us/history.html; accessed November 27, 2011). The emphasis on youth is critical. Latin@ FBOs work in urban contexts with the highest poverty rates in the country, including high rates of high school dropout, crime, and under- and unemployment, as well as the worst performing schools and least affordable housing in the country. These are direct consequences of persistent residential segregation and of the overrepresentation of Latin@s among the urban poor. Adding to the stress is the continual arrival of new immigrants who together with earlier established groups have limited civic skills to confront their communities' marginalization.

Latin@ FBOs are also "moral communities" (Wilson 2008, 221), meaning that Latin@ faith communities call on the collective conscience to invest, as the LPAC literature underscores, in the most vulnerable—the poor, the marginalized, the widow, the orphan, the stranger, and so on (Latino Pastoral Action Center, "About Us," http://www.lpacministries.com/365700.ihtml;

accessed February 25, 2010). One could simply be impressed by the fact that the Latino Pastoral Action Center in 2007 had total assets of $6.7 million and an operating budget of $2.5 million (Wilson 2008, 97), with access to approximately three hundred clergy in its immediate network and a mailing list of two thousand (ibid., 98). But as Wilson (2008) notes, this is only one side of what FBOs are about. A faith community that is truly engaged in its ethnic struggles does not come to substitute its religious identity with an ethnic one but rather reflects ethnicity as it becomes engaged in addressing its social and cultural concerns. Thus, ethnic communities, both immigrant and later generations, engage and claim for themselves a faith lived experience that blurs any notion of which generation has come to claim which, as each works to lift the other. We offer a perspective on the importance of FBOs in social contexts of ethnic communities and their generations in poor, gentrifying, and ever-growing ethnic neighborhoods, including an understanding of how their faith communities have been drawn into and shaped and transformed by their local narratives.

Empower the Urban: Moral Community

The Lower East Side of Manhattan, in another of the five boroughs that make up New York City, like the other boroughs has undergone tremendous change with the arrival of new immigrants and young professionals to the city. These changes have impacted established Latin@ neighborhoods such as the Lower East Side and transformed other neighborhoods. Janet Abu-Lughod, in her introduction to From Urban Village to East Village: The Battle for the Lower East Side (1994b), notes the population shifts and the impact of gentrification (which in this area has primarily served to displace much of the area's Latin@ population). Several Latin@ faith-based organizations in New York City work to confront the social problems created by gentrification. Empower the Urban, for example, is one of twelve organizations in the Lower East Side whose leadership is involved in working with Nueva Esperanza. Empower the Urban occupies the ground floor of a housing project and offers a number of social services particularly to the elderly, but its primary focus is the housing problem facing displaced Hispanics. Manhattan's District 3 covers an area that before World War II was populated mainly by European immigrants, mostly Jewish, Polish, and Ukrainian. By the 1950s, the neighborhood had experienced an influx of Puerto Ricans during their great migration from the island of Puerto Rico in search of work. Today this district is very diverse: there are still remnants of the older European immigrant children who stayed in the district, as well as the Puerto Ricans who

Table 5.2

Single Race, Nonhispanic: (by percentage)	Manhattan District 3	All of Manhattan	All of NYC
White	28.2%	45.8%	35.0%
Black / African American	7.1%	15.3%	24.5%
American Indian and Alaska Native	0.1%	0.2%	0.2%
Asian	35.2%	9.3%	9.7%
Native Hawaiian and other Pacific Islander	0%	0%	0.0%
Some other Race	0.4%	0.4%	0.7%
Two or More Races, Nonhispanic	2.1%	1.9%	2.8%
Hispanic Origin (of any race)	26.9%	27.2%	27.0%

came in the '50s and an ever-expanding Chinatown that also is included in the district. As table 5.2 shows, the ethnic and racial demographic shifts in this area of the city, particularly in the past decade, are reflected in the 2000 Census, which shows that Asians have overtaken Hispanics as the largest minority group in Manhattan's District 3.

What the U.S. Census is not designed to show, but what is still an important part of this community, is the religious ethnic presence in this area. Though we focus on the Latin@ faith communities and their connection to the neighborhoods across generations, when one walks the area, it is clear that Latin@ faith communities are not the only ethnic communities that continue to engage their communities beyond the first generation. Jewish synagogues, eastern European Christian churches, and Buddhist temples reflect the history of the ethnic diversity in the district. The synagogues, churches, and temples tell a similar story to the one Latin@s' second, third, and beyond immigrant generations share with regard to being engaged in faith communities embedded in the lives of their ethnic communities.

The present-day poverty of the Latino community poses one of the main challenges for Empower the Urban. Rev. Juan describes the reality of the Lower East Side in the following way:

> This area here is kind of mixed, though there is still a large presence of Hispanics. There is a larger presence of the Chinese. But there is also a large presence of the Jewish community. I mean, at one time it was all Jewish, and then that changed, and this area remains probably the last remnants of that Jewish community. But the Lower East Side, it kind of represents the city as a whole in terms of its ethnic makeup and ethnic groups, national groups, cultures and stuff like that. . . . But I would say that there's, you

know, again there's still a strong presence of the Hispanic community. The
Hispanics by and large live in the public housing projects. And the Lower
East Side has a lot of public housing.

Rev. Juan described the leadership of Empower the Urban as Hispanic,
emphasizing its importance as "probably in this area [meaning the immediate vicinity] the only Hispanic organization that exists." He added, "Most
of the programs that we have had have been around housing advocacy and
have been focused on working with the seniors and working with the youth."
He underscored that the outreach was intentionally focused on the Hispanic
community and its needs, particularly because the Lower East Side offers so
little to an already economically disenfranchised community. Empower the
Urban exemplifies a faith-based community outreach organization that gives
voice to two of the area's most vulnerable Latin@ populations in the city, the
elderly and youth. Empower the Urban not only bridges generational social
needs but positions itself as a voice for one of New York City's most vulnerable ethnic populations today.

The Future: Challenges of Limited Capital

Not too far from Empower the Urban in another section of the Lower East
Side is The Future, a street ministry that was begun in the early 1980s by
native New Yorker Rev. Jose, who is the son of parents who came from
Puerto Rico. In Rev. Jose's words, the ministry was started by his parents
"as an evangelistic outreach ministry. It was inspired by a verse in the book
of Romans. Romans 5:20 says, 'Where sin abounds, grace abounds much
more.'" Rev. Jose recalled,

> Their theory was to experience God's grace, [so] then they should find a
> lot of sin. And so their method of doing so was to ask the NYPD [New
> York Police Department] where the worst drug spots were in the city, and
> then they went there—figuring if they found a lot of drugs, they'd find a
> lot of sin and, by extension, experience God's abounding grace. And so we
> began in '82 as primarily a street ministry. Eventually their ministry grew
> to a point that they needed space where they in particular could engage in
> investing in transforming the lives of young people.

The need for space for their growing ministry led to renting from an old
immigrant Euro-ethnic church in the district. They became a Hispanic ministry housed within a Euro-ethnic church, where the relationship intersects

only at the level of renting space. This practice of ethnic churches selling space to other ethnic groups has become part of surviving, as church members move away from the neighborhood and thus away from the church.

Nancy Ammerman noted this phenomenon in the research she conducted for her book Congregation and Community (1996). In her research, she found some congregations being revived by the influx of new members, but those were congregations where new members became part of the church. Renting space establishes a different dynamic. The ministry of The Future, for example, exists separate and distinct from the Euro-ethnic church whose space it rents. Rev. Jose described the arrangement by saying, "Even though the church physically is here, most of the members of the church come from the Lower East Side or have roots in the Lower East Side." He explains that "because of the ongoing gentrification of the Lower East Side, a lot of people have been forced out of the community, and other people have voluntarily moved out as their economic realities have changed. But they still have roots and ties to the neighborhood, and so they come back to the church." By "church," Rev. Jose means the Hispanic church renting from the other ethnic group. This dynamic is important to note because it reflects a desire in the second generation to continue to pursue ministries and churches that are embedded in their communities. These ministries are a reflection of the fact that in a number of New York City Latin@ communities, the second and third generations still find themselves in highly segregated Latin@ poor communities.

According to Arun Peter Lobo et al.,

Between 1970 and 1990, Puerto Rican neighborhoods in the Bronx and Brooklyn expanded outward as adjacent areas experienced Puerto Rican for white replacement. But more than 40 years after Puerto Ricans initially began settling in New York City in significant numbers, two-thirds lived in all-minority tracts that were among the poorest in the city, resulting in continued high levels of segregation from whites. (2002, 721)

Today Dominicans and Mexicans are moving in large numbers to share in this formerly primarily Puerto Rican–dominant enclave and its challenges. However, Lobo et al. do note that "there is a substantial outflow of Puerto Ricans who leave the city for its suburbs and states such as Florida and Pennsylvania, and then tend to live in more integrated communities" (2002, 723). But as some Puerto Ricans are able to out-migrate, a majority remain, adding to a process of ethnic succession that is under way, "with Dominicans succeeding Puerto Ricans across the West Bronx, and Mexicans succeeding

Puerto Ricans in East Harlem and Sunset Park" (ibid.). These are also socioeconomically stressed areas of the city and places where Latin@ social capital is weak, which is why FBOs become critical to the first and second generations in the community.

We also highlight The Future to focus on the challenges faced by social ministries in Latin@-serving ethnic enclaves in mobilizing resources for their social ministries. Resources or social capital exist or are mobilized for social ministries in creative ways. However, the community's second and third generations that persist in socioeconomic marginalization face limits, as Rev. Jose noted:

> In terms of communicating to donors, fund development, administrative, bookkeeping, and everything else, it's the same three people pretty much that have to do everything. As a result, there are a lot of things that we believe strongly would be better done as a collaboration. But our collaborators are in the same boat, generally being underresourced and overstressed. So to be able to connect and find something where, you know, if we could pool all of our limited resources around a common issue, that would be a far greater benefit for all. It just requires intentionality, and it requires follow-up.

Rev. Jose cited the response to 9/11 by local churches, including his, as a shining moment for churches in a city that came together to face the city's needs. He said, "Organizing disaster relief response, that was really national in scope, but also for local community agencies that were very close to Ground Zero, we had the opportunity to take the lead on a lot of those programs." He also highlighted the effectiveness and the substance of the collaboration at the time. He felt he was part of a generation called to be about something more than succeeding in a career but rather to answer to a call to respond to the needs of his community.

Yet 9/11 did not change the fact that The Future's ministry is one that continues to rent space in another church and does not extend beyond that arrangement with that particular church. But the youth ministry of The Future appeals to non-Latin@ youth who have chosen to come to New York City as part of their church service. Rev. Jose sees himself as part of a Latin@ generation that can cross cultural divides, both in terms of his ethnicity and Pentecostal roots. Other Latin@ FBOs also show signs that greater collaborations across ethnic and racial divides do exist and in fact underscore one of the changes that second, third, and beyond generations have brought to their vision for a "lived faith."

La Posada: Inclusive and Collaborative

The second, third, and beyond generations see their social locations beyond themselves and their ethnic communities even as they articulate a Latin@ faith identity. In fact, miles from The Future is New York City's Brooklyn borough District 8 and La Posada. As shown in table 5.3, based on the 2000 U.S. Census, in this district, African Americans by far represent the largest constituency.

One could argue that the reality of this demographic in the district shapes how and why local churches approach their outreach ministries. La Posada's ministry focuses on moving individuals from substance dependency through spirituality/religious activity, individual and group counseling, psychological assessment, vocational counseling, and recreation. As one of the program's pamphlets notes, it addresses the whole person. There are programs for women as well as for men. Since 1997, La Posada realized one of its great-est goals: the men's program expanded from a twenty-resident facility to the current site, with a fifty-resident capacity. Rather than describe the ministry in terms of outreach to any one group, one member of the staff underscored the primacy of the ministry's mission as "faith-based, Christ-centered." The "faith-based, Christ-centered" call of this ministry is discourse driven by a targeted local social need but also reflects an articulated commitment to a multiethnic and racially diverse local faith community that makes up Brook-lyn's District 8, of which only slightly over 10 percent are Hispanic. Multilin-gual pamphlets, events, and religious services reflect the organization's diver-sity and cross-ethnic and racial collaborations.

Adding to this broader view of Hispanic ministries as entering into col-laborative social ministries is an FBO in the South Bronx that works as an indigenous, multicultural, cross-denominational urban youth ministry. It

Table 5.3

Single Race, Nonhispanic: (by percentage)	Brooklyn District 8	All of Brooklyn	All of NYC
White	6.8%	34.7%	35.0%
Black / African American	78%	34.4%	24.5%
American Indian and Alaska Native	0.2%	0.2%	0.2%
Asian	1.6%	7.5%	9.7%
Native Hawaiian and other Pacific Islander	0.1%	0%	0.0%
Some other Race	0.4%	0.7%	0.7%
Hispanic Origin (of any race)	10.4%	19.8%	27.0%

equips and empowers youth and youth workers to bring the transforming presence of the Gospel to urban high schools, colleges, and communities. It also envisions itself to be a model of how young lives and church communities living under its vision of Christianity can usher in "God's Kingdom" in urban centers in the United States and worldwide. The Coalition, as we refer to it here, serves as a network for several groups as part of its vision and work with local youth. It is housed on the top floor of a brownstone building that belongs to a Hispanic church that began the FBO. According to Pastor Maria, the immediate neighborhood is part of a district with the largest concentration of Hispanics in New York City, with about two-thirds of those being of Puerto Rican descent and the other third being made up of Dominicans and other Hispanics; there are also some African Americans and other economically marginalized whites. Pastor Maria described her ministry as serving an area of the South Bronx that has the poorest district in the United States, "with conditions you would find in the Third World." She added, "District 1, which is the district we're in right now, is the poorest district in the United States. There are more issues in this section of the city; they're likened to Third World country issues. I mean, it's really that bad. There are health issues, citizenship issues; I mean, there are a lot of issues." The 2000 U.S. Census ethnic and racial composition for District 1 is captured in table 5.4 and underscores the size of the Hispanic population in this district. Most of the residents have lived there for several generations, highlighting the social reality for the generations of Latin@s beyond their parents' initial arrival to these communities. Few have been able to change their social circumstances.

Despite the challenges that Hispanics face in the district, the social landscape for the collaborative and more inclusive strategies that Latin@ churches are embracing in this and other parts of New York City is part of a

Table 5.4

Single Race, Nonhispanic: (by percentage)	Bronx District 1	All of Bronx	All of NYC
White	1.3%	14.5%	35.0%
Black / African American	25.9%	31.2%	24.5%
American Indian and Alaska Native	0.3%	0.3%	0.2%
Asian	0.5%	2.9%	9.7%
Native Hawaiian and other Pacific Islander	0%	0%	0.0%
Some other Race	0.2%	0.6%	0.7%
Two or More Races, Nonhispanic	0.9%	2%	2.8%
Hispanic Origin (of any race)	70.8%	48.4%	27.0%

larger national trend involved not only in youth ministry but in other ministries, including work with the homeless, families in crises, and so on. In a report titled "Compassion on the Frontlines: An Assessment of Latino-Serving Faith-Based Organizations," published by the Institute for Latino Studies at Notre Dame, we found that 43 percent (or nineteen organizations in our national study) offer between 61–100 percent of their social services collaboratively, and 21 percent (or nine organizations) offer between 41–60 percent of their services in collaboration with other Hispanic and non-Hispanic FBOs (Grenier et al. 2008).

On average, Latin@ organizations do nearly half (48 percent) of their social service in collaboration with other organizations. The majority of organizations in our sample (thirty-one, or 72 percent) are based in communities with substantial Latin@ populations. But nearly a quarter (23 percent) operate in mixed ethnic neighborhoods, and just 5 percent said they work in a predominantly non-Latino area. Our larger sample of Latino-serving FBOs offer nearly half of their social services collaboratively, which indicates the importance that partner organizations and networks have to such groups. Nueva Esperanza has identified the need to train Latin@ religious leadership because they are at the front lines for mobilizing resources for the Hispanic community. Pastor Francisco, who provides another social services ministry not too far from Pastor Maria's ministry in the South Bronx, said the following about the importance of national organizations such as Nueva Esperanza:

> I think that Nueva Esperanza is what our people have been looking for, for years. And I think that if these folks stay on track, the Latino community is going to have a voice like never before over the next ten years. I think the black church is organized; I think that African Americans in this country have organized. It's time for our people to organize! You know, we're the least respected, least educated, most impoverished, and I think that that season and that age is changing now with organizations such as Nueva Esperanza.

Pastor Francisco points to the fact that the greatest barriers to developing more and effective collaborative relationships across Latin@ and other FBOs were lack of time by staff to dedicate to the task, a lack of contacts and opportunities, and difficulty accessing information about other organizations.

Final Comment

Latin@s, those who have newly arrived and those who have lived within U.S. borders for generations, are reshaping the U.S. cultural, political, economic, and social landscape. As faith engages the lives of individuals, religious institutions through their leaders become part of this dynamic. Thus, religious affiliation continues to provide a means by which ethnic groups articulate their ethnic identities by engaging their social locations. Recent demonstrations through-out the United States have unveiled the multigenerational and multiethnic face mobilizing against anti-immigrant and anti-ethnic legislation. Contributors to the book *Religion and Social Justice for Immigrants* (Hondagneu-Sotelo 2007) note in the collection of essays that organizing around immigrants' rights not only has become a matter of faith and justice called to action but is also as much about addressing racism, economic issues, and engaging the politics of diaspora and affirmation of ethnic communities. For many Latin@ religious community leaders who are the second, third, and beyond generation, their faith-ethnic identity is commingled into a self-identity that is nurtured in a continuum of family and local community that includes churches and faith-based organizations. As one pastor in an interview said in talking about what he thought good ministry looked like,

> Seeing my grandparents and my parents and their spiritual lives, their religious life, prayer, and talking about God . . .—so family is a given, but I think growing up poor, all our social activities when I was a child were evolved around the church. . . . My whole world aside from going to school was the church. . . . So good ministry I would think would imply that a service is going to be provided by individuals or by others who have an understanding of the cultural dynamic, the unique needs of that community with which it will serve.

In our view, this approach for good ministry reveals a faith path that is as much about identifying a connection to the Latin@ community as it is about being a person of faith.

NOTES

1. The use of the term "Latin@s" is gender neutral and refers to communities that include shared histories and cultures with Mexico, Central and South America, the Caribbean, and Spanish-speaking areas of the United States that were formed as part of U.S. expansion.
2. The research and analysis were funded by the Pew Charitable Trusts to complement their Networks of Faith (NOF) project—a two-year initiative designed to increase the capacity of Latin@-serving faith-based organizations through training sessions and networking events (Grenier et al. 2008).
3. The notable exceptions were the seven organizations in our sample whose chief purpose is evangelistic, most often involving religious or theological education.

4. The term "Hispanic" is used by the U.S. Census to denote people of Spanish ancestry. There is awareness among census takers of the limitations of this classification, in terms of both ethnic and racial identifications in the Latin@ communities. Also, some Latin@s identify as Hispanics, and others use multiple ways to self-identify. Throughout this chapter we primarily use "Latin@s" as part of recognizing a growing need to use better terminology to refer to Hispanics, but we also use the term "Hispanic," recognizing its multiple meanings within the communities.

5. "Lived religion" is understood here to mean faith in action. In Latin@ faith communities, the expectation for a "lived religion" is rooted in diverse articulations of liberation theology and the specific meanings it brings to local social realities and the struggles for justice that those social realities inspire. Benjamín Valentín (2002) provides a solid mapping of Latin@ U.S. theologies and their call for faiths in action and what it means in the U.S. Latin@ context. A collection of essays in Eldin Villafañe et al. (1995) urges specifically a reaffirmation to urban ministry—a persistent need in Latin@ communities.

6. Drawing on the Pew Hispanic Center's 2002 and 2004 surveys of Latino political attitudes, our research shows that in Latin@ faith communities, U.S.-born Latin@s are civically engaged at higher rates than their foreign-born counterparts are. We believe that some of these differences across the generations might be related to their comparative English-speaking skills (Hernández et al. 2007, 21). More important, the surveys show a commitment to a religious social teaching rooted in the liberation theologies and their encouragement to help the poor.

7. The names of individuals and organizations they work for have been changed to maintain their anonymity.

REFERENCES

Abu-Lughod, Janet. 1994a. The Battle for Tompkins Square Park. In *From Urban Village to East Village: The Battle for New York's Lower East Side*, by Janet Abu-Lughod et al., 233–261. Cambridge, MA: Blackwell.

———. 1994b. Welcome to the Neighborhood. In *From Urban Village to East Village: The Battle for New York's Lower East Side*, by Janet Abu-Lughod et al., 17–40. Cambridge, MA: Blackwell.

Ammerman, Nancy T. 1996. *Congregation and Community*. New Brunswick: Rutgers University Press.

Baia, Larissa Ruiz. 2004. Christianity and the Imagined Latino Self: The Emergence of Pan-Ethnic Identity Among Latinos in Paterson, New Jersey. Ph.D. diss., University of Florida.

Cnaan, Ram A., and Stephanie C. Boddie. 2002. *The Invisible Caring Hand: American Congregations and the Provision of Welfare*. New York: NYU Press.

Díaz-Stevens, Ana María. 1993. *Oxcart Catholicism on Fifth Avenue: The Impact of the Puerto Rican Migration upon the Archdiocese of New York*. Notre Dame, IN: University of Notre Dame Press.

Ebaugh, Helen Rose, and Janet Saltzman Chafetz. 2000. *Religion and the New Immigrants: Continuities and Adaptations in Immigrant Congregations*. Lanham, MD: AltaMira.

Espinosa, Gastón, Virgilio Elizondo, and Jesse Miranda. 2003. Hispanic Churches in American Public Life: Summary of Findings. *Interim Reports* 2:1–28. http://latinostudies.nd.edu/pubs/pubs.php?type=5.

Grenier, Guillermo, Rebecca Burwell, Edwin I. Hernández, Michael Mata, Milagros Peña, Marican Popescu, Aida Ramos, and Jeffrey Smith. 2008. Compassion on the Frontlines: An Assessment of Latino-Serving Faith-Based Organizations." Center for the Study of Latino Religion. http://latinostudies.nd.edu/publications/pubs/NOF_report_Final.pdf.

Hernández, Edwin I., Kenneth G. Davis, Milagros Peña, Georgian Schiopu, Jeffrey Smith, and Matthew T. Loveland. 2007. Faith and Values in Action: Religion, Politics, and Social Attitudes among US Latinos/as. *Latino Research* 1:1–41. http://latinostudies.nd.edu/pubs/pubs/RR_2007_11_1.pdf.

Hernández, Edwin I., Milagros Peña, and Kenneth Davis. 2006. *Emerging Voices Urgent Choices: Latino-a Leadership Development from the Pew to the Plaza*. Leiden, The Netherlands: Brill.

Hondagneu-Sotelo, Pierrette. 2007. *Religion and Social Justice for Immigrants*. New Brunswick: Rutgers University Press.

Lobo, Arun Peter, Ronald J. O. Flores, and Joseph J. Salvo. 2002. The Impact of Hispanic Growth on the Racial/Ethnic Composition of New York City Neighborhoods. *Urban Affairs Review* 37 (5): 703–727.

Lopez, Nancy. 2002. *Hopeful Girls, Troubled Boys: Race and Gender Disparity in Urban Education*. New York: Routledge.

Valentín, Benjamín. 2002. *Mapping Public Theology: Beyond Culture, Identity, and Difference*. New York: Trinity.

Villafañe, Eldin, Douglas Hall, Efraín Agosto, and Bruce Jackson. 1995. *Seek the Peace of the City: Reflections on Urban Ministry*. Grand Rapids, MI: Eerdmans.

Wilson, Catherine E. 2008. *The Politics of Latino Faith: Religion, Identity, and Urban Community*. New York: NYU Press.

CHAPTER 6

Latinos and Faith-Based Recovery from Gangs

EDWARD FLORES

> You guys are doing a great job. . . . Never stop what you're doing.
> Reach the gang members . . . because you guys are doing a work
> for God.
> —Ramon, twenty-five, from Victory Outreach, describing what a
> police officer told him

Ramon is an undocumented 1.5-generation immigrant and a former gang member and drug addict. He became addicted to crystal meth, running "missions with his homeboys" and selling drugs with his uncle. However, at the time of my interview with him, he had been involved with Victory Outreach for three years and was a self-described "baby Christian." Upon graduating from the one-year Victory Outreach men's recovery home, he moved to "re-entry," a small room in back of the Victory Outreach church, which he shared with two other men. During our interview, Ramon joyously recounted attending an evangelizing "handball tournament" in the Maravilla projects, a stronghold of East LA gangs. At the tournament, a police officer who self-identified as a Cavalry Chapel member—another Christian church—came up to him and told him not to be discouraged by racist police officers' harassment of Victory Outreach members. Ramon's described his reaction: "He came with the good message, . . . and it was a blessing to me because he was ministering to me, he was preaching to me, you know?" Ramon's involvement with Pentecostal evangelism kept him free from crystal meth addiction and out of gang life, integrating him with the broader East LA community in a sheltered way.

Through symbolically rich social interactions, recovering gang members not only exit gangs but also integrate into new groups. Pentecostalism is one route, in which the process of gang exit is undergirded by the theology of "evangelism through discipleship." Ramon, a baby Christian at a handball event, deepened his Christian faith while sharing it. Victory Outreach, a Pentecostal-evangelical ministry, facilitates recovery through ascetic religious practices and proselytism, such as highly ecstatic worship, fellowship events, and evangelizing missions. Ramon's experience with religion was different from most Mexican immigrants'. Ramon's religiosity was embedded not within a church dense with Mexican immigrants but rather within a Chicano-themed church.

In this chapter, I address the following questions: How do adult Latino men recover from gang life? What are the religious foundations of gang exit? How does this exit from gang life relate to acculturation? I contrast two sites, Victory Outreach, a Pentecostal-evangelical church, as I just described, and Homeboy Industries, a nondenominational nonprofit. I examine how theologies, religious practices, and the context of gang exit coalesce to construct Chicano-themed, faith-based communities into which exiting gang members can integrate. For example, in contrast to Victory Outreach's Pentecostal-evangelical approach, Homeboy Industries facilitates recovery from gang life through clinical rehabilitation, such as with Alcoholics Anonymous-style group therapy, and eclectic spirituality, such as yoga and Native American sweat lodges.

Victory Outreach and Homeboy Industries foster a process of social integration into spiritual communities through symbolic, religious practices.[1] Both Victory Outreach and Homeboy Industries construct Chicano cultural memory through faith-based performances of redemption.[2] However, this process differs markedly, based on the theological differences underpinning each organization. Victory Outreach's approach to gang exit can be characterized as "sheltered redemption," emphasizing ascetic religious practices and proselytism that seek to shelter members from segments of the local community.[3] On the other hand, Homeboy Industries' approach to gang exit can be characterized as "integrative redemption," emphasizing eclectic spirituality and clinical rehabilitation that seek to integrate members into segments of the local community.[4] I argue that recovery from gang life occurs by entry into both sheltered and integrative faith-based groups, offering rich cultural memory and resonating with the gang experience.

Literature Review

   Immigrant assimilation and delinquency have a long history in sociology, dating back to the early 20th-century era of European immigration. Scholars from the early Chicago School of sociology suggested that second-generation immigrant males were at heightened risk for delinquency and street gang membership (Thrasher 1963 [1927]; Whyte 1943). Scholars contended that pockets of concentrated poverty create spaces that give rise to delinquent collectivities of marginalized boys and men. As street gangs became institutionalized in urban America, following the 1970s, scholars working within the Chicago School began to argue that gang activity flourishes within a context of drug markets and lack of social controls (Anderson 1976; Wilson 1987; Taylor 1990; Padilla 1992; Fagan 1996; Venkatesh 1996, 1997; Hagedorn 1998). Second-generation immigrants were especially prone to gang membership, fully integrated into neither their parents' home society nor mainstream American institutions, in a situation called "multiple marginality" (Vigil 1988).
   The segmented assimilation paradigm suggests that racism and increasingly polarized labor markets have detrimentally affected immigrant assimilation more so today than in previous eras (Gans 1992; Portes and Zhou 1993). Today, nonwhite second-generation immigrants are exposed to adolescent countercultures and are vulnerable to downward assimilation into gangs and street life (Zhou and Bankston 1998; Portes and Rumbaut 2001; Lay 2004; Vigil, Yun, and Cheng 2004; R. Smith 2006). However, segmented assimilation theory also contends that immigrant parents can leverage a coethnic community's resources to foster upward assimilation. Immigrants can blend together American educational practices with traditional immigrant values through what is termed "selective acculturation." The immigrant church fosters social cohesion among coethnics, anchoring selective acculturation and upward mobility.
   Immigrant religion takes two general forms: "linear religion," which refers to immigrants' traditional religious practices transported from a home country, and "reactive religion," which refers to religious conversion after immigration and settlement (Portes and Rumbaut 2006 [1990]). These trends in immigrant religiosity flourish in the context of a competitive religious marketplace in America; religious institutions have historically competed for immigrants' membership by providing resources that assist with integration (Hirschman 2004; Sánchez-Walsh 2003; Espinosa, Elizondo, and Miranda 2005; Badillo 2006). In the early 20th century, Protestants such as Jane Addams engaged in philanthropic missions to help disenfranchised

immigrants, while the Catholic Church countered the spread of Protestantism and "Americanization" of immigrants with its own programs to aid homeless and alcoholic immigrants (Moloney 2002). European immigrant integration and religion also had a gang component. For example, Italian parents often sent their boys to Catholic school for disciplinary purposes (Gans 1962). Within America's competitive religious marketplace, the Catholic Church offered European immigrants resources, such as parochial schools and health care, which then facilitated their integration to American society (Lopez 2009). The example of early 20th-century Italian Americans in the Catholic Church illustrates how social integration occurred through linear religion.

In contrast, the example of U.S. Latinos in Pentecostal churches illustrates how social integration occurs through reactive religion. Marginalized from the U.S. Catholic Church and blocked from ascending its ranks, many Latinos turned to Pentecostalism, where they did not experience barriers for advancement (Sánchez-Walsh 2003; Lopez 2009). Storefront Pentecostalism has since become a growing phenomenon among marginalized U.S. and Latin American communities (Stohlman 2007). A recent survey found that for every Latina/o converted to Catholicism, four have converted away from it and that Pentecostalism has won the largest share of converts (Espinosa 2006). Just as with earlier European immigrants, today's Latino and Asian immigrants settle in low-income, marginalized communities but also experience religion as an integrating force. Such religious conversion from Catholicism to evangelical Christianity is an example of reactive religion, or religious conversion after immigration and settlement.

Recent empirical data on immigration and religiosity reveal that "downwardly acculturated" second-generation immigrants experience increased religiosity in adulthood (Portes and Rumbaut 2006 [1990]). Initially, segmented assimilation scholars theorized the beneficial effect of religiosity on immigrant integration by drawing from research on dense coethnic churches (Zhou and Bankston 1998; Zhou, Bankston, and Kim 2002; Chong 1998; Ng 2002; Kim 2004; Cao 2005). However, recent segmented assimilation research has found that low-income, downwardly assimilated second-generation immigrants practice reactive religion through Wicca, Rastafarianism, and evangelical practices (Portes and Rumbaut 2006 [1990]; Fernández-Kelly 2007). Portes and Rumbaut describe "the failure of religious traditions brought from the home country to meet immigrants' needs and the presence of more attractive alternatives" (2006 [1990], 326).

How do second-generation immigrants who previously engaged in delinquency as adolescents experience reactive religion in adulthood? Zhou et al.

(2008) suggest that second-generation immigrants' socioeconomic trajectories may shift as they experience assimilation in adulthood. This process is grounded, in part, through cultural memory that serves as a "dual frame of reference" (Zhou et al. 2008, 51). Zhou et al. state, "Having experienced or being told of economic hardships in the homeland, traumatic escape from war, hunger, and political/religious persecution . . . many children of immigrants, regardless of national origin, can become self-motivated and resilient" (2008, 58). Somewhat similarly, scholars have found that Pentecostal conversion can facilitate Latino men's exit from gang life, even in adulthood (Vigil 1982; León 1998; Vásquez and Marquardt 2003; Sánchez-Walsh 2003; Wolseth 2010). Pentecostal conversion offers a sense of belonging to Chicano gang members who have failed to acculturate to American society and traditional Mexican culture (Vigil 1982). Pentecostalism replaces the gang (Vigil 1982; Vásquez and Marquardt 2003; Wolseth 2010).

This chapter explores two processes central to reactive religion among adult second-generation immigrants with a gang background. First, I explore how recovering gang members seek redemption and social integration, away from gangs and toward a conventional lifestyle. This process is synonymous with segmented assimilation scholars' interest in assimilation in adulthood. Second, I explore how religious conversion centrally organizes this process of reintegration, through the construction of cultural memory and social cohesion with a faith-based group. As the vignette of Ramon illustrated, the themes touched on in Chicano recovery from gang life are the same as those conceptualized by Zhou et al. (2008) as being part of immigrant cultural memory: economic hardship, trauma from violence, persecution, and resilience. However, Chicano recovery from gang life is situated neither in traditional immigrant religion nor in immigrant-centered cultural memory of hardship. Rather, Chicano gang recovery takes place through urban America and Chicano cultural memory of hardship. It is situated within the barrios of East LA—not Mexico or Guatemala.

In this chapter, I argue that gang recovery occurs by integration into cohesive faith-based groups, offering rich cultural memory and resonating with the gang experience. I describe my methods in the following section, before describing the theological differences between the two organizations I observed. I then examine how these differences affect the nature of gang recovery within each organization. I find that the theological differences between Victory Outreach and Homeboy Industries shape their approach to redemption, facilitating the process of gang exit and broader social integration.

Methods

I used qualitative methods to compare faith-based outreach to former or transitioning gang members in a city with the highest rate of gang activity in the United States: Los Angeles. I spent eighteen months observing gang outreach at a Jesuit-based nonprofit, Homeboy Industries—in downtown Los Angeles—and a Pentecostal-evangelist church, Victory Outreach–Eastside. I shadowed my subjects in their everyday lives and conducted thirty-four interviews with persons who were or had been gang members. Of the thirty-four respondents, eighteen were from Homeboy Industries, fourteen were from Victory Outreach, and two were members of both organizations. There were leaders in my sample; five were leaders at Homeboy Industries, and five were leaders at Victory Outreach. Regarding the origins of my respondents, all respondents were Mexican or Mexican-origin, except for one who was of Guatemalan descent. Nine were "1.5 generation," born in Mexico but brought to the United States before the age of thirteen; seven of these respondents were undocumented. Fourteen were second generation, many born to at least one undocumented parent, and eleven were third-plus generation.

The Jesuit Catholic–based Homeboy Industries and Pentecostal-evangelical Victory Outreach both grew out of the city of Boyle Heights. In fact, both organizations grew out of the Pico-Aliso housing projects, which have the highest concentration of poverty west of the Mississippi (Vigil 2007). Sonny Arguinzoni moved to Los Angeles from New York to attend Latin American Bible Institute, used his apartment on Gless Street to house recovering heroin addicts, and then founded the first Victory Outreach church in 1967. Father Gregory Boyle started his outreach to gang members upon arriving at Dolores Mission, also on Gless Street, in 1986; he offered work to gang members before starting Jobs For a Future (JFF), which then turned into a storefront nonprofit, Homeboy Industries. Both organizations have outreach ministries designed to help gang members transition out from gang lifestyle. Victory Outreach now has over six hundred churches, most of them storefront churches in urban areas, around the world. Homeboy Industries now employs five hundred gang members every year and has developed a model emulated by gang outreach organizations across the country. Whereas Victory Outreach is Pentecostal-evangelist and draws from a larger network of American Christianity for culture—music, film, and literature—Homeboy Industries is nondenominational, offering group therapy classes similar to Alcoholics Anonymous and spiritual classes that draw on Eastern and Native American spirituality.

At both sites, barrio symbols were visible on flyers that were handed out, with air-brush artwork and low-riders promoting events. Many, if not all, male members groomed themselves and wore clothes according to what was popular in the barrio. Such a style included thick moustaches, shaved heads, old gang tattoos, oversized clothes, and white sneakers. Men at both sites spoke using East Los Angeles barrio slang such as heina (girlfriend), homeboy (close male friend), and ranking out (deciding to not participate in something after committing to it). Leaders at both sites drew on life in the barrio in order to give examples for lessons that they taught.

I explained the purpose of this project as one in which I was seeking to learn more about the meaning of faith-based outreach to transitioning gang members. I asked some subjects if they were willing to be interviewed. Despite the fact that I am not a former drug addict or gang member, there was little discomfort for either subjects or myself when I conducted observation or interviews. Homeboy Industries is a large nonprofit, and Victory Outreach is an evangelist organization. Members at both sites dedicate much of their free time to meeting new persons. Homeboy Industries survives on public fund-raising efforts, and one of Victory Outreach's main goals is to proselytize evangelicalism. Both organizations have already gotten significant exposure to the public through major news organizations, newspaper articles, and books.

I followed the extended case method in the process of collecting data and writing analyses (Burawoy et al. 1991). I sought to integrate the anomalous cases of two inner-city ministries into segmented assimilation theory, which has largely overlooked the presence of religiously based urban reform institutions in immigrant neighborhoods. I also sought to integrate the experiences of my previously downwardly mobile subjects into segmented assimilation theory, which focuses largely on adolescent acculturation. The theoretical impetus for my decision to examine cases of young adults follows from Herbert Gans's (2007) call to immigration scholars to conceptualize acculturation as a process occurring over the life course.

Theological Differences

Victory Outreach and Homeboy Industries compete in a religious marketplace, selling "recovery from gang life" in ways that are influenced by the theological differences between Catholicism and Pentecostalism. Homeboy Industries reflects the tendencies of the Catholic Church toward centralized hierarchy. Catholicism is saddled with a rigid and dense social hierarchy; social integration into it takes place through spiritual intermediaries and traditional rituals (i.e., sacerdotalism, or praying to saints, and repentance or absolution, which requires praying through priests). Father Greg first started Homeboy Industries' precursor, Jobs For a Future (JFF), by forming Christian base communities through Dolores Mission Church. However, in the last year of my study, Father Greg raised $5 million from donors and foundations to keep Homeboy Industries running. Although Homeboy Industries is nondenominational, the most popular spiritual practices are yoga and meditation; these spiritual practices Father Greg claimed to find highly compatible with Catholicism (Boyle 2010). On the other hand, Pentecostalism is marked by decentralizing tendencies; social integration takes place through ecstatic altar calls and "evangelism through discipleship." Victory Outreach reflects the decentralizing tendencies of the Pentecostal church; its social structure is very tied to its ascetic and evangelistic theological foundations.[5] Sonny Arguinzoni, Victory Outreach's founder, preaches a vision to evangelize and start churches in urban areas worldwide.[6] Victory Outreach is a rapidly growing church that encourages members to do missionary work abroad and to ascend in leadership.

Gang exit at Victory Outreach is shaped by the theologies of "evangelism through discipleship" and its decentralizing tendencies, while gang exit at Homeboy Industries is shaped by spiritual ecumenism and dense social hierarchies. Victory Outreach's approach to gang exit can be characterized as "sheltered redemption," emphasizing ascetic religious practices and proselytism that seek to shelter members from the local community's negative influences.[7] Homeboy Industries' approach to gang exit can be characterized as "integrative redemption," emphasizing eclectic spirituality and clinical rehabilitation that seek to integrate members into the labor market and into broader local communities.[8] In the following section, I describe how these two approaches create cohesive social groups, foster cultural memory of hardship in distinctive ways, and resonate with the Chicano gang experience.

Sheltered Redemption

Victory Outreach facilitates members' sheltered reintegration into their families and the local labor market. Victory Outreach's (2010a) mission statement calls for evangelism and instilling within members "the desire to fulfill their potential in life with a sense of dignity, belonging, and destiny." Worship sermons, small-group Bible studies, and evangelism at informal gatherings constituted the infrastructure of community and belonging. The church hosted weekly worship services on Fridays and Sundays, at a storefront off a major street in the East Los Angeles area. Tuesday Bible-study groups congregated in members' homes, and members ate homemade Mexican food after worshiping. Several ministries, such as youth ministries and music practice, met throughout the week. Sunday-morning service usually drew the largest attendance, with about 130 adults. The pastor led most sermons, while other leaders "took the pulpit" to give announcements and lead prayers at the start of service, and sometimes members from other Victory Outreach chapters visited to give guest sermons. Members of Victory Outreach called each other "brother" and "sister," terms popularly used in the wider Christian community, and used call-and-response to shape the intensity of the speakers' messages.

Members of Victory Outreach engage in what María Patricia Fernández-Kelly (2007) has defined as religiously based "oppositional" acculturation: marginalized second-generation immigrants regain their honor by ascribing to values deemed more moral than those in mainstream society. Not to be confused with the way in which immigration scholars often use the term "oppositional culture," religious oppositional acculturation refers to a moral "one-upsmanship" that marginalized immigrants and men of color engage in so as to reclaim honor that is lost by not fitting in with mainstream society's ideals (ibid.). For immigrant men, racism is experienced as emasculation and is reacted against through "protest masculinity" (Poynting, Noble, and Tabar 1999). Protest masculinity "restores a feeling of power to a less powerful social group" through the "withdrawal of respect" (ibid., 74). Victory Outreach leaders spoke out against the materialism and pursuit of wealth rampant in mainstream America. They asserted that events related to Christian worship and evangelism—especially events at their own church—were inspired by God, while everything that was not was "worldly" and "evil."

Victory Outreach leaders' dichotomization of social life inside the church as good and that outside the church as evil constructed the church as a "sanctuary" space. This protected members from "the world," but it also imposed strict demands on their schedules. Instead of allowing members to celebrate holidays outside the church, which leaders saw as sinful, the church arranged its own celebrations. For example, Victory Outreach celebrated Halloween as a "harvest festival" at the local Boys and Girls Club, hosted a Thanksgiving dinner and a Christmas dinner at the church, organized a collective viewing of the Super Bowl as a fund-raiser at a member's house, and arranged a regionwide Valentine's Day dinner for single men and women. Worship services that emphasized the "holy ghost" charisms—speaking in tongues, prophecies, spiritual healings—defined Victory Outreach as on morally higher ground than dominant society.

Victory Outreach's stance against nonstandard, low-wage labor protected members from the emasculating effects of poverty and racism. Members were encouraged to quit any job that required one to work Sundays or overtime. At one worship service, Pastor Raul said, "Abraham didn't go to a place God sent him, out of fear of the famine. Maybe he was unemployed. He went to Egypt. But God didn't bring them out to send them back. Egypt was bondage, slavery. . . . There's some people like that. . . . 'I didn't come to church 'cause I gotta work.' . . . They go to places they're not supposed to be, and they're not at places they're supposed to be." In this quotation, the pastor was making a parallel between Abraham leaving Egypt and returning and members missing church because they had to work. The pastor dichotomized church and the world, implying that one finds sanctuary in the church but bondage outside the church. He reasoned that Abraham might have returned to Egypt for the same reason that some members might leave church, for fear of not having employment and income. The pastor strongly critiqued this behavior and urged members to demand a standard work schedule. The pastor said, "Some of you are like this." He then spoke in a meek voice, unintelligibly. The pastor yelled, "No! You have to learn to speak up!" The congregation cheered. The pastor then said, "They used to ask me to have to work triple overtime, Tuesday, Friday, but I don't even work for regular time on Sunday. . . . They even say, 'You know you don't have to stay,' and some of you are just like, 'Okay,' and you still stay! Why you working like a slave?! It's LA, not Mexico or Chihuahua!" This display of Pentecostal protest masculinity sought to ground members' sense of cultural knowledge in Christianity; the pastor drew on biblical symbolism, Abraham's return to Egypt, to frame his concern with members missing church due to oppressive working conditions.

Despite the construction of rigid boundaries between the church and dominant society, Victory Outreach members periodically left their sanctuary to proselytize in neighborhoods with drug addicts and gang members. They promoted the idea that every person needs to be saved and that the best way to accomplish this is through personalized interactions. This idea is characteristic of the "absolute voluntarism" and "personal influence strategies" that are at the heart of the American evangelical movement (C. Smith 1998). Due to Victory Outreach's location in the U.S.-Mexico borderlands, such approaches are culturally pluralistic (León 1998, 2004; Sánchez-Walsh 2003). At activities such as "street evangelism," members performed Christian rap at corner malls in low-income Latino communities. At "feed my sheep" gatherings, members distributed pozole and refreshments in gang-ridden neighborhoods. Members also handed out blankets on skid row and baskets to needy families on the weekend before Christmas. In members' social interactions with non-Christians, they passed out flyers, prayed for strangers, and said good-bye to everyone with the words "God bless." These outreach efforts combined elements of Mexican, American, and Mexican American culture, and members alternated between English, Spanish, and the Mexican American argot Caló. While members rapped with an inner-city style of oversized clothes and exaggerated mannerisms, they also listened to Christian worship music in their cars and made light-hearted Christian jokes about being "saved" or "rebuked" during social outings to restaurants.

Through these evangelizing efforts, Victory Outreach members created a self-enclosed community. For example, when one member and the pastor's son rapped to customers at a Fourth of July fund-raising fireworks stand in the East LA area, many members ate and socialized with their spouses, children, and other members. When Cecilia, a young, single female member of Victory Outreach, asked to go to skid row in order to practice evangelizing techniques she would use in missionary work abroad, Tony, an older member who always tried to attract her attention, offered to be her escort. And when Ramon and Susana gave soup and prayed for a homeless, drug-addicted woman, the woman shed tears; Susana then cheered her up by giving her several compliments, telling her that her hair was beautiful, asking questions about her "cute" pet dog, and offering to take both in at the women's recovery home.

Victory Outreach members integrated into this tight community through the opportunities for advancement that opened up through the decentralized church structure. This experience was shared by Rick, a tall, fair-skinned, twenty-seven-year-old recovered gang member from the East Los Angeles area. Rick was raised by his mother, a second-generation Mexican American, and his grandmother, from Mexico. After getting involved with street gangs and becoming a crystal meth addict, Rick's mother took him to the Victory Outreach men's recovery home, where Rick was forced to throw away his rap CDs. Rick recovered and became heavily involved with the church, performing "Christian rap" for Victory Outreach at street rallies and even running the men's home for a few months. Rick's ambition was one day to pastor a new chapter in Victory Outreach, a goal that seemed likely considering the church had grown to over six hundred chapters in forty years. This ambitious, but likely unprofitable, career path led to an argument between Rick and his mother, who wanted him instead to begin seeking a career path in the formal labor market.

> She doesn't really understand. . . . It's kind of addicting for me to help people now, see the wonderful power of God. And she, she would rather me

working, making money, and doing other stuff. When I told her I wanted to be a pastor, the first thing she said was, "Well, there's not too much money in that." God's not gonna let me starve, and he's not gonna let me fall off. He's gonna take care of me, 'cause my main goal in life is not like a lot of a percentage of America, which is get all money and that, you know. I don't, I don't—my drive is not that. That's not what I wake up to all "Aw, man." My drive, like I told you, is to see people get changed, to help people out.

Here we see that Rick felt that Victory Outreach sheltered him from participating in street life and filled his life with meaning by helping others. He hoped one day to become a pastor, to have a family, and to support that family. He juxtaposed these goals against the materialism and pursuit of wealth rampant in mainstream America. Victory Outreach's ascetic and evangelistic theological principles created a community, with rigid social boundaries, that quickly grew and provided Latino men with opportunities for advancement.

Integrative Redemption

In contrast to Victory Outreach's (2010a) mission statement, which calls for evangelism and advancement within the organization, Homeboy Industries' mission statement emphasizes integration into society, broadly conceived.[9] Members are critical of the aggressive approach that the legal system has taken toward incarcerating low-income youth of color and of the lack of employment opportunities found in the inner city following incarceration. In 2008, Homeboy Industries employed roughly five hundred gang members at any given time through the Homeboy Industries nonprofit, Homeboy Bakery, Homegirls Café, Homeboys Silkscreen, and Homeboys Landscaping. Legal services, tattoo removal, and self-help workshops were available to gang members in recovery. Members attended an array of group therapy classes such as Criminal and Gang Members Anonymous, Anger Management, Relapse Prevention, and Yoga. However, members referred to each other as "homeboys" and "homegirls," terms that reveal the porous boundaries between Homeboy Industries and the broader urban community. Homeboy Industries, unlike Victory Outreach, is influenced by ecumenism; gang exit takes place in a spiritually eclectic context. For example, fourteen years ago, Mario was released from the courts to Father Greg's authority and then sent to live in a Christian men's recovery home. Despite the fact that Father Greg is Catholic and that Pentecostals usually do not see Catholics as practitioners of the same faith, Mario explained to me that both he and Father Greg supported any form of spiritual development, or "whatever works."

Homeboy Industries' ecumenical leanings have allowed therapeutic models of clinical rehabilitation to be used in gang exit. Group therapy classes at Homeboy Industries often ended with the serenity prayer, a simple prayer that makes no preference for religion. The moderator would simply ask someone to "close us out with a prayer." As everyone formed a big circle, joined hands, bowed their heads down, and closed their eyes, the handpicked volunteer would say, "God, grant me the serenity to accept the things I can't change, the courage to change the things I can, and the wisdom to know the difference." Members would say "Amen" and open their eyes, and the meeting would be adjourned. This type of reintegration with dominant society is spiritually more inclusive than are the localizing tendencies observed in Pentecostalism and gangs.

However, members of Homeboy Industries, like Victory Outreach, did engage in a moral one-upsmanship that placed themselves over dominant institutions. Evo, organizer of the Spreading Seeds program, would take members of his class out to the historical park across the street, to teach meditation and breathing exercises. One day he described how a circular plaque on the ground contained the history of different groups that had inhabited the space. Under the warm summer sun and the sound of tree leaves rustling in the breeze, Evo told the story of how the indigenous Tongva, the Chinese, and Blacks were all pushed into this same physical space, albeit at different times in history. He then asked if it was not merely a coincidence that Homeboy Industries, an organization helping recovering gang members, was now across the street. Evo created a parallel between the past and present, between groups oppressed in the United States and urban gang members, situating them with cultural knowledge of hardship, trauma, and persecution in the United States. Evo instructed the members in breathing exercises and talked about the concepts of Yin and Yang and positive and negative energy. Evo said that the U.S. government's hegemonic tendencies—here, with the police in our streets, and abroad, through our continuing wars—are part of the negative energy. He encouraged members not to get "caught up in that" but to be part of the positive force, which could be experienced through spirituality.

Homeboy Industries also drew on Native American spiritual practices to facilitate gang exit. At a daily morning meeting, where all members congregate before work, I once heard Father Greg give his "thought of the day" to everyone by telling a Native American parable. In the parable, a grandson tells his grandfather that he feels he has two wolves inside of him, one full of anger and resentment and the other with love, kindness, and compassion. The grandson asks the grandfather, "Which one wins?" The grandfather responds, "The one that you feed, that one wins." Father Greg related this parable to recovering gang members' experiences with feelings of relapsing into drug abuse or gang violence, suggesting that "feeding" feelings of drug use or gang violence would encourage one to act on those same feelings. This spiritually eclectic approach creates rich symbolic imagery that not only facilitated the process of gang exit but also allowed members to reconstruct their foundation of cultural knowledge, from street gang life to Native American culture. Whereas Victory Outreach reconstructed members' cultural knowledge through Christian symbolism, Homeboy Industries did so, in part, through ancient Native American symbolism.

A few members of Homeboy Industries attended a "sweat lodge," a traditional Native American faith ritual of cleansing, about once a month. I once joined members of Spreading Seeds for a sweat behind an urban, Victorian-styled halfway house in the San Fernando Valley. When we arrived at the house, we went to the backyard, which had grass over most of the yard, except for a patio area with a concrete floor and a few wooden benches. Three long-haired, soft-spoken, middle-aged, Native American "elders" told us in a whisper that the ceremony was already beginning. We worked together to unfold a stack of blankets and place them over the tent's straw frame. The elders gave us instructions about the four directions painted on the wall and explained how each person's path was different. We stood around the pit, feeling the sting and breathing the smoke of the hot burning rocks, while someone walked around and gave us leaves. We held them in the palms of our wet, sweaty hands. The elders explained that we were to move around the pit clockwise, each individually throw leaves to the center, and pray; and then we were to go to the tent, kneel down, ask for permission to enter, and crawl in clockwise. The "umbilical cord" that connected the pit and the tent would be broken if we did not proceed behind the altar. Inside, we could barely see. The elders explained that we could pray to whomever we wished; the sweat lodge was inclusive of all religions, including Christianity. We were told we would do four rounds, and if we had to leave, it would have to be between the rounds. When the rocks were brought in, I did not think I could survive the heat. During the first round, I managed to sing along to the words, but I felt my face and lungs burning up. The elders said that we could put our face on the ground, that it would cool it off, or we could put mud on our faces. I found no mud and felt like I was about to pass out. I went outside after the first round ended, staggering, unable to walk properly. I searched for water, trying to replenish myself, as I was already drenched in sweat.

Between the third and fourth round, Jaime, an undocumented 1.5-generation immigrant, and Evo came out together. Jaime whispered to Evo in the cold dark of the night, that inside the unbearable sweat he thought about what it must be like for people coming from Mexico to the United States, having to cross through the desert in such heat. Jaime's words spoke deeply to me; I was born into an undocumented family, given an English name, and told not to speak Spanish at school. My earliest memories are of my mother instructing me every morning, as she dressed me, what would happen if she or my father did not come home that day. Jaime's words immediately drew a cathartic feeling in me, and I thought of this as I prayed for mothers, children, and others when we returned to the sweat.

Over the next year, I led a class at Homeboy Industries called College 101, designed with the aim to get Homeboys into college. I was delighted when my normally apathetic students would suddenly become interested in learning about "our history." This always referred to Spanish and English colonization of the Americas or pre-civil-rights treatment of Latinos in the United States. I treated these sessions as teachable moments to educate them on related sociological concepts, such as Marxism or feminism. This phenomenon was not unique to my class. In the Find a Tree or Spreading Seeds programs, I saw instructors calm students' anger toward the police and court system by reminding them that in traditional Native American or African cultures, humility is a virtue and anger is frowned upon. Homeboy Industries' use of Native American or other non-Western cultures, as repositories for symbolism, suggested that cultural knowledge is not just a resource that Latino immigrants do or do not have but can be constructed to undergird the process of gang exit.

Summary

Recovery from gang life occurs by integration into cohesive social groups, which offer rich cultural memory and resonate with the gang experience. Because of religious tolerance in America, American gang members experience gang exit in a context of a free "religious marketplace." Faith-based urban-American ministries and organizations compete for recovering gang members' membership and offer models of gang exit based on theologies and religious practices. Victory Outreach's decentralizing and ascetic model was influenced by Pentecostal-evangelist theology, while Homeboy Industries' centralized and spiritually inclusive model was influenced by Catholic theology. Both approached gang recovery as a process of redemption and reintegration. Victory Outreach offered a model of sheltered redemption, in which exiting gang members experienced recovery through activities meant to shelter them from the broader local community. Recovering gang members attended church activities, such as services and evangelism events, and abstained from drug and alcohol use and nonchurch activities. Homeboy Industries offered a model of integrative redemption, in which exiting gang members experienced recovery through activities meant to integrate them within the broader local community. Exiting gang members were encouraged to work and participate in spiritually inclusive prayers and meditations, although they left this setting and returned to their local neighborhoods when they were not working for Homeboy Industries.

The theologies, religious practices, and approaches to redemption offered by each organization undergirded the construction of cultural memory that exiting gang members experienced through recovery. Exiting gang members experienced racism, poverty, violence, drug addiction, and incarceration, and some were undocumented. These experiences were understood through parables or stories of Christians as religiously persecuted or of minority groups oppressed by racism and colonization. The two organizations created understandings of urban life, and gang exit, through Sunday-morning church services, street evangelism, prayer, and meditations. Some of these religious practices were reactive, or in other words, contrasted with religious practices originating in members' parents' countries of origin. Furthermore, social groups did not have to present immigrant gang members with cultural memory of hardships situated in a foreign country, so long as cultural memory resonated with their experiences as gang members. Recovering Latino gang members integrated into socially cohesive groups, offering rich cultural memory and resonating with the gang experience.

This study of gang recovery would seem to support William Herberg's thesis, that race has declined in significance and that religion is now much more salient in immigrants' children's lives. At Victory Outreach, recovering Latino gang members experienced social reintegration by accepting Jesus and casting out the devil. At Homeboy Industries, recovering gang members experienced reintegration through a faith-based "Jobs Not Jails" campaign. However, just because race is not explicit does not mean that it does not affect immigrants' children's outcomes.

Latino gang members struggle to leave gangs amid a backdrop of racial inequalities in poverty, violence, incarceration, and employment. Such recovery from gangs occurs within the American context of post-civil-rights "color-blind racism." Just like overt, Jim Crow–style racism, color-blind racism has reproduced growing racial disparities across schools, neighborhoods, labor markets, and prisons (Bonilla-Silva 2003). Young, poor, Black, and Latino men are disproportionately represented in America's growing prison population (Rios 2009). Current projections predict that one in six male Latinos and one in three male Blacks will someday experience incarceration (Bonczar 2003, 1).[10] However, this study suggests not only how the corrections system institutionalizes practices that target Black and Latino men but also how faith-based groups aim to offset some of the most deleterious consequences of racism. Nonetheless, unless we address the underlying structural factors giving rise to social inequality, and incarceration, cyclical patterns of gang initiation and gang recovery will simply crystallize color-blind racism.

NOTES

1. Durkheim (1965 [1915]) suggested that society was represented through symbols used in religious worship and that social actors were bonded together through the "collective effervescence" of worship. A Durkheimian perspective would thus suggest that recovery from gangs, and social integration into new social groups, can be facilitated through religious performance.
2. I use a concept of performance in line with Bettie's (2003) definition of performance, as situated within what Sheri Ortner (1996, 12) calls "structurally embedded agency."
3. Another example of sheltered redemption might be the Black Islamic movement within United States prisons. About 6% of roughly 150,000 federal prison inmates are Muslim, as well as 18% of the 63,700 state prisoners in New York; these prisoners are deeply concerned with slavery, segregation, and the history of U.S. racism (Zoll 2005). However, little academic research exists on Black Muslim prisoners.
4. Another example of integrative redemption might be the Chicano self-help movement within the California state prison system in the 1970s (Moore 1978).
5. See Victory Outreach (2010b).
6. Victory Outreach's website proclaims, "To maximize its potential for growth around the globe, Victory Outreach has in place a structure that decentralizes the decision-making processes, empowering local churches to meet the needs of their communities, utilizing their own distinctive approach. . . . By operating ministries independently, new leadership will develop to propel this fellowship into the new millennium" (Victory Outreach 2010b).
7. See note 3.
8. See note 4.
9. The Homeboy Industries (2010) mission statement declared, "Jobs Not Jails: Homeboy Industries assists at-risk and formerly gang-involved youth to become positive and contributing members of society through job placement, training and education."
10. The state prison population grew from 196,092 in 1972 to 1,596,127 in 2007 (Maguire 1995, 556; Pew Center on the States 2008, 5)

REFERENCES

Anderson, Elijah. 1976. *A Place on the Corner*. Chicago: University of Chicago Press.
Badillo, David. 2006. *Latinos and the New Immigrant Church*. Baltimore: John Hopkins University Press.
Bettie, Julie. 2003. *Women without Class: Girls, Race, and Identity*. Berkeley: University of California Press.

Bonczar, Thomas P. 2003. "Prevalence of Imprisonment in the U.S. Population, 1974–2001." Special Report. Washington, DC: Bureau of Justice Statistics.

Bonilla-Silva, Eduardo. 2003. *Racism without Racists: Color-Blind Racism and the Persistence of Racial Inequality in the United States*. Lanham, MD: Rowman and Littlefield.

Boyle, Gregory. 2010. *Tattoos on the Heart: The Power of Boundless Compassion*. New York: Free Press.

Burawoy, Michael, Alice Burton, Ann Arnett Ferguson, Kathryn J. Fox, Joshua Gamson, Nadine Gartrell, Leslie Hurst, Charles Kurzman, Leslie Salzinger, Josepha Schiffman, and Shiori Ui. 1991. *Ethnography Unbound: Power and Resistance in the Modern Metropolis*. Berkeley: University of California Press.

Cao, Nanlai. 2005. "The Church as a Surrogate Family for Working Class Immigrant Chinese Youth: An Ethnography of Segmented Assimilation." *Sociology of Religion* 66 (2): 183–200.

Chong, Kelly H. 1998. "What It Means to Be Christian: The Role of Religion in the Construction of Ethnic Identity and Boundary among Second Generation Korean Americans." *Sociology of Religion* 59 (3): 259–286.

Durkheim, Émile. 1965 [1915]. *The Elementary Forms of the Religious Life*. Translated by Joseph Swain. 1912. New York: Free Press.

Espinosa, Gastón. 2006. "Methodological Reflections on Social Science Research on Religions." In Miguel A. De La Torre and Gastón Espinosa, eds., *Rethinking Latino(a) Religion and Identity*. Cleveland: Pilgrim.

Espinosa, Gastón, Virgilio Elizondo, and Jesse Miranda. 2005. "Introduction: U.S. Latino Religions and Faith-Based Political, Civic, and Social Action." In Gastón Espinosa, Virgilio Elizondo, Jesse Miranda, eds., *Latino Religions and Civic Activism in the United States*. New York: Oxford University Press.

Fagan, Jeffrey. 1996. "Gangs, Drugs and Neighborhood Change." In C. R. Huff, ed., *Gangs in America*, 2nd ed. Thousand Oaks, CA: Sage.

Fernández-Kelly, María Patricia. 2007. "Religion and the Divided Self among Second-Generation Immigrants in the United States." Paper presented at the Eastern Sociological Society Meetings, Philadelphia.

Gans, Herbert J. 1962. *The Urban Villagers: Group and Class in the Life of Italian-Americans*. New York: Free Press.

———. 1992. "Second-Generation Decline: Scenarios for the Economic and Ethnic Futures of the Post-1965 America Immigrants." *Ethnic and Racial Studies* 15 (2): 173–192.

———. 2007. "Acculturation, Assimilation, and Mobility." *Ethnic and Racial Studies* 30 (1): 152–164.

Hagedorn, John M. 1998. *People and Folks: Gangs, Crime, and the Underclass in a Rustbelt City*. Chicago: Lake View.

Hirschman, Charles. 2004. "The Role of Religion in the Origins and Adaptation of Immigrant Groups in the United States." *International Migration Review* 38 (3): 1206–1233.

Homeboy Industries. 2010. "Mission Statement." Retrieved online from http://www.homeboy-industries.org (June 1, 2010).

Kim, Rebecca Y. 2004. "Second-Generation Korean American Evangelicals: Ethnic, Multiethnic, or White Campus Ministries?" *Sociology of Religion* 65 (1): 19–34.

Lay, Sody. 2004. "Lost in the Fray: Cambodian American Youth in Providence, Rhode Island." In Jennifer Lee and Min Zhou, eds., *Asian American Youth: Culture, Identity, and Ethnicity*. New York: Routledge.

León, Luis D. 1998. "Born Again in East LA: The Congregation as Border Space." In R. S. Warner and Judith G. Wittner, eds., *Gatherings in Diaspora*. Philadelphia: Temple University Press.

———. 2004. *La Llorona's Children: Religion, Life, and Death in the U.S.-Mexican Borderlands*. Berkeley: University of California Press.

Lopez, David. 2009. "Whither the Flock? The Catholic Church and the Success of Mexicans in America." In Richard Alba, Albert J. Raboteau, and Josh DeWind, eds., *Immigration and Religion in America: Comparative and Historical Perspectives*. New York: NYU Press.

Maguire, Kathleen. 1995. *Sourcebook of Criminal Justice Statistics: 1995*. Darby, PA: Diane.

Moloney, Deirdre M. 2002. *American Catholic Lay Groups and Transatlantic Social Reform in the Progressive Era*. Chapel Hill: University of North Carolina Press.

Moore, Joan W. 1978. *Homeboys: Gangs, Drugs, and Prison in the Barrios of Los Angeles*. Philadelphia: Temple University Press.

Ng, Kwai Hang. 2002. "Seeking the Christian Tutelage: Agency and Culture in Chinese Immigrants' Conversion to Christianity." *Sociology of Religion* 63 (2): 195–214.

Ortner, Sheri. 1996. *Making Gender: The Politics and Erotics of Culture*. Boston: Beacon.

Padilla, Felix. 1992. *The Gang as an American Enterprise*. New Brunswick: Rutgers University Press.

Pew Center on the States. 2008. *One in 100: Behind Bars in America*. Retrieved online from http://www.pewcenteronthestates.org/uploadedFiles/One%20in%20100.pdf (June 1, 2010).

Portes, Alejandro, and Rubén G. Rumbaut. 2001. *Legacies: The Story of the Immigrant Second Generation*. Berkeley: University of California Press.

———. 2006 [1990]. *Immigrant America: A Portrait*. Berkeley: University of California Press.

Portes, Alejandro, and Min Zhou. 1993. "The New Second Generation: Segmented Assimilation and Its Variants." *Annals of the American Academy of Political and Social Science* 530 (1): 74–96.

Poynting, Scott, Greg Noble, and Paul Tabar. 1999. "'Intersections' of Masculinity and Ethnicity: A Study of Male Lebanese Immigrant Youth in Western Sydney." *Race, Ethnicity, and Education* 2 (1): 59–77.

Rios, Victor M. 2009. "The Consequences of the Criminal Justice Pipeline on Black and Latino Masculinity." *Annals of the Academy of Political and Social Sciences* 623 (1): 150–162.

Sánchez-Walsh, Arlene. 2003. *Latino Pentecostal Identity: Evangelical Faith, Self, and Society*. New York: Columbia University Press.

Smith, Christian. 1998. *American Evangelicalism: Embattled and Thriving*. Chicago: University of Chicago Press.

Smith, Robert C. 2006. *Mexican New York: Transnational Lives of New Immigrants*. Berkeley: University of California Press.

Stohlman, Sarah. 2007. "At Yesenia's House . . . : Central American Immigrant Pentecostalism, Congregational Homophily, and Religious Innovation in Los Angeles." *Qualitative Sociology* 30 (1): 61–80.

Taylor, Carl S. 1990. "Gang Imperialism." In C. Ronald Huff, ed., *Gangs in America*. Newbury Park, CA: Sage.

Thrasher, Frederic. 1963 [1927]. *The Gang: A Study of 1,313 Gangs in Chicago*. Chicago: University of Chicago Press.

Vásquez, Manuel A., and Marie Friedmann Marquardt, with Ileana Gómez. 2003. "Saving Souls Transnationally: Pentecostalism and Youth Gangs in El Salvador and the United States." In Manuel A. Vásquez and Marie Friedmann Marquardt, *Globalizing the Sacred*. New Brunswick: Rutgers University Press.

Venkatesh, Sudhir Alladi. 1996. "The Gang and the Community." In C. Ronald Huff, ed., *Gangs in America*, 2nd ed. Newbury Park, CA: Sage.

———. 1997. "The Social Organization of Street Gang Activity in an Urban Ghetto." *American Journal of Sociology* 103 (1): 82–111.

Victory Outreach. 2010a. "Mission Statement of Victory Outreach International." Retrieved online from http://www.victoryoutreach.org/aboutus/victory-outreach-mission.asp (July 12, 2010).

———. 2010b. "Structure of Victory Outreach." Retrieved online from http://www.victory-outreach.org/aboutus/victory-outreachstructure.asp (June 1, 2010).

Vigil, James Diego. 1982. "Human Revitalization: The Six Tasks of Victory Outreach." *Drew Gateway* 52 (3): 49–59.

———. 1988. *Barrio Gangs: Street Life and Identity in Southern California*. Austin: University of Texas Press.

———. 2007. *The Projects: Gang and Non-gang Families in East Los Angeles*. Austin: University of Texas Press.

Vigil, James Diego, Steve C. Yun, and Jesse Cheng. 2004. "A Shortcut to the American Dream? Vietnamese Youth Gangs in Little Saigon." In Jennifer Lee and Min Zhou, eds., *Asian American Youth: Culture, Identity, and Ethnicity*. New York: Routledge.

Whyte, William F. 1943. *Street Corner Society: The Social Structure of an Italian Slum*. Boulder, CO: Westview.

Wilson, William J. 1987. *The Truly Disadvantaged*. Chicago: University of Chicago Press.

Wolseth, Jon. 2010. "Safety and Sanctuary: Pentecostalism and Youth Gang Violence in Honduras." *Latin American Perspectives* 35 (4): 96–111.

Zhou, Min, and Carl L. Bankston. 1998. *Growing Up American: How Vietnamese Children Adapt to Life in the United States*. New York: Russell Sage Foundation.

Zhou, Min, Carl L. Bankston, and Rebecca Y. Kim. 2002. "Rebuilding Spiritual Lives in the New Land: Religious Practices among Southeast Asian Refugees in the United States." In Pyong Gap Min and J. H. Kim, eds., *Religion in Asian America*. Lanham, MD: AltaMira.

Zhou, Min, Jennifer Lee, Jody Agius Vallejo, Rosaura Tafoya-Estrada, and Yang Sao Xiong. 2008. "Success Attained, Deterred, and Denied: Divergent Pathways to Social Mobility in Los Angeles' New Second Generation." *Annals of the American Academy of Political and Social Science* 620 (1): 37–61.

Zoll, Rachel. 2005. "American Prisons Become Political, Religious Battleground over Islam." *SignOnSanDiego.com*, June 4. Retrieved online from http://legacy.signonsandiego.com/news/nation/20050604-0928-struggleforislamii.html (June 1, 2010).

PART III

Hybridized Ethnoreligion

CHAPTER 7

Racial Insularity and Ethnic Faith

The Emerging Korean American Religious Elite

JERRY Z. PARK

Korean Americans are currently the fourth or fifth largest Asian group in the United States by population, but within the sociological study of Asian American religion, the Korean American case is clearly the dominant group of study.[1] Through this one group, scholars have studied sociological theories and concepts that deal with contemporary immigration and the role that religion plays in it. Religion for contemporary immigrant Koreans tends to reflect the ways that religion has functioned in previous generations of new Americans. Religious communities act as sites of social, psychological, and spiritual support, as well as provide access to coethnic networks and institutions such as health care and legal services. To the extent that religion and religious community are central to most Korean immigrants, their children share a similar background that couples religious faith with ethnic solidarity. Unlike their parents, however, this "new second generation" has a different view of reality due to growing up here in the United States (Portes and Zhou 1993). They inhabit a world where their ethnicity is subsumed under a larger racial label, but even that label refers to a minority group in the American social landscape. Thus, most second-generation Korean Americans emerge from an ethnically and religiously homogeneous environment as well as a racially heterogeneous societal environment in which they are not in the majority.

This chapter focuses on the Korean American second generation by exploring the changes in religiosity that happen in college for "elite" Korean Americans.[2] In a sample of elite college students, I show that Korean Americans sociologically resemble African Americans in their religious affiliations and degree of observance and are much less like their Asian peers. Unlike nearly all other Asian and non-Asian members of this sample, a larger proportion remains quite active in their faith during college. Importantly, too, a much larger portion of the active religious Korean American college students participate in religious organizations that are predominantly Asian, compared to other Asian college students. This is apparently stable across campus environments regardless of the proportion of Asian students. It suggests that elite Korean Americans are strongly inclined toward coethnic solidarity, and as such their postcollege outcomes such as marriage and employment opportunities may rely more heavily on their Korean and Korean American circles compared to other Asian groups.

Immigrant Korean American Protestantism:
A New Case Study of Traditional Sociology

Individuals and groups are a product of their circumstances and social backgrounds, and emerging Korean Americans are no exception. The experience of immigration remains an essential element in the narratives of young Korean Americans today. While the Korean presence in the United States began as early as the start of the 20th century, it was not until the changes in immigration law in 1965, along with the new social, economic, and political conditions of Europe, Asia, and Latin America that their numbers grew significantly, totaling today over 1.5 million (U.S. Census Bureau 2008). Korean immigrants, like many other newcomers, arrived in the United States due to a variety of pull factors that have been mainstay explanations of American immigration history. Many sought new opportunities to prosper economically, while others came to gain a better education or simply to be closer to other family members who had already migrated here. Push factors such as political unrest, famine, or persecution were not as salient for Koreans from 1965 onward. The unique combination of influences in migration for Korean immigrants creates a specific framework of experiences that emerging

Korean Americans share as children who grow up in these particular households. And for the purposes of this chapter, this framework specifies the role
that religion plays in their personal and communal lives.

Uniquely and Predominantly Protestant

Immigration research over the past decade has paid some attention to the
role of religion in the lives of today's immigrants (Cadge and Ecklund 2007).
In the Korean case especially, the place of religion, and specifically Protestantism, cannot be ignored. Regional studies of Korean Protestant religious
participation in the 1990s estimate that between 50 and 80 percent of Korean
Americans are members of these communities. In lay circles, the ubiquity of
Korean-immigrant churches has created its own popular idiom: "When the
Chinese go abroad, they open a restaurant. When the Japanese go abroad,
they open a factory. When the Koreans go abroad, they start a church" (as
noted in Kim 1998). Further, my analysis of data derived from the New Immigrant Survey (NIS), which collected the first and largest representative sample of immigrants applying for citizenship, reveals that Korean immigrants
applying for citizenship in 2002 were largely Protestant (between 55 and 57
percent, depending on use of survey weighting procedures). In addition,
analysis of the Pilot National Asian American Politics Survey (PNAAPS),
which collected responses from Asian Americans in multiple metropolitan
cities in 2000, shows that 66 percent of the immigrant generation of Korean
respondents were Protestant as well.

Therefore the majority of research on Korean American religion has
focused on the Protestant and immigrant experience.[3] To underscore the
magnitude of the "Protestantness" of Korean Americans, we might consider
comparing them to other Asian American groups. The NIS shows that no
other Asian group applying for citizenship had a majority Protestant presence among them. Chinese and Filipino immigrants, for example, are nearly
tied with the second-largest Protestant shares within their ethnic group, at
13.6 and 13.2 percent, respectively. The PNAAPS places Chinese Protestant
immigrants as the second-largest Asian American Protestant group, at 20
percent, over 45 percentage points lower than Korean immigrants in that
same sample. This is noteworthy too when considering that Protestantism
is not the dominant religion of South Korea. Put simply, Korean immigrants
are far more Protestant than any other Asian American ethnic group is, and
this unique attribute implies that one of the central contexts for most emerging Korean Americans, relative to other Asian groups, is the immigrant ethnic Protestant religious community.

Sacralizing the Ethnic or Purifying the Faith?

Religion has been an important carrier of ethnic culture and a source of support for all immigrants regardless of faith tradition and ethnic background (Ebaugh 2003; Smith 1978; Warner and Wittner 1998). While fewer Asians than other groups cite religious freedom as a reason for immigration, religious identity and association are still significant factors in the decision to emigrate for many.[4]

Earlier theories argued by Will Herberg (1955) and Oscar Handlin (1951), among others, posited that religion becomes more important to the immigrant ethnic community relative to its role in their lives in their former homelands. These sojourners can take few things for granted since they are entering a context where they are not fluent in the main language of the receiving country, they do not yet have employment, and they will no longer be a part of the ethnic-racial majority. Given these realities, the opportunity to gather with coethnics who understand their cultural language and customs for a brief time in an ethnic congregation is highly welcome (Hurh and Kim 1990). Additionally, the opportunity for intraethnic networking in turn leads to entrepreneurial opportunities or access to health-related and legal services (P. Min 1991, 1992; Yoo 2002; Zhou and Bankston 1998; Zhou, Bankston, and Kim 2002). For example, Victoria Kwon's ethnography of a Korean church in Houston noted the importance of cell group ministries as a means by which Korean immigrants obtained same-ethnic business contacts (Kwon 1997, 2000; Kwon, Ebaugh, and Hagan 1997). Participation in an ethnic church, then, is socially and psychologically beneficial for Korean immigrants, as has been the case for many other groups in previous generations. In this sense, Korean-immigrant Protestant religion acts as a modern example of traditional patterns evidenced in other migrating groups.

Given the positive functions that religious congregations have in the lives of Korean immigrants, immigrant parents and anyone involved in the lives of the younger generation work proactively in transmitting their ethnic culture through these organizations. Through language classes, informal conversation, and congregation-endorsed ethnic celebrations, emerging Korean Americans inherit the beliefs and practices of their parents. The degree of success and exact content of this transmission, however, is under some debate. On the one hand, sociologist Kelly Chong (1998) argued that second-generation Korean American evangelicals in Chicago adhere to their ethnic culture within a religious context as a result of racial marginalization in American culture. Put differently, the religious environment sacralizes Korean ethnic culture for the second generation. By elevating ethnicity as God given, young Korean

Americans can better respond to the racial marginalization they encounter. On the other hand, sociologists Pyong Gap Min and Dae Y. Kim (2005) found that many second-generation Korean Americans in New York City participate in near-exclusive worship gatherings of same-ethnic and same-age peers, with little interaction from the immigrant generation. They argue that little ethnic identity is cultivated in the context of second-generation religious-ethnic communities. Sociologist Karen Chai Kim argues similarly. In her study of a Boston-area congregation of emerging Korean Americans, she notes that Protestant religious identity can function as a way to maintain distinction from the previous generation. They do so specifically by critiquing the religious practice of the immigrant church as "less Christian" and "too Korean" (K. Kim 2001a). From this perspective, religion does not reify ethnicity but rather redefines it. While both perspectives demand further study, what seems clear is that religious and ethnic identities are coupled together for many Korean American Protestants as they participate in these religious contexts.

Emerging Korean American Protestants and
the Continuing Significance of Race

The popularity of Protestantism for immigrant Koreans brings two important tensions for the emerging generation. One tension is the role of ethnic culture in a racialized society, as in the United States. Sociologists Michael Omi and Howard Winant (1994) have argued that the United States undergoes a variety of racial projects whereby in every generation the social structure uses racial categories to distribute limited resources and social or political power unequally. While these categories vary from generation to generation, intellectual historian David Hollinger (1995) has argued that five labels dominate contemporary cultural discourse on race: white, black, Asian, Hispanic, and Native American. Korean ethnicity, then, is subsumed within the larger category of "Asian" as one of several cultures that share some presumed core values and beliefs in common. Asian Americans then join with African, Latino, and Native Americans as racial minorities who participate in a multicultural America that is dominated largely by white Americans with varying degrees of European heritage. From this perspective, Korean immigrants and their children inhabit a context where their culture is not an equal partner alongside African Americans and Latinos in the discussion of racial difference and tolerance but rather is a part or fraction of Asian Americans who collectively form one racialized group. Thus, a Korean religious community in conveying its beliefs and traditions to the next generation is doing so within a cultural context where they are aware that they are viewed as bit players.

The other tension that many religious immigrant and emerging Korean American Protestants experience is the universality of their faith tradition and the particularity of their ethnic-religious community. Protestantism as a branch of Christianity espouses universal accessibility, regardless of cultural heritage. This very message of "going out into the world" and "sharing with all the Good News of Jesus Christ" served as the historical impetus for European and American missionary work in places such as Korea (K. Min 2005 [1972]). But while this universal message has been shared throughout the world, it too interacts with the social realities created through racial projects. Just after the conclusion of the Civil War, American religious congregations had the opportunity to join together freed Christian African Americans and their white counterparts. But this was often not the path chosen by many Christian groups, which led inevitably to the development of Christian (i.e., Protestant) congregations organized and sustained by blacks and others by whites (DeYoung et al. 2003; Lincoln and Mamiya 1990). Ethnic-specific Chinese and Japanese congregations, for their part, also formed through separate worship services, which resulted in "de facto congregations" (Jeung 2005; J. Kim 2002; Tseng 2003; Warner 1994; Yi 2007). And while most Korean congregations today feel little to no connection to the complex history of racial segregation in American Christianity, the unquestioned ethnic homogeneity of their communities testifies to the implied cultural norms of racial segregation in contemporary American religious life.

In sum, when we consider the case of emerging religious Korean Americans, we must keep in mind that they were socialized (1) by immigrant parents who predominantly ascribed to and participated in Protestant churches, more so than any other Asian immigrant group; (2) in a religious context that bundles together ethnic and religious identities in a variety of ways; (3) in a societal context that places their ethnicity within a larger socially constructed category called "Asian"; and (4) in a religious faith tradition that espouses an unconditional and universal message but is practiced within communities that remain largely segregated by race. Add to this the reality that most of these young men and women attended schooling environments where they were at best a sizable minority, and we gain a better picture of what the emerging generation views as "the way things are." They carry these impressions, intuitions, and experiences with them as they leave their parents' homes and the church communities that raised them and enter into the world of university education.

Race, Religion, and the Parachurch College Campus Ministry

Emerging Korean Americans today enter the world of the university at an interesting moment. Given the relatively small numbers of Asian Americans (recent U.S. Census estimates put the Asian population between 4 and 5 percent), one would expect the proportion of college-attending Asian Americans to be similarly low. But journalists have pointed out since the 1980s that Asian Americans are overrepresented in America's universities (Brand 1987). Campuses such as the University of California–Berkeley have an Asian population that makes up a 40 percent share of the student body. While the largest Asian student populations are primarily in California, schools such as Cornell University and the Georgia Institute of Technology have Asian populations of 17 and 12 percent, respectively. Considering the higher proportions of Asian Americans with college degrees in the population overall, we should expect that the disproportional rate of attendance should continue for the foreseeable future.[5]

The implication of this high rate of college attendance among Asian Americans is that college is a normative path to take after high school for the emerging generation. While many Asian Americans flock to schools with higher proportions of Asian students, most college attenders do not always have the option to do so. This means that most Asian Americans in college are engaged in environments that resemble their high school contexts, where they are a visible minority on the campus.

The experience of being in the minority is not new to many emerging Asian Americans, but they do experience it without the support of their family and the presence of their coethnic friends. The college context invites young adults to fashion their own support system in any way they deem worthwhile. But apart from students developing friendships through interactions in dormitory hallways and class projects, universities often house a wide array of student-led organizations that provide opportunities for friendship, career counseling and direction, and purposeful activity. And among the plethora of available organizations are ones that represent the many facets of American religion. Put together, the university context is in some ways a microcosm of life in American society. Relationships are developed through interactions built on sharing institutional or organizational settings, and the wide array of organizations implies a marketplace from which individuals choose how and with whom they will connect or commune.

Emerging Korean Americans, as one important subset of emerging Asian Americans, enter into the university setting with the opportunity to make decisions about how they will make use of their time. These decisions occur within a context where they are an ethnic minority within a larger racial minority. And they occur within a context of legions of organizations coexisting with the aim of supporting students in different ways. Given the typical background of emerging Korean Americans, many of them must then ask themselves which religious organizations to choose among an array of options.

Sociologist Rebecca Kim (2004a) has noted the importance of race in the decision-making process of college-attending Korean American evangelicals.[6] Drawing from her ethnographic and interview work with undergraduate second-generation Korean American evangelicals (SGKAEs) in an urban public university in Southern California, Kim illustrated the complex and seemingly paradoxical ways that these young adults choose to participate in a religious organization. She noted that despite an awareness among SGKAEs that they profess a universal faith, they opt to participate in ethnically homogenous organizations. The tendency to participate in such groups is a function of having a diverse supply of religious student organizations from which to choose and the American racial structure in which their minority status is made salient. Put differently, when faced with the choice to participate in any type of religious group, SGKAEs will opt for the one that serves as an ethnic haven in a college context that marginalizes their ethnic-racial status (R. Kim 2004b).

This observation is not lost on many Protestant ministry leaders who help establish Asian American and church-based and non-church-based Christian groups (Lum 2007; Richards 2008; Stafford 2006). Through these groups, religious students and those who are interested in religion find opportunities to develop friendships and a new sense of community in the absence of familial ties. This is particularly true for the second-generation children of immigrants who were raised within an ethnic church. Absent the availability of their home congregations, campus religious groups can in some ways replicate these familiar structures with an added emphasis on meeting the specific needs of the college students.

In view of the contextual differences that emerging Korean Americans experience compared to their immigrant forebears, what kinds of religious choices do they make while in the university context? Do the observations made by Rebecca Kim in her study of a Southern California public university apply more broadly through other contexts? Are those who claim a religious heritage maintaining their faith? Are their choices to participate in religious communities affected by race?

Emerging Korean American Religion: A View from the NLSF

Using data from the recently completed National Longitudinal Survey of Freshmen (NLSF), we can for the first time examine some of the broad trends at work in the cultural world of undergraduates. The NLSF is a completed five-year study of elite colleges and universities (see the appendix, p. 150) that included large samples of nonwhite students in order to understand how America's "best and brightest" experience the world of higher education and whether such experiences have any bearing on their racial attitudes (http:// nlsf.princeton.edu/). Included in this data is a subsample of over one hundred Korean American elite college students.[7] While findings from analyzing this data are not representative of all colleges, we have a rare opportunity to compare Korean American religion among the emerging generation with other Asian Americans and members of other racial groups at the elite levels of higher education. And from this we can understand better how religion functions for these young adults and whether their patterns resemble other religious Asian Americans or other young American elites in general.

The first observation about these elite college-age Korean Americans revealed that they remain uniquely and predominantly Protestant, much like their immigrant parents' generation. Put differently, they did not resemble their Asian racial peers and instead were more similar to African American freshmen in their proportional distribution of religious affiliations. Korean elite freshmen are largely Christian (about 87 percent), as are African American elite freshmen (85 percent). A majority of both Christian groups profess a Protestant faith (66 percent of Korean Americans and 68 percent of African Americans). By way of contrast, only 38 percent of other Asian freshmen in the sample affiliated with the Christian tradition, and the majority

Table 7.1. Religious Affiliations of Korean and other American Elite Freshmen (National Longitudinal Survey of Freshmen 2001)

	Korean Freshmen	Asian Freshmen (non-Korean)	African American Freshmen	Hispanic Freshmen	White Freshmen	Total
Catholic	21.0	16.9	17.2	67.9	29.3	32.2
Protestant	65.5	21.1	68.1	14.2	38.2	37.8
Muslim		6.2	1.8		0.3	1.9
Hindu		17.0	0.1	0.3	0.1	3.8
Buddhist	2.5	9.6	0.3	0.3	0.2	2.3
Other	0.8	4.8	4.4	7.9	21.5	9.5
Agnostic/ Ref/DK		2.7	1.8	1.4	1.5	1.8
None/ Blank	10.1	21.7	6.3	8.0	8.9	10.8
Total	100.0	100.0	100.0	100.0	100.0	100.0

within the tradition was still Protestant (21 percent). At the other end of the religious spectrum, a higher proportion of Korean American elite freshmen claimed no religious affiliation (10 percent) compared to students in other racial groups. However, they remain distinct even from other Asian American freshmen, for whom the proportion of nonaffiliation is highest (over 21 percent).[8] In sum, Korean elite freshmen were more Christian and more Protestant than were their other Asian peers (and resembled their African American peers more so), and they were proportionally less likely to report nonaffiliation.

When responding to a survey question on religious observance, Korean American elite freshmen again more resembled their African American elite counterparts than they did other Asian Americans. Students who reported a religion (88.8 percent of all surveyed freshmen) were asked to rate their religious observance on a scale of 0 to 10, where 10 was labeled "extremely observant."[9] Korean elites rated themselves more religiously observant than the sample average (6.4 compared to 5.6). Again, their mean level of observance was very similar to that of religious African American elite freshmen (6.2) and was higher than other religiously identified Asian American elite freshmen (5.5).[10]

In view of Korean elites' professed religious adherence, how does this background influence their religious choices on campus? Two years after the questions of affiliation and religiosity were asked, respondents were surveyed about their extracurricular group participation. In the third interview of these elite students (spring of the students' sophomore year), they were asked whether they participated in a variety of organizations during their second year, and among these was listed "religious group."[11] Further, for each group that students reported involvement, they were asked a follow-up question on the group's majority racial composition. Students were given the choice to mark "White," "Black," "Hispanic," "Asian," "Equally integrated," or "Don't

Table 7.2. Religious Group Involvement During Second Year of College (NLSF)
N = 3398

Is R involved in a religious group?	Korean Freshmen	Asian Freshmen (non-Korean)	African American Freshmen	Hispanic Freshmen	White Freshmen
Yes	48.0	22.2	27.2	18.3	18.4
No	52.0	77.8	72.8	81.7	81.6
Total	100.0	100.0	100.0	100.0	100.0
N	102	724	919	788	865

Table 7.3. Current Religious Group Involvement and Previous Church Attendance (NLSF) N = 3390

| | Currently involved in religious org? | Church Attendance Prior to Entering College | | | | | |
		No religion reported	Never	Rarely	Often but not every week	Once a week	More than once per week
Korean	yes	0.0	25.0	31.6	21.1	59.3	95.7
N = 102	no	100.0	75.0	68.4	78.9	40.7	4.3
Other Asian	yes	5.0	1.5	11.8	28.8	56.6	79.2
N = 723	no	95.0	98.5	88.2	71.2	43.4	20.8
African American	yes	3.6	0.0	9.0	26.4	52.7	74.4
N =915	no	96.4	100.0	91.0	73.6	47.3	25.6
Hispanic	yes	1.6	2.0	7.0	25.4	38.8	77.3
N = 787	no	98.4	98.0	93.0	74.6	61.2	22.7
White	yes	5.1	0.0	7.6	25.4	46.8	75.0
N = 863	no	94.9	100.0	92.4	74.6	53.2	25.0

Column percentages add up to 100 per racial/ethnic group.

Know." With this pair of questions, we can examine whether Korean American elite college students resemble their Asian peers in terms of participation in religious groups of different racial compositions. As a proxy for religious observance, this question also allows us to see whether self-reported faith at time 1 is associated with faith observance at time 2.

Of the respondents, Korean American elite freshmen again show greater religious involvement, and in fact they outpace all groups in this sample: 48 percent reported involvement in a religious organization in their second year at college. About 22 percent of other Asian American sophomores answered similarly. Unlike earlier analyses of religiosity, however, Korean American sophomores were more involved than were African Americans (27 percent) and much more than were Hispanics and non-Hispanic whites (each about 18 percent).[12]

Not only are Korean American elite college students unique in their previous and current religious participation, but they also maintain their faith practice at higher rates than other groups do and successfully recruit the religiously inactive. Nearly 96 percent of Korean college elites who attended church more than once a week prior to college participated in a religious organization during their second year. Between 75 and 79 percent of other racial groups reported the same involvement at this level of religious activity. Coupled together with the previous finding that young Korean Americans in this sample are generally more religious, we see not only some indirect support of earlier research that estimated a strong majority of Korean Americans as religiously active (Hurh and Kim 1990) but also some of the net consequences of the active participation of their faith.

At the other end of the spectrum, about 32 percent of Korean American elite college students who rarely attended church prior to college were currently involved in a religious organization. This may not seem surprising, especially since this implies that the majority of infrequent church attenders are not involved in a religious group currently. The difference is in comparison to other racial groups: only 12 percent of other Asian elite college students reported similarly, and the proportions are even lower for other groups. While we should take heed that these differences may be an artifact of low sample sizes, the finding does raise the question as to why Korean American young adults who did not grow up attending church are more likely to report being involved in a religious organization while at college. One possible explanation might be that Korean American networks in college have a religious bent owing to the influence of religious participation of so many who grew up in the ethnic church (Abelmann 2009). It may also suggest that perhaps religious community plays a more significant role for Korean Americans. Or it may be that the tie of ethnicity and religion is much

Table 7.4. Racial Composition of Religious Group Involvement During Second Year of College (NLSF) N= 760Attendance (NLSF) N = 3390

Majority Race of Religious Group	Korean Freshmen	Asian Freshmen (non-Korean)	African American Freshmen	Hispanic Freshmen	White Freshmen
White	24.5	35.4	24.0	75.9	90.6
Black	2.0	1.2	58.0	2.1	1.3
Hispanic				4.3	1.3
Asian	67.3	57.8	8.8	5.7	2.5
Equally Integrated	6.1	5.6	9.2	12.1	4.4
Total	100.0	100.0	100.0	100.0	100.0
N	49	161	250	141	159

stronger for Korean Americans, such that coethnic community is found in some college religious communities especially in the absence of a secular ethnic alternative group.

While Korean American college-student religious involvement is unique among Asian Americans, they follow a larger pattern among religious Asian Americans and members of other racial groups: racial insularity. When responding to the question of religious group racial composition, Korean American juniors involved in religious organizations were more insular than were other Asian Americans involved in similar religious organizations (about 67 percent, compared to 58 percent). Indeed, their insularity was higher than that of religiously involved African Americans but was less than that of Hispanics and whites.

This observation is relatively stable even when we limit the analysis to the Protestant college students: 66 percent of Korean Protestant sophomores were involved in Asian-majority religious groups, while 52 percent of other Asian Protestant sophomores reported similarly. Among other groups, 65 percent of African American Protestants and 86 percent of white second years were involved in religious groups in which their race was in the majority. Only Hispanic Protestants varied in this pattern: 46 percent were involved in a white-majority religious organization, and another 30 percent reported participation in a group that was "equally integrated" (table available from author upon request).

Based on what we know in the extant research, some of the explanation for this preference for same-race group participation rests with experiences of racial composition growing up and in feelings of prejudice from one's social surroundings. To further test these relationships, I conducted associational modeling in which I accounted for several of these factors to see whether they better explain the likelihood of a respondent participating in a religious organization in which the respondent's race was the dominant group. I included a measure for the percentage of Asian Americans in the undergraduate population at the student's university. This range was between 1 and 40 percent. A greater proportion of Asian American students should increase the likelihood that religious Asian respondents will participate in religious groups with a majority of Asians. The NLSF also asked respondents what was the majority race of the high school they attended as well as the racial composition of the three-block radius around the home in which they grew up. In addition, respondents were asked a battery of questions on their perceptions of prejudice on the campus. The answers to these questions were highly correlated, so I reduced them into a simpler single variable that accounted for the respondent's perception of campus prejudice.

The resulting logistic regression analysis predicting the likelihood of "Asian-majority" religious group participation showed that Korean Protestants were 180 times and other Asian Protestants were 76 times more likely than whites to be involved in such an organization. When we account for the concentration of Asians in the neighborhood in which one grew up and the concentration of Asians in one's last high school of attendance, neither of these had a significant influence in predicting participation in a racial-majority religious group. However, a higher percentage of Asians on campus was significant in predicting group participation, which supports the proposition that larger concentrations of minorities on campus should result in more opportunities for same-race group participation, which includes religious group participation (R. Kim 2006). Finally in subsequent analysis, I also included a control variable for perceived prejudice against the respondent on campus, and this measure was not significant. In other words, participants in Asian-dominant religious organizations were not influenced by feelings of prejudice against them. This does not support the argument that a climate of prejudice influences insularity among second-generation Korean evangelicals.

Emerging Korean American Exceptionalism?

In sum, many young religious Korean American elites are socialized in ethnic immigrant communities that are organized around the life of a religious (most often Protestant) church. Their predecessors founded these communities for social, cultural, and spiritual support through the tumultuous experience of surviving in a new world where language and customs are no longer taken for granted. Transmitting the culture of their homeland through a religious community has been a mainstay strategy for thousands of American immigrants for hundreds of years. In this sense, emerging second-generation Korean Americans resemble certain familiar patterns observed across many voluntary immigrant groups.

But emerging Korean Americans experience American culture in some ways that differ from that of other previous generations of emerging children of immigrants. They stand apart from other Asian Americans and the white mainstream in their higher degrees of religiosity upon entering the hallowed halls of higher education. Their faith is resilient through the first few years in college. As such, perhaps it is not surprising that they might gravitate toward religious organizations, especially ones that have a critical mass of religious Asian Americans. The idea of ethnic and racial homogeneity is not altogether new; indeed it is part of the makeup of the American religious marketplace. Christian racial minorities in the United States have sometimes been forced into single-race congregations, and sometimes it has been a preferred context for those who feel a subtle but ever-present stigma or penalty for not being white. If religious community is the site for rest and spiritual freedom, perhaps for some this means separation.

In this sense, emerging Korean Americans may find solace and comfort in homogeneous religious groups partly as a reminder of the world that helped raise them and partly to experience rest from minority status in a way that is analogous to other Christian minorities. To some degree also, racial homogeneity for religious Korean Americans might be preferred especially if their faith has in some ways been integrated into their ethnic identity. In other words, their worldview may indeed be Christian, but it is an identity that is interwoven with being Korean in a world that is categorized as both secular and not Korean. This coupling prevents these faithful followers from finding fellowship with others of minority and majority racial groups who might otherwise identify with them. As noted earlier, the initial religious profile of Korean American elite college students is similar to African American elite students, indeed more so than to other Asian students. And to the extent that the worldview of religious Korean Americans interprets their experiences through a theological lens, they probably share more in common with other religious students who share the same religious traditions.

What are the consequences of this racial insularity? If these findings are predictive of long-range postcollege behavior, we might expect that emerging Korean American Christians will congregate in churches and religious communities with those who most resemble themselves. It would not be surprising to find that it is these students who form the leadership of new pan-Asian religious organizations such as those documented by Russell Jeung in the San Francisco Bay Area (Jeung 2005). While the college campus may have provided a golden opportunity for the followers of this global faith to experience a multicultural religious community, many forgo this opportunity in favor of racial insularity. For reasons of comfort or ethnic-religious identity, emerging religious Korean Americans both reflect continuity with their immigrant forebears, who have transmitted their culture and faith to them, and change as they must negotiate that identity in a world where they have a greater stake in moral trends of mainstream society. Those trends focus not only on the politics of family formation but also on how we reckon with socioeconomic differences and the pernicious interconnections of race with inequality.

Appendix: National Longitudinal Survey of Freshmen List of Colleges

Barnard College
Bryn Mawr College
Columbia University
Denison College
Emory University
Georgetown University
Howard University
Kenyon College
Miami University
Northwestern University
Oberlin College
Penn State University
Princeton University
Rice University

Smith College
Stanford University
Swarthmore College
Tufts University
Tulane University
University of California, Berkeley
University of Michigan, Ann Arbor
University of Notre Dame
University of Pennsylvania
Washington University
Wesleyan University
Williams College
Yale University

NOTES

Special thanks to Sam Stroope for assistance in editing this chapter and to Julie J. Park for very helpful comments toward improving the argument.

1. Not only is the research disproportionate to the population, but much of this research has appeared only in the past decade. While Korean Americans are the fourth or fifth largest Asian ethnic group in recent decades, in my review of over 160 articles and books published between 1975 and 2008 on Asian American Christianity, almost 30 percent (N = 48) focus specifically on the Korean American Protestant case, and the majority of these studies (about 81 percent) appear after 2000.

2. I use the term "elite" to refer to the class of respondents on which this study is based. Since the sample was obtained from twenty-seven of the most prestigious universities in the United States today, the sample of Korean Americans forms one part of the new emerging elite.

3. As of this writing, there are no sociological studies of Korean American Catholics save one (A. Min 2008) and no treatment of Korean American Pentecostalism, which is reportedly the fastest growing segment of Christianity all over the Asian continent (Cox 1995; Pew Forum on Religion and Public Life 2006; Yang and Tamney 2006). And while Buddhism has been one of the largest religions in Korea, analysis of the first wave of the New Immigrant Survey (completed in 2003) suggests that less than 8 percent of Korean immigrants identify as Buddhist. Nevertheless, research on Korean American religion has only recently included Buddhist groups and is relatively scarce (B. Kim 2001; K. Kim 2001b; O. Kwon 2003, 2008; Suh 2003, 2008; Sunim 2001; Yu 2001).

4. Recently, historians' studies have begun the important task of documenting and narrating the earlier Asian-majority congregations. These include Chinese, Japanese, and Korean Baptists, Methodists, and Presbyterians (see Ch'oe 2007; Hayashi 1995; Jeong and You 2008; Jeung 2005; Tseng 1996, 1999, 2002, 2003; Yi 2007; Yoo 2002). These histories

are essential in understanding the ways in which religion has played an important role among immigrant communities. However, the overwhelming numerical increase among these ethnic groups suggests that many of them are most likely unaware and perhaps not strongly influenced by the presence and memory of these congregations.

5. The Census Bureau's 2007 American Community Survey reported that 50 percent of Asians age twenty-five or older had a bachelor's degree, compared to 28 percent of all Americans.

6. Evangelicals form one wing of the family of theologically conservative Protestants who all share a high view of the Christian Bible, the importance of belief in the historical figure of Jesus Christ, and the importance of transmitting the message of Christianity to others (Marsden 1991; Woodberry and Smith 1998).

7. In this study, a Korean American respondent was identified using the following classification. The respondent must identify him- or herself as Asian and report that both biological parents originated from Korea (either North or South). Respondents who identified only one parent of Korean origin were identified as "mixed Asian." In this approach, the other major Asian American ethnic groups are proportionally represented in the following way: Chinese = 25.2 percent, Filipino = 4.3 percent, Asian Indian = 19.5 percent, Japanese = 1.1 percent, Vietnamese = 6.4 percent, other Southeast Asian = 3.1 percent, other South Asian = 0.6 percent, and mixed Asian = 27.3 percent. Korean respondents made up the remaining 12.4 percent of the Asian respondents. Given the absence of a majority subethnic group, the comparison group can sufficiently be labeled as "other non-Korean Asian Americans."

8. Even differentiating between foreign-born and native-born, Korean American elite freshmen show no differences between generations and remain distinct from other Asian Americans (table available from author upon request).

9. The question read, "On a scale of 0 to 10, how observant would you say you are of your religion's customs, ceremonies, and traditions? Zero is extremely unobservant and 10 is extremely observant."

10. Bivariate regression analysis confirms that Korean respondents in the sample were significantly more observant compared to all other groups (non-Korean Asian, Hispanic, and white) except for African Americans. Figure available from author upon request.

11. The first wave of the NLSF consists of baseline information surveyed in the fall of their freshman year, whereas the second and subsequent waves were conducted in the spring. The third wave then refers to the end of the sophomore year for the respondents.

12. Logistic regression analysis also demonstrates that Korean American students were nearly three times more likely than other students to be involved in religious organizations, after controlling for observance levels.

REFERENCES

Abelmann, Nancy. 2009. *The Intimate University: Korean American Students and the Problems of Segregation.* Durham: Duke University Press.

Brand, David. 1987. "Education: The New Whiz Kids." *Time,* August 31.

Cadge, Wendy, and Elaine H. Ecklund. 2007. "Immigration and Religion." *Annual Review of Sociology* 33:359–79.

Ch'oe, Yong-ho, ed. 2007. *From the Land of Hibiscus: Koreans in Hawai'i, 1903–1950.* Honolulu: University of Hawai'i Press.

Chong, Kelly H. 1998. "What It Means to be Christian: The Role of Religion in the Construction of Ethnic Identity and Boundary among Second-Generation Koreans." *Sociology of Religion* 59:259–86.

Cox, Harvey. 1995. *Fire from Heaven: The Rise of Pentecostal Spirituality and the Reshaping of Religion in the 21st Century*. Cambridge, MA: Da Capo.

DeYoung, Curtiss P., Michael O. Emerson, George Yancey, and Karen C. Kim. 2003. *United by Faith: The Multiracial Congregation as an Answer to the Problem of Race*. New York: Oxford University Press.

Ebaugh, Helen R. 2003. "Religion and the New Immigrants." Pp. 225–39 in *Handbook of the Sociology of Religion*, edited by Michele Dillon. New York: Cambridge University Press.

Handlin, Oscar. 1951. *The Uprooted: The Epic Story of the Great Migrations That Made the American People*. Boston: Little, Brown.

Hayashi, Brian M. 1995. *"For the Sake of Our Japanese Brethren": Assimilation, Nationalism, and Protestantism among the Japanese of Los Angeles, 1895–1942*. Stanford: Stanford University Press.

Herberg, Will. 1955. *Protestant, Catholic, Jew*. Garden City, NY: Doubleday.

Hollinger, David A. 1995. *Postethnic America: Beyond Multiculturalism*. New York: Basic Books.

Hurh, Won M., and Kwang C. Kim. 1990. "Religious Participation of Korean Immigrants in the United States." *Journal for the Scientific Study of Religion* 29:19–34.

Jeong, Yu-Jin, and Hyun-Kyung You. 2008. "Different Historical Trajectories and Family Diversity among Chinese, Japanese, and Koreans in the United States." *Journal of Family History* 33:346–56.

Jeung, Russell. 2005. *Faithful Generations: Race and New Asian American Churches*. New Brunswick: Rutgers University Press.

Kim, Bok I. 2001. "Won Buddhism in the United States." Pp. 259–72 in *Korean Americans and Their Religions: Pilgrims and Missionaries from a Different Shore*, edited by Ho-Youn Kwon, Kwang C. Kim, and R. S. Warner. University Park: Pennsylvania State University Press.

Kim, Jung H. 2002. "Cartography of Korean American Protestant Faith Communities in the United States." Pp. 185–213 in *Religions in Asian America: Building Faith Communities*, edited by Pyong G. Min and Jung H. Kim. Lanham, MD: AltaMira.

Kim, Karen C. 1998. "Competing for the Second Generation: English-Language Ministry at the Korean Protestant Church." Pp. 295–331 in *Gatherings in Diaspora: Religious Communities and the New Immigration*, edited by R. S. Warner and Judith Wittner. Philadelphia: Temple University Press.

———. 2001a. "Beyond 'Strictness' to Distinctiveness: Generational Transition in Korean Protestant Churches." Pp. 157–80 in *Korean Americans and Their Religions: Pilgrims and Missionaries from a Different Shore*, edited by Ho-Youn Kwon, Kwang C. Kim, and R. S. Warner. University Park: Pennsylvania State University Press.

———. 2001b. "Intra-ethnic Religious Diversity: Korean Buddhists and Protestants in Greater Boston." Pp. 273–94 in *Korean Americans and Their Religions: Pilgrims and Missionaries from a Different Shore*, edited by Ho-Youn Kwon, Kwang C. Kim, and R. S. Warner. University Park: Pennsylvania State University Press.

Kim, Rebecca Y. 2004a. "Negotiation of Ethnic and Religious Boundaries by Asian American Campus Evangelicals." Pp. 141–59 in *Asian American Religious: The Making and Remaking of Borders and Boundaries*, edited by Tony Carnes and Fenggang Yang. New York: NYU Press.

———. 2004b. "Second-Generation Korean American Evangelicals: Ethnic, Multiethnic, or White Campus Ministries?" *Sociology of Religion* 65:19–34.

———. 2006. *God's New Whiz Kids? Korean American Evangelicals on Campus.* New York: NYU Press.

Kwon, Okyun. 2003. *Buddhist and Protestant Korean Immigrants: Religious Beliefs and Socio-economic Aspects of Life.* New York: LFB.

———. 2008. "The Religiosity and Socioeconomic Adjustment of Buddhist and Protestant Korean Americans." Pp. 60–80 in *Religion and Spirituality in Korean America*, edited by David K. Yoo and Ruth H. Chung. Urbana: University of Illinois Press.

Kwon, Victoria H. 1997. *Entrepreneurship and Religion: Korean Immigrants in Houston, Texas.* New York: Routledge.

———. 2000. "Houston Korean Ethnic Church: An Ethnic Enclave." Pp. 109–23 in *Religion and the New Immigrants: Continuities and Adaptations in Immigrant Congregations*, edited by Helen R. Ebaugh and Janet S. Chafetz. Lanham, MD: AltaMira.

Kwon, Victoria H., Helen R. Ebaugh, and Jacqueline Hagan. 1997. "The Structure and Functions of Cell Group Ministry in a Korean Christian Church." *Journal for the Scientific Study of Religion* 36:247–56.

Lincoln, Eric C., and Lawrence H. Mamiya. 1990. *The Black Church in the African American Experience.* Durham: Duke University Press.

Lum, Lydia. 2007. "The 'Asianization' of Campus Fellowships: Student Flock to University Christian Groups to Find Solidarity and Acceptance, Say Educators." *Diverse Issues in Higher Education*, October 4.

Marsden, George M. 1991. *Understanding Fundamentalism and Evangelicalism.* Grand Rapids, MI: Eerdmans.

Min, Anselm K. 2008. "Korean American Catholic Communities: A Pastoral Reflection." Pp. 21–39 in *Religion and Spirituality in Korean America*, edited by David K. Yoo and Ruth H. Chung. Urbana: University of Illinois Press.

Min, Kyong-bae. 2005 [1972]. *A History of Christian Churches in Korea.* Seoul, South Korea: Yonsei University Press.

Min, Pyong G. 1991. "Cultural and Economic Boundaries of Korean Ethnicity: A Comparative Analysis." *Ethnic and Racial Studies* 14:225–41.

———. 1992. "The Structure and Social Functions of Korean Immigrant Churches in the United States." *International Migration Review* 26:1370–94.

Min, Pyong G., and Dae Y. Kim. 2005. "Intergenerational Transmission of Religion and Culture: Korean Protestants in the U.S." *Sociology of Religion* 66:263–82.

Omi, Michael, and Howard Winant. 1994. *Racial Formation in the United States: From the 1960s to the 1990s.* New York: Routledge.

Pew Forum on Religion and Public Life. 2006. "Spirit and Power: A 10-Country Survey of Pentecostals." Washington, DC: Pew Research Center. Retrieved February 2007 from http://pewforum.org/publications/surveys/pentecostals-06.pdf.

Portes, Alejandro, and Min Zhou. 1993. "The New Second Generation: Segmented Assimilation and Its Variants among Post-1965 Immigrant Youth." *Annals of the American Academy of Political and Social Science* 530:74–96.

Richards, Kathleen. 2008. "Young, Asian American, and Christian: UC Berkeley Is Home to Some of the Brightest Young Minds in the Country, and Many of Them Are Increasingly Drawn to Evangelical Christianity." *East Bay Express*, April 2.

Retrieved November 14, 2008, from http://www.eastbayexpress.com/gyrobase/ young__asian_american__and_christian/Content?oid=673924&page=7.

Smith, Timothy B. 1978. "Religion and Ethnicity in America." *American Historical Review* 83 (December): 1155–85.

Stafford, Tim. 2006. "The Tiger in the Academy: Asian Americans Populate America's Elite Colleges More than Ever—and Campus Ministries Even More than That." *Christianity Today*, April, 70–73.

Suh, Sharon A. 2003. "'To Be Buddhist Is to Be Korean': The Rhetorical Use of Authenticity and the Homeland in the Construction of Post-immigration Identities." Pp. 177–92 in *Revealing the Sacred in Asian and Pacific America*, edited by Jane N. Iwamura and Paul Spickard. New York: Routledge.

———. 2008. "Asserting Buddhist Selves in a Christian Land: The Maintenance of Religious Identity among Korean Buddhists in America." Pp. 40–59 in *Religion and Spirituality in Korean America*, edited by David K. Yoo and Ruth H. Chung. Urbana: University of Illinois Press.

Sunim, Samu (Kim, Sam-Woo). 2001. "Turning the Wheel of Dharma in the West: Korean Son Buddhism in North America." Pp. 227–58 in *Korean Americans and Their Religions: Pilgrims and Missionaries from a Different Shore*, edited by Ho-Youn Kwon, Kwang C. Kim, and R. S. Warner. University Park: Pennsylvania State University Press.

Tseng, Timothy. 1996. "Religious Liberalism, International Politics, and Diasporic Realities: The Chinese Students Christian Association of North America, 1909–1951." *Journal of American–East Asian Relations* 5:305–30.

———. 1999. "Chinese Protestant Nationalism in the United States, 1880–1927." Pp. 19–51 in *New Spiritual Homes: Religion and Asian Americans*, edited by David K. Yoo. Honolulu: University of Hawai'i Press.

———. 2002. "Unbinding Their Souls: Chinese Protestant Women in Twentieth-Century America." Pp. 136–63 in *Women and Twentieth-Century Protestantism*, edited by Margaret L. Bendroth and Virginia L. Brereton. Urbana: University of Illinois Press.

———. 2003. "Trans-Pacific Transpositions: Continuities and Discontinuities in Chinese North American Protestantism since 1965." Pp. 241–72 in *Revealing the Sacred in Asian and Pacific America*, edited by Jane N. Iwamura and Paul Spickard. New York: Routledge.

U.S. Census Bureau. 2008. "S0201. Selected Population Profile in the United States. Korean Alone or in Any Combination." Retrieved September 8, 2009.

Warner, R. S. 1994. "The Place of the Congregation in the American Religious Configuration." Pp. 54–99 in *American Congregations*, vol. 2, edited by James P. Wind and James W. Lewis. Chicago: University of Chicago Press.

Warner, R. S., and Judith Wittner. 1998. *Gatherings in Diaspora: Religious Communities and the New Immigration*. Philadelphia: Temple University Press.

Woodberry, Robert D., and Christian Smith. 1998. "Fundamentalism et al.: Conservative Protestantism in America." *Annual Review of Sociology* 24:25–56.

Yang, Fenggang, and Joseph B. Tamney. 2006. "Exploring Mass Conversion to Christianity among the Chinese: An Introduction." *Sociology of Religion* 67:125–29.

Yi, Mahn-Yol. 2007. "Korean Immigration to Hawai'i and the Korean Protestant Church." Pp. 41–52 in *From the Land of Hibiscus: Koreans in Hawai'i, 1903–1950*, edited by Yongho Ch'oe. Honolulu: University of Hawai'i Press.

Yoo, David K. 2002. "A Religious History of Japanese Americans in California." Pp. 121–42 in *Religions in Asian America: Building Faith Communities*, edited by Pyong G. Min and Jung H. Kim. Lanham, MD: AltaMira.

Yu, Eui-Young. 2001. "The Growth of Korean Buddhism in the United States with Special Reference to Southern California." Pp. 211–26 in *Korean Americans and Their Religions: Pilgrims and Missionaries from a Different Shore*, edited by Ho-Youn Kwon, Kwang C. Kim, and R. S. Warner. University Park: Pennsylvania State University Press.

Zhou, Min, and Carl L. Bankston. 1998. *Growing Up American: How Vietnamese Children Adapt to Life in the United States*. New York: Russell Sage Foundation.

Zhou, Min, Carl L. Bankston, and Rebecca Y. Kim. 2002. "Rebuilding Spiritual Lives in the New Land: Religious Practices among Southeast Asian Refugees in the United States." Pp. 37–70 in *Religions in Asian America: Building Faith Communities*, edited by Pyong G. Min and Jung H. Kim. Lanham, MD: AltaMira.

CHAPTER 8

Second-Generation Filipino American Faithful

Are They "Praying and Sending"?

JOAQUIN JAY GONZALEZ III

Dolly, a petite first-generation migrant from Cebu City, worked long hours in two nursing jobs to afford sending her two kids, Kuya Karl and Shal, through Catholic elementary, middle, and high schools in San Francisco. The tuition and expenses were prohibitive, especially for a single parent, but receiving a Catholic education was a tradition in her family she intended to keep.

Every Sunday evening, her only time off, they would all go as a family to nearby Saint Ignatius Church to attend the nine-o'clock-in-the-evening student mass. I caught up with them in their living room after. Both born at San Francisco General Hospital in 1980s, Kuya Karl, a Catholic University of San Francisco (USF) alumnus, and his sister, Shal, grew up watching and eventually helping their mother fill up balikbayan boxes destined for relatives and friends in the Philippines every six months. "Eto ang role ko sa buhay—taga-dasal at taga-padala" (This is my role in life—prayer and sender), Dolly revealed in a serious tone. "Panganay kasi ako eh" (Because I'm the eldest child), she added. Smiling, I responded, "Ako rin" (Me too). We felt an instant bond.

Boisterously reminiscing together with Shal and Kuya Karl, we traded descriptions of our common packing ritual. Wrapping breakables in bubble-cushioned plastic and then applying thick brown masking tape on Old Navy tank tops and Capri khakis sandwiching packs of Spam, corned beef, Vienna sausage, Ivory soap, Hershey chocolates, Aquafresh toothpaste, Oral B tooth-brush, toys, shoes, pictures, among others. Then came the hilarious black Sharpie labeling of each item: "Nanay," "Tatay," "Kuya Boyet," "Ate Baby," "Donoy," "Manang." Kuya Karl, who did most of the loading into their car, lifted a corner of the almost full box and exclaimed, "Dude, you know each one weighs more than a hundred pounds!" Nodding my head in sympathy, I said, "I know!" I looked at Dolly and asked why she needs to send them. She smiled. But before their mother could respond, Shal and Kuya Karl inter-rupted her and chimed in unison, "Utang na loob!" (Debt from within).

Is Dolly's balikbayan box ritual still typical of first-generation Filipino Catholic migrants? What is the likelihood of Kuya Karl and Shal continu-ing their mother's utang na loob? How do first-generation migrants such as Dolly keep their second-generation children engaged in ethnicity- and faith-driven activities such as remitting money and sending care boxes to the Phil-ippines? What are the demographic, historical, sociological, and economic underpinnings of the prayer and sender behavior? Sociological studies done in the 1990s of second-generation children support the conventional think-ing, that they will not "pray" and "send" as much to their country of ethnic origin as much as their parents did (Pearlman and Waldinger 1997; Portes and Zhou 1993; Rumbaut 1994; Zhou 1997). This chapter examines the extent to which these findings are still valid, including what variants may be found among the turn-of-the-millennium second-generation migrants.

Empirical data for this chapter was derived from a combination of archi-val research, blog analysis, ethnographic work from a larger USF study called The Religion and Immigration Project (TRIP), and some preliminary trends and patterns from the San Francisco Bay Area Philippine Religion, Migra-tion, and Philanthropy Survey, as well as what I learned from talking with Dolly, Kuya Karl, and Shal.

Filipino American Catholics and the Global Philippine Diaspora

Products of Philippine Studies programs at USF and City College of San Francisco (CCSF), respectively, Kuya Karl and Shal learned in the classroom that their family's San Francisco, California, sojourn is just a small square patch stitched to a larger quilt of stories from more than two million Filipino and Filipina migrants in the United States, which in turn is simply the corner weave of a larger blanket called the global Philippine diaspora—a saga covering eight million people in over 180 countries. Thus, there is a high likelihood that Kuya Karl and Shal could bump into second-generation Filipino migrants like them if ever they traveled to Detroit or Dubai, to San Francisco or Sydney, to Los Angeles or London, to Toledo or Toronto, and to New York or New Delhi. They also read from the assigned historical texts that the Philippine migration to the United States is more than a hundred years old. Although Filipino Indios were documented to have been brought to coastal towns of California and Louisiana by the trans-Pacific Manila-Acapulco galleon trade (1565–1815), which connected the Americas with Asia, the systematic growth in the number of Philippine migrants to the United States began only in the 1910s. Many Filipinos who came to America were Catholics who helped increase church attendance rates, especially among Catholic churches in the major gateway cities of San Francisco, Honolulu, Los Angeles, Seattle, New York, and Chicago. In Hawaii and on the West Coast, they were mainly agricultural laborers, while on the East Coast, they were hotel, restaurant, commuter train, recreational hall, and odd-job workers. This trend spread to other U.S. cities, big or small.

The end of World War II and the passage of the 1965 Immigration Act further increased immigration to the United States and thus helped fill Catholic churches in the vast ecclesiastical territory or dioceses of San Francisco (counties of San Francisco, San Mateo, and Marin), Oakland (counties of Alameda and Contra Costa), and San Jose (county of Santa Clara). By the 1960 census, there were 12,327 Filipinos in the city of San Francisco alone. This figure more than tripled by the 1990 census. According to United States Catholic Conference of Bishops (USCCB), there are more than one hundred thousand registered Filipino Catholics in the Archdiocese of San Francisco out of an estimated population of more than four hundred thousand Catholic residents. From the 1980s to the 1990s, many San Francisco Bay Area Catholic churches filled up with devoted Filipino parishioners, especially south of San Francisco and across the bay in the neighboring Catholic dioceses of Oakland, San Jose, and even Sacramento. Kuya Karl and Shal's mother, Dolly, just like many of the current first-generation migrants to San Francisco, came during this post-1965 wave that saw a shift in labor-market needs to professionals such as nurses, doctors, architects, engineers, accountants, and teachers. Saint Andrew's Church and the Our Lady of Perpetual Help Church, both in Daly City, and Saint Augustine's Church in south San Francisco all have Filipino priests preaching to memberships that are more than 80 percent Filipino. Tagalog masses are held at Saint Patrick's Church and Saint Boniface Church in downtown San Francisco as well as at Holy

Angels Church in the heart of Colma (San Buenaventura 2002; Gonzalez 2009; Lorentzen et al. 2009).

For most first-generation Filipinos, being proud of where they came from is apparent, from the ethnic attire they wear to the food they bring to public gatherings. But declaring an ethnicity in multicultural America has only become trendy among many second-generation Filipinos in the past couple of decades. The situation in San Francisco nowadays is not like the earlier one, in which you were expected to assimilate by forcing yourself into one American melting pot, an idea still promoted by federal immigration authorities. I came to San Francisco in 1988, ten years after Dolly's arrival. As a first-generation migrant like her, I did not think of myself immediately as "American" or "Filipino American." For me, it took about a decade of soul searching and attending a combination of Philippine community events and San Francisco Giants baseball games before I comfortably settled into my duality as a Filipino and an American. Dolly still considers herself as simply Filipino and refers to her kids and mine as the ones who are "Filipino American." This multiple interpretation is common in the large Filipino community. Picking up "Asian American" as another layer of my ethnic identity only came about two decades later. It actually sunk in when I started attending Asian American studies meetings and Asian American community events. Over the years, I simply thought of myself as "Asian." Dolly feels that she is Asian only when she is asked to fill in government forms and select an ethnicity. She also added, smiling, "When I am at Ranch 99 Oriental supermarket in Daly City." Many Filipinos, and a majority of Filipino American Catholics, in San Francisco who are first-generation migrants could probably relate to Dolly or me. Kuya Karl, Shal, and my daughter, Elise, picked up these layers of ethnic identification from their elementary, secondary, and tertiary schools, as well as from the media. Some Filipino American youth have even said in previous studies that they always indicate "Pacific Islander" in forms asking them to self-identify their ethnicity. Some said they do so because they are Filipinos from Hawaii, while others said because the "P.I. [Philippines Islands] are islands in the Pacific Ocean."

Praying and Sending?

Kuya Karl and Shal learned from their USF and CCSF Philippine Studies lectures that two of the world's top praying and sending countries are Mexico, which is 89 percent Catholic, and the Philippines, which is 84 percent Catholic. They are also the top countries of origin of San Francisco Bay Area migrants. Hence, the spiritual and religious practices of these huge Catholic populations are naturally reflected in the activities—financial and other-wise—of Mexican and Filipino migrants globally. Comparatively, however, almost all of Mexico's migrant population live and work in the neighboring United States, while the more than eight million overseas Filipinos are dis-persed to 180 countries, as mentioned earlier. More than two million Fili-pinos are based in the United States, translating to (even with conservative estimates) more than a million Filipino migrants filling up Catholic, Prot-estant, and Independent church pews on a weekly basis. Globally, Filipino migrants sent more than US$12 billion to the Philippines in 2004, while Mexican migrants remitted more than US$18 billion to Mexico in the same year. More than US$5 billion of Filipino migrant remittances originated from the United States, US$2 billion from California-based Filipinos alone. More than one-quarter of the parishioners in the vast dioceses of Oakland, San Jose, and San Francisco are Filipino and Mexican first-generation and second-generation Catholics, and their church contributions are quite sig-nificant and needed for the survival of Catholicism in Bay Area cities. But do both first-generation and second-generation Catholic migrants pray and send—help families, communities, and churches back in their Philippine hometowns flourish with their utang na loob–driven remittances?

My answer is based on findings from an ongoing large-scale project, the Philippine Religion, Migration, and Philanthropy Database, with seed fund-ing from the USF Religion and Immigration Project, USF Faculty Devel-opment Funds, USF Yuchengco Philippine Studies Program, Golden Gate University's Mayor George Christopher Endowment, and the Asian Develop-ment Bank. The survey contains more than two thousand randomly sampled responses from first-generation and second-generation Catholic migrants from fifty churches in the ecclesiastical dioceses of San Francisco, Oakland, and San Jose; the survey was administered in 2005–2007.

I was not surprised to find that out of 1,674 Filipino Catholics who declared themselves prayers and senders in the database, 1,231, or 78 per-cent of the survey respondents, were first-generation migrants (see table 8.1). They were like Dolly and me—arrivals, most likely, at San Francisco Interna-tional Airport (SFO) during the 1980s and at the time of the survey in their forties, averaging forty-four years old. But based on the wide age range of the first-generation respondents, who were between their twenties and their eighties, our 1980s migration wave was preceded by 1950s, 1960s, 1970s waves and succeeded by 1990s and even 2000s prayers and senders. Nevertheless, what surprised me after aggregating and examining the survey results further was finding that a notable proportion, almost a quarter, of the respondents were second-generation migrants. This is the clearest evidence that there are

Table 8.1. Demographic Distribution of Filipino Prayers and Senders

	Age	Female	Male	Number	Percent
First-generation	44	656	575	1231	78
Second-generation	32	170	173	343	22
Total		876	798	1674	100

Source: San Francisco Bay Area Philippine Religion, Migration, and
Philanthropy Survey, 2005-2007.

second-generation Filipino Catholic migrants who continue the practice of
praying and sending. The average age of the second-generation prayers and
senders was thirty-two years old, ranging from late twenties to sixties. They
were sons and daughters of first-generation migrants who came before the
1970s. There was no gender difference: they were split evenly one-half male
and the other half female.

So based on these demographic trends, it is still possible for Kuya Karl or
Shal to change their mind as they get older and eventually send back to their
less fortunate cousins in Cebu or their mother's other charities. They just
need to cultivate a deeper connection with their family in the Philippines
through periodic Christmas or summer visits through their church or school
or even through the Internet via Facebook and Skype. After all, their hometown is the second-largest remittance destination province for second-generation prayers and senders and is the place where Catholicism was founded
in the Philippines, home of the oldest churches and the most recognizable
religious icon, the Santo Niño de Cebu. Kuya Karl and Shal know this fact,
not from their Philippine studies classes but from the small altar at the corner of their living room. Their mother is a devotee and strong believer in the
miracles of their hometown's patron saint. Some of the many miracles Dolly
attributes to the Santo Niño's many intercessions are her passing the tough
Philippine nursing board exams and subsequently successfully hurdling
the grueling NCLEX (National Council Licensure Examination), which
made her a licensed U.S. registered nurse (RN), her coming to the United
States on an automatic immigrant visa (green card), and her finding work
at a San Francisco hospital. Many of the first-generation Catholic migrant
survey respondents whom I followed up with interviews explained to me
their similar heartfelt belief—that their jobs, salaries, home, health, and savings are all from the "grace of God" (biyaya ng Dios). These are the Lord's
answers to their prayers. Thus, they have asked their U.S.-born children and

grandchildren to do the same—"Invest in miracles!" Further results of the survey are reported in table 8.2.

The second-generation Filipino Catholics surveyed seem to have respected and followed the first generation in terms of their San Francisco prayers. Thus, they mirror the first generation's capacity to create miracles across the Pacific, in their ancestors' hometowns. Even though they may not be as experienced as the first generation, they are in relatively well-paying occupations in managerial, sales, and service professions; their home-ownership rate is higher than the national average for their age group; they have a high rate of health insurance coverage; and they have relatively healthy savings. The second-generation Filipino Catholic prayers and senders from San Francisco remit money and ship balikbayan boxes to the same provinces as the first generation does. Comparatively, however, they only remit money, on average, in the amount of US$100–US$500 once a year, while the first-generation wire transfers the same amount on average every month. Remarkably, 40 percent of second-generation Filipino Catholic migrants compared to 65 percent first-generation Filipino Catholic migrants also ship a balikbayan

Table 8.2. Investing in Transnational Miracles

	First-generation	*Second-generation*
Praying in San Francisco:		
Top three occupations	Managerial, Service, Technical	Managerial, Sales, Service
Average working years	10-20 years	1-10 years
Range annual salary	$30k-$60k	$30k-$60k
Own home	55%	42%
Health insurance	86%	86%
Savings from income	81%	86%
Sending to the Philippines:		
How often	once a month	once a year
How much	$100-$500	$100-$500
What for	household maintenance	medical expenses
Send balikbayan box	65%	40%
Top three provinces	Manila, Pampanga, Cebu	Manila, Cebu, Pampanga
Philippine retirement	41.5%	17.5%

Source: San Francisco Bay Area Philippine Religion, Migration, and Philanthropy Survey, 2005-2007.

box on average annually. The rate of the second generation is a lower than that of the first generation, but it is still noteworthy.

The homeland ties of the second-generation Filipino Catholic migrants are definitely in the United States, as evidenced by their response to the question "Where do you wish to retire?" Only 17.5 percent said that it would likely be the Philippines, compared to 41.5 percent of first-generation migrants who said they would likely go back to their hometown. During the follow-up interviews and ethnography, I found out that the philanthropy of the second generation is focused on addressing issues of first- and second-generation Filipinos and Filipinas who are at risk. Thus, some of the second-generation Filipino Catholics I talked to sit on the boards of nonprofits in San Francisco, including the Veterans Equity Center, South of Market Community Action Network, South of Market Employment Center, Filipino Community Center, Filipino American Development Foundation, West Bay, United Playaz, South of Market Senior Nutrition Program, Bindlestiff Studio, Manilatown Heritage Foundation, and the Filipino Education Center. They do not just sit on the boards; many also help run them.

Second-generation Filipino American Catholics may not be praying and sending as much as the first generation, but this does not mean that they are not doing transnational civic work. My follow-up interviews and participant observations also revealed that they are active in Philippine causes through hometown associations, Philippine aid agencies (e.g., Ayala Foundation, Gawad Kalinga, Philippine International Aid, Books for the Barrios, Pusod, and REEF, or Reaching Out through Environmental Education for Filipinos), Filipino American Coalition for Environmental Solidarity, Young Filipino Professionals Association, Chevron Filipino Employees Association, and PG&E Filipino Employees Association. I did not have to look far for examples; two second-generation Filipino American professors at two San Francisco universities and their families validated this point. For the past decade, San Francisco State Asian American studies professor Dan Gonzales and his wife, Linda, have given back by "adopting" a number of elementary school children in Manila and paying for their educational needs through San Francisco–based Philippine International Aid. And USF sociology professor Evelyn Rodriquez and her sister, Vicky, decided to endow her late mother's high school in Leyte province.

Filipinization of San Francisco—Kasamahan and Bayanihan

Filipinization, akin to Americanization, is the process of Filipino influence brought about by varying degrees of Philippine cultural, political, and economic interaction. While the Americanization of the world is driven by pop culture, the media, the Internet, the military, and business, the Filipinization of the world is propelled predominantly by transnational movement and the resulting kinship multiplication and growth.

Based on aggregated data from the U.S. Census, the largest Asian population in the United States is Chinese. But Filipinos would outnumber Chinese if the figure for Chinese were accurately disaggregated by national or regional origin—that is, from Taiwan, Singapore, Hong Kong—and if the large number of undocumented Filipinos were counted. Nevertheless, because of the Philippines' long Spanish and American colonization, first-generation Filipinos feel that they are the most American and Latino among America's Asian migrants. Dolly, Kuya Karl, and Shal were actually taken by surprise when I told them that the total Filipino American population in the United States is larger than the Japanese American and Korean American populations combined. They quickly followed up with the typical question I get when I tell people this fact: "Then why are there more Japanese and Korean restaurants than Filipino restaurants? Why is there no Manilatown in San Francisco?"

Generally, Filipino migrants do not make themselves visible in American cities through the number of Philippine restaurants or by clustering themselves into a Pinoy enclave. Specifically, first-, second-, and third-generation Philippine Catholic migrants consciously or subconsciously help Filipinize or establish themselves in the San Francisco Bay Area visibly through Catholic churches, Catholic schools, Catholic events, and Filipino clubs, as well as through their cross-memberships in formal and informal San Francisco social organizations. Filipinization in the Bay Area is produced via two means, by kasamahan (socially) and bayanihan (civically). It is how temporary and permanent Philippine migrants and their families pray, get together, and earn money in their new homeland or country of destination (kasamahan) as well as how they provide assistance among themselves, contribute to their host or new communities, and send back to families and hometowns in the Philippines (bayanihan). Filipinization by kasamahan is the mostly inward-focused kinship, ethnic ties, bonds, and relationships. These include forming formal and informal groupings such as a Filipino church choir, prayer or Bible-study group, bingo socials, mahjong sessions, and regional societies—leading to communal feelings of togetherness, companionship, fraternity or sisterhood, solidarity, pride, and competitiveness. Filipinization by bayanihan is the predominantly outward-oriented linkages, associations, bridges, and connections. These involve transforming kasamahan to volunteer activities, civic involvement, community partnerships, political advocacy, protest marches, clean-up drives, money sending, disaster relief

Table 8.3. Filipino population compared to U.S. population, 2004

	U.S. Filipinos	U.S. Population
Education		
High school graduate	90.8%	83.9%
Bachelor's degree	47.9%	27.0%
Masters, Doctorate degree	8.2%	9.9%
Employment rate	68.8%	65.9%
Income		
Median family income	$72,165	$53,672
Individual per capita income	$25,534	$24,020

Source: U.S. Census Bureau (2004).

work, donating, and fund-raising. Filipinization may be more pervasive in some countries than in others, depending on many factors including the number of migrants, their status and standing, and their homeland or home-base context. Their capacity to make significant bayanihan and kasamahan contributions to America is anchored on their being highly educated and employable, resulting in higher individual and family incomes compared to the average for the total U.S. population, as illustrated in table 8.3. They are a young and highly productive segment of the U.S. population—63 percent of them are Generation Yers.

In my San Francisco field work, I found out that most first-generation Filipino Catholic migrants emphasize to the next generation that they should be able to blend in with whatever (bahala na) or any (kahit ano) ethnoscape they face, especially since in their psyche they think that a Filipino is European, Asian, and American enough to do so. For instance, I did not find contemporary Philippine migrants in San Francisco, unlike their Asian and other migrant ethnic counterparts, centering their associational life in highly visible ethnic business and linguistic enclaves like a Chinatown, a Japantown, a Little Italy, or a Latino District. It is not a necessity for them. It is good if there is a Filipinotown or a Philippine grocery or a Filipino restaurant, but they can survive without one. After all, Philippine cuisine relates to Spanish/Latino, American, and Asian food. They eat Spanish paella, American hamburger, and Chinese siopao. They feel comfortable shopping at Japantown in San Jose, Chinatown in downtown Oakland, the Mission District's Latinotown, or their neighborhood Safeway. To most new migrants, these enclaves play a major role in their sociocultural networking and civic connections to mainstream society. They also seek to draw the mainstream into their "ethnictowns" for business and social life. The Filipino and Filipina migrant "centers" or "spaces" for associational Filipinization via kasamahan and bayanihan in which I immersed myself were much more interwoven with whatever mainstream or minority neighborhood they were in. There are clusters, but they do not have the size and scale of your typical ethnic town.

Hence, the neighborhood Catholic church is what a Filipino American community historian and Saint Patrick's parishioner observed as one of Filipino Americans' most important centers of gravity, or the focal point of their "barrio" mental construct in San Francisco (Canlas 2002). So how pervasive is their presence in San Francisco's Catholic ethnoscape? And what is the typical dynamic between first- and second-generation parishioners, such as Dolly and her children? Let us examine their activities inside and outside their churches.

According to the United States Catholic Bishops Conference, the three San Francisco Bay Area Catholic dioceses—Oakland, San Francisco, and San Jose—are ranked fourth, fifth, and sixth in Filipino parishioner population size after the massive dioceses of Los Angeles (first), Honolulu (second), and San Diego (third) (www.usccb.org). The Bay Area dioceses are teeming with Filipino attendees, their voices, their songs, and the indigenous practices that the first generation brought with them from the Philippines. Established in 1853, the Archdiocese of San Francisco is one of the oldest ecclesiastical dioceses in the western United States. It is home to more than one hundred churches and religious sites, including the Cathedral of Saint Mary of the Assumption, the National Shrine of Saint Francis of Assisi, Missions Dolores and San Rafael, Saint Patrick Seminary and University, and Holy Cross Cemetery. There are also more than eighty Catholic elementary, middle, and high schools as well as colleges in its jurisdiction. In this vast geography, as table 8.4 shows, one out of every four Catholics in the archdiocese is Filipino. Thus, Tagalog masses, Philippine feast days, novenas, and devotions are held all over the archdiocese. The popular charismatic renewal movement

Table 8.4. Filipinos in San Francisco Bay Area Catholic Dioceses

Diocese	Filipinos	Percent of total Catholic population
Oakland (4th)	103,722	19%
San Francisco (5th)	100,519	25%
San Jose (6th)	76,060	13%
	280,301	18%

Source: United States Catholic Conference of Bishops (2003).

El Shaddai meets every week at the Star of the Sea Church in the Richmond District (www.sfarchdiocese.org).

The Diocese of Oakland is home to 560,000 Catholic residents in the East Bay region of San Francisco. Of this number, more than 103,000 are Filipino Catholics, or one out of every five. Catholic schools administers over forty-seven elementary and middle schools as well as nine high schools, serving over nineteen thousand students. There are also seven Catholic colleges and seminaries in the diocese's ecclesiastical jurisdiction, including Graduate Theological Union, Holy Names University, Queen of the Holy Rosary College, and Saint Mary's College of California. Tagalog Sunday masses are held at Cathedral of Christ the Light in Oakland, Our Lady of Good Council Church in San Leandro, and Saint Paul Church in San Pablo (www.oakdiocese.org). Although formalized by the Vatican only in 1981, Catholic evangelization and mission work in the Diocese of San Jose is as old as the ones in neighboring San Francisco and Oakland. The ecclesiastical Diocese of San Jose is the largest among the three dioceses in population, serving a very ethnically and socioeconomically diverse community of over six hundred thousand Catholics. In this diocese, which lies south of San Francisco, roughly seventy-six thousand are Filipino Catholics, or one out of every ten. It is the home to fifty-two parishes and missions, three university campus ministries, and thirty-eight schools. It is the second-largest education provider in the county after the San Jose Unified School District. The diocese has a large and active office of Filipino ministry, which organizes novenas, masses, and fiesta celebrations for the Our Lady of Antipolo (also known as Our Lady of Peace and Good Voyage) in the month of July, the San Lorenzo Ruiz in the month of September, and the Santo Niño de Cebu in the month of January (www.dsj.org).

The churches in the San Francisco Bay Area, including the more than fifty sampled for USF's The Religion and Immigration Project, represent the diverse socioeconomic backgrounds of Filipino Catholics, from recent first-generation migrants living in the poorer South of Market and Tenderloin districts of the City of San Francisco and attending services at Saint Patrick's and Saint Boniface to the more settled middle- to upper-class second- and third-generation Filipinos going to Our Lady of Angels in the affluent Silicon Valley area.

Inside Saint Patrick's Catholic Church in San Francisco and Saint Augustine's Catholic Church in south San Francisco, where my research team and I spent a considerable amount of time doing participant observation, we experienced many encounters between the first- and second-generation Filipino parishioners. The intergenerational interaction closely resembles those we have seen at Catholic churches in the Philippines. Youth members participate in liturgy (as altar servers, members of the young-adult choir, and in other roles), while adult members regularly perform the duties of ushers, lectors, and Eucharistic ministers. Because many adults and seniors started out in these youth roles, they have a natural connection with their young counterparts. The youth, in turn, respect their elders. The relative status of older and younger parishioners at Saint Patrick's can be seen in the interactions among the many parish organizations. Of the twenty-five different parish organizations, only four are geared toward younger parishioners. However, the presence of independent youth organizations is significant in that it addresses the question of legacy. Given the advanced age of many of the parishioners, the youth represent the future lay leaders of the parish, and their involvement in parish activities prepares them for the future assumption of leadership roles. There are special connections between the older and younger groups—the younger members of the adult organizations serve as informal mentors to the youth parishioners, and the younger members often address their elders as ate (older sister) or kuya (older brother) as if they were kin, rather than merely fellow church members.

Similar generational dynamics exist among adult parishioners, with younger adults showing deference to older adults. Though most call each other either "brother" or "sister," there are times when persons are addressed as either kuya, ate, manong (elder man), manang (elder woman), tita (aunt), tito (uncle), or kabayan or kababayan (countryman/countrywoman), usually in more informal settings. This is another example of the prevalence of fictive kin relationships that are brought over from the Philippines, much like the relationship between the youth parishioners and their mentors.

Besides the home, the Catholic church is a venue where first-generation Filipino migrants have a strong tendency to exhibit and try to pass on religion-reinforced Filipino traits, values, and actions to the next generations. It is where Dolly is able to make the important connections between the teachings of Jesus Christ and utang na loob (debt of gratitude) to Kuya Karl and Shal. Through Bible study, rosary sessions, devotional meetings, Sunday school, teach-ins, meditations, weddings, baptisms, funerals, and confirmations, as well as other rites and rituals, she and many other first-generation adult and senior migrants are able to explain and exemplify to second-generation youth the mix of faith and ethnicity underpinnings of the following traits and behaviors: samba (worship), dasal (prayer), panata (vow), bahala na (leave up to God), makisama (get along with others), pasalamat (thankfulness), damay (sympathy), galang (respect), awa (mercy), patawad (forgiveness), sakripisyo (sacrifice), tulong (help or contribution), lingkod (serve), pagmamahal (care), magbigay (to give), maintindihin (understanding), bigay (give), pasensiya (patience), and hiya (embarrassment). When practiced by Filipino migrant faithful in everyday life, these have led to varying manifestations of kasamahan and, thereafter, bayanihan for the benefit of their church, the San Francisco community, and the U.S. and Philippine homelands.

Filipino Catholic migrants also use their church as a space for intergenerational reflection via public performances such as the one I witnessed many years ago. I have always known Filipinos, young and old, to adore basketball, and they are serious worshipers of the warm California sunshine. So it came as a surprise when on May 20, 2001, many of them gave up the chance of watching the NBA finals and the opportunity to savor the record-breaking Sunday-afternoon heat by heading for the beach. Instead, more than two hundred of them, joined by friends and relatives from all over San Francisco, gathered under the towering dome roof of All Souls Catholic Church in south San Francisco. They came to watch Handog, an emotionally moving Filipino American migration story told in Tagalog and English songs and performed in classic folk dances by young and old parishioners. The altar area of the beautiful church became the stage for the intergenerational cultural show's dramatic interpretation of the journey to America. Handog illustrates that many first-generation migrants come unprepared for the harsh realities that they must face in their quest to build a new home in a foreign land. Discrimination, culture shock, abuse, and strained family ties are just some of the "social costs" that they had to deal with. Nevertheless, first-generation Filipinos and their children drew strength from their own adaptive and resilient nature, fortified by their deep religious faith, to survive and eventually succeed. This is when one realizes how embedded faith is in both generations.

But not all second-generation youth, such as Shal and Kuya Karl, enjoy participating in Handog productions or could connect to their parents' devotional prayer meetings to San Lorenzo Ruiz, the first Filipino saint, or to the Santo Niño de Cebu, the most recognizable religious icon in the Philippines. Some are also not as enthusiastic about Tagalog Bible study or joining the Salubong procession during Holy Week. Some might start out as altar servers or choir singers, but then they get bored and look for a more engaging and dynamic connection to their faith. This is when they seek and create faith gatherings and relationships outside their parish churches. As young adults, they also need a new spiritual space to process their lives, including some intragenerational and intergenerational frictions and conflicts as well as their own ethnic identity. This is where their Catholic schooling and youth ministries come in.

Outside of Sundays, many first-generation Filipino migrants would like to entrust their children's education to a faith-based institution. Dolly, like many of them, feels that a Catholic school is a place where respect, discipline, and Christian values would continue to be reinforced. As a result, aside from Catholic churches, another major beneficiary of Filipino Catholic inflow into the San Francisco Bay Area is the dioceses' many Catholic primary, secondary, and tertiary schools. As early as September 1963, thirty-eight of the forty-five elementary schools in the downtown San Francisco area already reported a total of 680 Filipino children in attendance. The schools with the largest numbers were Sacred Heart Elementary (78), Saint Paul (42), Star of the Sea (41), Saint Peter (38), and Saint Monica (28). In the 1980s and 1990s, San Francisco's religious elementary and high schools experienced surges in Filipino enrollment as the children of migrants from the 1960s and 1970s reached school age. New arrivals and their families also contributed to the increase. By 2000, the student body of Corpus Christi Elementary School had become more than 75 percent Filipino. Several other San Francisco elementary schools have student populations that are close to 50 percent Filipino; these include the Church of the Epiphany, Church of the Visitacion, Saint Elizabeth, Saint Emydius, Saint Finn Barr, Saint John the Evangelist, Saint Kevin, Holy Angels, and Our Lady of Perpetual Help. Not too far away, in the city of Vallejo, there are three Catholic schools—Saint Catherine of Siena Elementary School, Saint Basil's Parish School, and Saint Vincent Ferrer.

Some of the Catholic elementary and high schools in the San Francisco Bay Area currently have student populations that are between 20 and 25 percent Filipino, including in the nearby Diocese of Oakland Our Lady of the Rosary, Saint Leander, and Saint Joachim, as well as high schools such as Saint Ignatius College Preparatory, Archbishop Riordan, Mercy High, Bishop O'Dowd, Sacred Heart Cathedral Preparatory, Saint Mary's College High School, De La Salle High School, Moreau Catholic High School, and Immaculate Conception Academy. These Catholic high schools are the main feeder schools to Catholic colleges and universities, including the University of San Francisco, Santa Clara University (SCU), Holy Names University (HNU), Dominican University (DU), and Notre Dame de Namur University (NDMU). Hence, there is corresponding rapid growth in Filipino second-generation student enrollments at these tertiary institutions. Saint Patrick's Seminary and University in Menlo Park and Graduate Theological Union in Berkeley also report a significant number of students of Filipino descent who are training for the priesthood or enrolled in graduate theological and religious programs.

San Jose State University (SJSU), San Francisco State University (SFSU), University of California–Berkeley (UCB), and California State University–East Bay (CSUEB) are public universities that have also experienced a surge in Filipino American second-generation, and consequently Filipino Catholic, registrations. Community colleges such as De Anza, Skyline, and City College of San Francisco (CCSF), as well as private universities such as Stanford University, Golden Gate University, Devry University, in the San Francisco Bay Area also report similar trends. The number of Filipino American students has led to the demand for and consequent creation of Philippine and Filipino American studies programs and course offerings, covering social justice, culture, politics, economics, society, history, arts, law, and the interests of both first-generation and second-generation migrants. This allows these students to bridge both geographic and mental divides and barriers.

The Catholic education, including required theology and ethics classes, at the University of San Francisco leads many Filipino Catholics, first and second generation, to send their children there. At USF, the decade-old Maria Yuchengco Philippine Studies Program (YPSP) offers both a minor and major concentration in Philippine studies. YPSP caters to the academic needs of the more than four hundred second-generation Filipino and Filipina American students who enroll every year, as well as non-Filipinos who are interested in preparing themselves for careers and interactions with the fast-growing Asia Pacific and Asian America. Kuya Karl received a bachelor's degree in business with a minor in Philippine studies. To quench students' thirst for kasamahan or cultural knowledge, there are courses in Philippine and Filipino American history, culture, politics, spirituality, sports, arts, and Tagalog language. To satisfy their hunger to do bayanihan or volunteer work with the Filipino American and Philippine community, students take service-learning courses such as "Knowledge Activism" and "Summer Immersion in the Philippines." For instance, Kuya Karl took my "Filipino Culture and Society" course for his kasamahan teachings and my "Filipino Politics and Justice" course for his bayanihan experience.

The second-generation Catholic faithful at these Catholic, private, and public colleges and universities have active clubs that do cultural awareness (kasamahan) and social justice (bayanihan) activities. At USF, Kasamahan, the Filipino American student club, is the largest, with more than two hundred members, and the most active student organization on campus. Thousands of second-generation student club members have danced, acted, and sung at the annual USF Philippine Cultural Night (PCN), entitled "Barrio Fiesta," in the past thirty-six years. Kuya Karl was an active Kasamahan member who participated in Barrio Fiesta from his freshman to senior years. Some male Kasamahan members are also brothers at Chi Upsilon Zeta (XYZ), an equally energetic Filipino American service fraternity. Kasamahan has been recognized as Club of the Year, while Chi Upsilon Zeta has been awarded Greek of the Year. Second-generation Filipino Catholics are also USF professors and administrators. They join their first-generation colleagues in hosting an annual Simbang Gabi mass—a Filipino Christmas mass complete with Filipino songs, readings, and food.

Outside of churches and universities, Filipino and Filipina second-generation Catholic migrants provide spiritual energy to a number of youth ministries of faith-based Catholic organizations and movements. One of these, Singles for Christ (SFC), is a second-generation adult youth ministry of a larger umbrella, Manila-based organization called Couples for Christ, which began in 1981. SFC is joined by Kids for Christ, Youth for Christ, Handmaids of the Lord, and Servants of the Lord. SFC has grown into a global movement, with chapters in 160 countries and more than three hundred thousand members. SFC's San Francisco Bay Area chapter is intended for single men and women who are at least twenty-one years old and not more than forty years old. The heart and soul of SFC is the "household," with around five to eight men or women who meet weekly for mutual support and encouragement in their Christian life. A SFC household's purpose is to build an environment for the support of the Christian life of the individual—a venue for encouraging and hastening spiritual growth. It provides friendship, brotherhood, and sisterhood that is Christ-centered. SFC helps individuals overcome obstacles in their Christian journey. Highly energetic communal worship, prayer, singing, sharing, discussion, and fellowship characterize their many gatherings all over the San Francisco Bay Area. In August 2008, chapter members participated in the fourteenth CFC Singles for Christ USA National Leaders Conference at the Town and Country Rest and Convention Center in San Diego, California. SFC's national leaders' conference is one of the largest Catholic singles conferences in the United States and Canada.

Banal Na Pagaaral (Holy Study), or BNP, is a Filipino religious movement that began forty years ago. It is led and founded by Ate Salve, who is a charismatic leader and first-generation Catholic migrant who settled in California. BNP San Francisco Bay Area members profess to be a community of people who have been touched by Jesus Christ. Most of them come from local public and private high schools and colleges, and many are socialized Catholic and educated at Catholic institutions. The mission of BNP's youth ministry is to spread the divine message of salvation to all young people through retreat classes, apostolic work, and panawagan (calling) classes. The goal is self-reflection and transformation in their lives. At the retreats and panawagan classes, powerful testimonies are given by peers who have experienced hope and transformation. BNP Youth Ministry in San Francisco is an active group but is not as vibrant as the ones in Southern California and New York. There are five thousand BNP members in Los Angeles. In August 2007, they sponsored a BNP Youth Day and Sportsfest in Ontario. In 2008, BNP New York, which was celebrating its twentieth anniversary, sponsored Holy Week and Christmas activities and parties as well as get-togethers on Central Park and bowling. BNP youth members from San Francisco supported their brothers and sisters in Los Angeles and New York.

Transnational intrigue always sprouts among the Filipino faithful globally. There are accusations from Catholic Church leaders in the Philippines and California that the BNP movement promotes activities and evangelization not in line with the teachings of the Roman Catholic Church. Thus, the Archdiocese of Los Angeles and several in the Philippines have banned the BNP. But the charismatic appeal and trendiness of the BNP continues among the young second-generation Filipino Catholics in San Francisco, New York, Los Angeles, London, Sydney, and other cities all over the world who are seeking alternatives from the first generation's church-based and passive approach, as alluded to in their many recent blog statements, including the following:

Anyhow, I am a devout Catholic and am also active with the BNP (Banal Na Pag-aaral). I've been with the BNP for about 15 years now and here are my impressions of the movement. Prior to 1994, my faith in God and my knowledge about the Catholic religion was little to none, even though I did call myself a Catholic since that's how my parents raised me. After attending the BNP retreat my curiosity opened up more about my religion, and through time, I was able to learn more and even help some people who have been in the same situation I was in. For me, being active in the BNP and going to the activities has definitely increased my service to God and the Catholic faith. The Mass means so much more to me, prayers, the Rosary, and so much has changed in my life ever since I was made aware of the great things that I did not see before in my faith. I guess that's it for now—but if you have any questions or anything that I might be able to help clear up, please do ask and I'll answer the best I can. All I know is that through the BNP, my relationship with God has been stronger than ever. ("Sraymundo," posted in forums.catholic.com, August 28, 2007, 1:26 p.m.)

I'm not Filipino, I'm very much Caucasian American, free thinking and definitely not superstitious when it comes to faith. I avoided Christianity until not too long ago. I came to the Lord based on what I experienced in the BNP, and what I saw and heard and so now I am Catholic and so very happy to be one. ("BigJ73," posted in forums.catholic.com, August 28, 2008, 6:57 p.m.)

Summary and Conclusions

Filipinization through kasamahan and bayanihan is an ongoing process. On the surface, it seems the combined praying and sending of balikbayan boxes and remittances might end with first-generation Filipino Catholic migrants such as Dolly and myself. Second-generationers Kuya Karl and Shal candidly admitted to me that, at the moment, they do not have the strong ties that their mother has for the relatives back in the Philippines. But Shal adds, "This does not mean that we do not love our lola [grandmother], lolo [grandfather], titos [uncles], titas [aunts], and our cousins. They are in our thoughts and prayers, and we will definitely visit them, . . . not as often as mom though." Kuya Karl looks at Dolly and quips, smiling, "Hey, Mom, . . . but we will always help you pack those heavy boxes!"

However, praying and sending might not end with the first generation. Most likely the beneficiaries will change, but the cardinal behavior of praying and transnational giving will not end with Kuya Karl and Shal. This is thanks to role models such as Dolly and many other first-generation migrants, whether they are Catholic or not Catholic, whether they are Filipino or not Filipino. The seeds of kasamahan and bayanihan have been planted. The next generation will continue the Filipino behavior of utang na loob and many other traits influenced by their family and religious socialization through other forms of kasamahan and bayanihan. Kuya Karl has already started by doing hours of volunteer work with at-risk first-generation kids at West Bay Pilipino Multi-services Agency. Shal has also shared some of her precious Friday afternoons with South of Market's Filipino Seniors Nutrition Program. The last time I checked, the family was busily preparing to ship a second balikbayan box filled with Kuya Karl's and Shal's hand-me-down clothes for their younger cousins in Cebu.

REFERENCES

Canlas, M. C. (2002). *SOMA Pilipinas Studies 2000*. San Francisco: Arkipelago.
Gonzalez, J. (2009). *Filipino American Faith in Action: Religion, Immigration, and Civic Engagement*. New York: NYU Press.
Lorentzen, L., Gonzalez, J., Chun, K., and Do, H. D. (2009). *Religion at the Corner of Bliss and Nirvana: Politics, Identity, and Faith in New Migrant Communities*. Durham: Duke University Press.

Pearlman, J., and Waldinger, R. (1997). "Second Generation Decline? Children of Immigrants, Past and Present—A Reconsideration." *International Migration Review* 31, no. 4: 893–922.

Portes, A., and Zhou, M. (1993). "The New Second Generation: Segmented Assimilation and Its Variants." *Annals of the American Academy of Political and Social Science* 530, no. 1: 74–96.

Rumbaut, R. G. (1994). "The Crucible Within: Ethnic Identity, Self-Esteem, and Segmented Assimilation among Children of Immigrants." *International Migration Review* 28, no. 4: 748–794.

San Buenaventura, S. (2002). "Filipino Religion at Home and Abroad: Historical Roots and Immigrant Transformations." In Min, P. G., and Kim, J. H. (eds.), *Religions in Asian America*. Lanham, MD: AltaMira.

United States Conference of Catholic Bishops. (2003). *Office for the Pastoral Care of Migrants and Refugees Report*. Washington, DC: USCCB.

U.S. Census Bureau. (2004). *American Community Survey*. Washington, DC: U.S. Census Bureau.

Zhou, M. (1997). "Growing Up American: The Challenge Confronting Immigrant Children and Children of Immigrants." *Annual Review of Sociology* 23:63–95.

CHAPTER 9

Second-Generation Korean American
Christians' Communities

Congregational Hybridity

SHARON KIM AND REBECCA Y. KIM

Wherever Koreans settle in the United States, they invariably start an ethnic church or join and faithfully attend a preestablished one. Researchers have shown that the majority of Koreans regularly attend the 4,000 or so Korean churches every Sunday in the United States (Kang 2008; S. Kim 2009; Min and Kim 2005). In Los Angeles alone, there are over 1,000 Korean churches, and eight of them are megachurches with an average attendance exceeding 3,000 members. Furthermore, among post-1965 immigrants, Koreans have the highest percentage of Protestant affiliation—over 70 percent of Koreans attend church weekly, and these churches are not simply religious organizations servicing the spiritual needs of Korean Americans. Rather, they function as central "hubs" of the immigrant community that provide a myriad of services that range from economic to cultural interests (Hurh and Kim 1990; Kwon, Kim, and Warner 2001; Min 1992; Min and Kim 2002). The primacy of the ethnic church is well documented for the first generation of Koreans, but what about the second generation? What happens to the second generation's religious participation once they come of age? This chapter addresses

this question using existent research and our own data gathered from interviews and participant observations in a variety of Korean American campus
ministries and churches in the past 10 years.[1]

Focusing on Korean American Christians, we review the different models
of the second generation's religious participation and argue that the second
generation, in cities across the United States, is actively constructing their
own emergent ethnic religious space. Rather than inheriting the churches
of their immigrant parents or joining preestablished mainstream churches,
they are creatively fashioning their own houses of worship. Moreover, within
their newly formed churches, they are actively and intentionally reaching out
to all Americans, regardless of their ethnicity and race.

Models of Transition

Churches are dynamic, and models of church transition can overlap. With
this in mind, we can look at five main models of church transition for the
second generation.[2] The first is the classic model of the ethnic church as a
source of cultural retention and group solidarity (Dolan 1975; Ebaugh and
Chafetz 2000; Greeley 1972; Guest 2003; Herberg 1955; Mol 1976; Warner and
Wittner 1998; Zhou, Bankston, and Kim 2002). From this perspective, one
option of church transition is that the second-generation Korean Americans
(SGKAs) will remain in their parents' church and more or less carry on the
first generation's ethnic religious tradition. For example, Kelly Chong (1998)
finds that participating in Korean churches reinforces a distinct Korean ethnic identity for SGKAs. The Christian faith in the Korean American evangelical Protestant community supports the construction of a strong ethnic identity among SGKAs. The ethnic church ideologically defends and legitimates
a "set of core traditional Korean values and forms of social relationships" and
serves "as an institutional vehicle for the cultural reproduction and socialization of the second generation into Korean culture" (Chong 1998, 262). With
such a transmission of culture, the second generation can continue their religious participation within the immigrant church. But it is not clear how long
this may last, particularly if the second generation cannot speak Korean.

At the other end of the ethnic-retention model is the "assimilated" or
accommodated church model. To persist over generations, the ethnic church
must make room for the more acculturated second generation (Fishman
1972; Mullins 1987; Palmer 1972; Steinberg 1981). To accommodate more culturally and socioeconomically assimilated, English-speaking members and
mixed-marriage couples who have more options in the religious marketplace, the church must transition into a multiethnic church. Unless there is a

significant number of new immigrants or a renewed wave of racial discrimination, deethnicization of the church is the future. As Mark Mullins puts it,
the essential decision that the aging immigrant church faces is one between
"accommodation," and therefore a transformation into a multiethnic organization, or "extinction" (1987, 323). As the first generation age and the second generation come of age, the immigrant church must transition to a more
inclusive, ethnically nondescript, multiethnic congregation to survive.

There is still a sizable foreign-born population in the Korean American
community. In 1990, 82.2 percent of the Korean population in the United States
was foreign-born. Estimates drawn from the 1998 and 2000 Current Population Surveys, however, show that foreign-born Koreans now make up approximately 52.4 percent of the population. Meanwhile, the second generation make
up 21.9 percent and the third and later generations make up 25.7 percent of
the Korean population (Logan et al. 2001). Given this, the immigrant church
can stay alive with existent immigrants and renewed immigration from Korea.
Immigrant Korean churches continue to fill their leadership positions with
first-generation Korean Americans and pass on leadership positions to immigrants from Korea rather than the second generation. Thus, transition into a
more assimilated congregation is not currently necessary for the survival of the
Korean-immigrant church. This is especially the case considering that most of
the medium to large immigrant churches have separate ministries for the more
acculturated second generation within the congregation.

With a sizable first-generation as well as a growing second-generation
population, many Korean-immigrant churches have adopted a de facto congregational mode of transition, whereby two congregations exist within one
physical church space (Chai 1998; Warner and Wittner 1998). The two generations may worship in the same church building, but they do so independently of one another and in separate worship services with "different styles,
priorities, and visions for the future" (Chai 1998, 302).[3] The second-generation congregation, otherwise known as the English Ministry (EM), holds its
worship services in English and is often led by young pastors, sometimes not
even Korean, trained in American seminaries. The English Ministry is considered a separate department of the immigrant church and enjoys its own
senior pastor as well as a degree of autonomy over its own governance. However, the final decisions and control over the governance of the ministry still
remains within the hands of the immigrant leadership. Although the English
ministries enjoy a level of autonomy within their separate de facto congregations, they still remain largely dependent on the immigrant congregation for
their continued survival. Hence, they exist in a state of frustration, of wanting, on the one hand, freedom and respect from the first generation yet, on

the other hand, due to their dependent status, being perceived and treated as juvenile second-class citizens.

Outside of the immigrant church, there are also independent panethnic Asian American congregations. Different Asian ethnic groups develop solidarity based on their dawning recognition that they are treated by others as different primarily because of their physical appearance (Alumkal 2002; Emerson and Smith 2000; Jeung 2002). Continuing racial divisions in the broader society lead to the construction of separate Asian churches that join together ethnic groups such as Chinese Americans, Korean Americans, and Japanese Americans (Jeung 2005; Iwamura 2003; Min and Kim 2002). In a study of Asian American churches in the Bay Area, Russell Jeung (2005) found that Japanese and Chinese churches evolved into panethnic congregations within two generations. Rather than continuing to target one ethnic group, these churches began to target various Asian ethnic groups for the sake of institutional survival. What once started out as a monoethnic church eventually transitioned into a panethnic church with its own distinct Asian American subculture. Jeung argues that "Chinese and Japanese American churches are not dying out or becoming open to all but are adapting by becoming Asian American" (2005, 2). Rather than joining mainstream denominations or remaining ethnic specific, the churches in his study established themselves through embracing a racialized Asian American identity.

Beyond these four models of ethnic church transition, we find that the second generation, particularly in ethnically diverse cities such as Los Angeles, are carving out an alternative path that is distinct from mainstream churches, immigrant churches, de facto congregations, and panethnic churches. They are creating and inhabiting newly formed hybrid churches that are shaped by multiple frames of reference. Founded by the second-generation Korean Americans themselves, these emerging churches offer the second generation a unique ethnic and cultural religious space that reflects their unique experiences of growing up in America. The churches also have a distinct Korean Christian imprint, reflecting the second generation's experiences of growing up in Korean-immigrant churches. Nevertheless, these new churches are reaching out to all Americans. The churches cater to the unique generational and cultural experiences of second-generation Korean Americans while inviting all Americans, irrespective of their ethnicity or race, into their churches.

Methods

We interweave existent studies on the second generation with our own research within the second-generation Korean American Christian community in the past ten years. Rebecca Kim conducted research on Korean American and other Asian American college-campus ministries for two years in Southern California. She conducted field research in a variety of campus ministries for Korean American college students and conducted 100 personal interviews. Sharon Kim has conducted participant observation for ten years (1996–2006) at 22 of the 56 different Korean American churches that are presently in the Los Angeles area. She has also interviewed 108 Korean American Christians in Southern California who are involved in a variety of Korean American churches. Our data also include Sharon Kim's survey of five large Korean American churches in Southern California that together have more than 700 members: Faith Church, Fruitful Church, Family Church, Flowing Life Church, and University Church. In this survey, 510 surveys were administered, with a 67 percent response rate (340 completed surveys).[4]

The SGKA churches in our study are not a monolithic group. They are an emerging congregation and have group boundaries that are in flux. The churches vary in the extent to which they are ethnic specific, in the numbers of Korean Americans versus other ethnic groups. Thus, for us, what makes these churches SGKA is not necessarily the numerical demographic makeup of the church or even the visible cultural markers of the church, such as language or food. We define the churches as SGKA congregations because they are founded by SGKAs, embrace the unique hybrid experiences of the second generation, and have the imprint of Korean Christianity.

Impetus for Hybrid Communities of Worship

When we ask the second generation why they are in separate ethnic congregations, they tell us that it is "just more comfortable" to do so. Nearly everyone in our interviews talks about being comfortable in separate SGKA ministries relative to the other religious community options that they have.

Breaking down this issue of comfort, research on the second generation points to the reality of their being border Americans stuck between the immigrant generation and the broader American community. On the one hand, they grew up in homes with immigrant Korean parents, with unique cultural traditions and struggles (Chai 1998; Kim and Pyle 2004; R. Kim 2006). On the other hand, they continue to be an ethnic and racial minority, misunderstood as perpetual foreigners in the broader society. These two sources of tension help explain why SGKAs are drawn together in the emerging second-generation congregations.

Growing Up with Korean-Immigrant Parents

One of the most common themes that emerge when SGKAs talk about how they found themselves in the new churches is the shared experience of growing up in immigrant-parent homes. Karen Chai finds that the chance to be with those who share similar cultural background and experiences is one of SGKAs' main motives for attending the separate SGKA English-language ministries. "The most consistently cited reason was the opportunity to be with people who share their cultural background. . . . They are able to form close relationships with others who have been shaped by the same Korean cultural forces" (1998, 311). As one of the SGKAs in our own study similarly explains, "Most of us have first-generation parents. We know what goes on in a Korean house: . . . parents' pressure; study, study, study; marry a Korean; don't talk back. So it is easier to get closer with other Koreans. They know where you are coming from."

Among the shared experiences that Korean American students mention, pressures to excel in school are the most common, as a SGKA explains: "Korean parents are like, 'You have to do this, this, this to be successful. . . . You have to go to medical school or law school and study, study, study.' They think the best colleges are Harvard, Yale, Princeton. I am not saying white people don't stress education, but Koreans, they take it to another level." Another SGKA shares, "If I bring home my report card, and I have all As with one B, my parents will focus on that B and ask me why I got that B. They never talk about all the As I got." These pressures can even start before birth. A SGKA pastor in our study shared that he personally knows three people whose names are "Harvard, Yale, and Princeton." Not surprisingly, a simple Google search of "Harvard, Yale, or Princeton Kim" yields several hits. The pressures to excel were also the first explanations that many Korean Americans used to understand the case of Azia Kim, a SGKA who posed as a Stanford student in 2006–2007. Even though she was not admitted to the school, she pretended to be a student at Stanford for eight months, taking classes, sleeping in dorms, and studying for final exams.

The immigrant generation's more "collective" orientation amplifies these pressures to excel. Studies of immigrant families show that conflicts between parents and their children oftentimes arise over value contrasts between individualism and collectivism (Min 1998; Zhou and Bankston 1998). Decisions over issues such as one's major in college or occupational and marriage selection can involve entire families. Related to this, SGKAs feel a tremendous level of stress over not failing or shaming their families or parents.

These pressures are compounded by a cultural affection disconnect between the two generations. SGKAs want their parents to be openly expressive, communicating love, affection, and affirmation like "typical" American families. Their immigrant parents, however, shy away from public displays of affection and believe that they are expressing their love for their children by sacrificing, working hard, and providing financially. A first-generation Korean American parent explains, "We Koreans are not good at openly showing our love. We don't know how to because our parents were not like that with us. If we put food on the table and a roof over our family, that's how we show love. That's the Korean way. We feel uncomfortable kissing, hugging, and saying 'I love you' to our children. I wish our children could understand that." This cultural disconnect is amplified by language barriers. Most Korean Americans born in the United States cannot speak Korean well or cannot speak it at all. Meanwhile the first-generation parents have difficulty speaking English. The disconnect at home is reflected in SGKAs' religious participation in immigrant churches. Language and cultural barriers between the two generations fuel SGKAs' longing for their own religious space. In fact, independent SGKA congregations stem from the underlying conflict that the second generation had and continue to have with the first generation within the church context. The generational, linguistic, and cultural barriers, along with the treatment of the second generation's English or young-adult ministries as essentially second-class ministries for children, fuel SGKAs' desires to branch out and form their own independent congregations.

Growing Up Second Class

As in other studies on Asian Americans (Alumkal 2003; Ecklund 2006; Jeung 2005; Kibria 2002; R. Kim 2006; Min 2002; Tuan 1998), SGKAs tell stories of being racialized, marginalized, and made to feel like foreigners and incomplete Americans. A SGKA reflects, "Growing up, I never thought that I was that different. But I remember kids telling me, because they tend to be very honest and direct, . . . they would ask, 'Why is your face so flat? How can you see from your eyes?'" This kind of ethnic and racial categorization and grouping coincides with racism.

Danny, a SGKA who grew up in Long Beach, California, remembers the racism that he experienced growing up in a largely Latino neighborhood: "I was living in Lakewood. I remember we used to go to the park nearby, and there were a group of Hispanics, and they would always push us around and take away our lunch money. They used to call us names. I remember that my friends and I would try to not walk that way. They would pull their eyes and call us 'chinks,' 'china boys,' 'japs,' and some other bad names." Racialization against Korean Americans by others is commonly expressed as their being foreigners, strangers in their own land. A SGKA who spent years practicing medicine in the U.S. Air Force in Mississippi shared how he repeatedly encountered white Americans who saw him as an alien:

> When I practiced in Mississippi, a lot of my patients were retirees and predominately Caucasians. They'd come in and want to know whether I was Japanese or Chinese. After that, they'd say, 'You know, I helped your people during the Korean War.' Here I am a member of the U.S. Air Force in uniform treating them, and they keep insisting that they helped my people. They saw me simply as a Korean—a foreigner.

Racialized as different, treated and viewed by others as the perpetual foreigner, generalized as "chink," "jap," or "gook"—no matter what their level of acculturation—leads the second generation to feel incompletely part of the world outside their parents' home.

This racial reality makes it relatively more comfortable for SKGAs to take part in their own ethnic congregations in lieu of predominantly white or multiracial congregations. As a SGKA explains, "My race is a nonissue when I am in [my Korean American church]; that is one less thing that I have to worry about." You may be a racial minority in the broader society, but within the SGKA congregation you are the majority; your cultural generational experiences are part of the unstated normative culture. Faces that look like yours are reflected in the leadership and most of the church membership. You are not the racial minority and, in many cases, not the ethnic minority either.

SGKAs' frustration with the immigrant Korean church and their hybrid experiences growing up in immigrant families as second-class citizens in America fuel their participation in SGKA congregations.

Emergent Communities of Faith

Korean Americans are the largest nonwhite group in American evangelical seminaries. For example, they make up over 25 percent of the student body at Fuller Theological Seminary in California. Coming out of these seminaries, Korean Americans are not just setting up immigrant churches or finding positions in white mainstream churches. Many of the Korean American seminary graduates themselves are a stuck generation, incompletely accepted in the minority and the mainstream Christian communities. These 1.5- and second-generation Korean Americans, spurred by their own frustrations with the first-generation church and the larger mainstream, are starting their own independent churches, where they can meet the needs of the emerging generation and integrate their own multifaceted identities.

The creation of a religious space that caters to a particular population is part of a broader and popular church-development movement that capitalizes on the importance of homogeneous group associations. Instead of trying to reach out to diverse populations, the successful and rapidly growing churches in contemporary America are tailoring their religious institutions to meet the specific needs of particular homogeneous populations (Wagner 1990; Warren 1995). It is understood that people want to become Christians "without having to cross racial, linguistic, or class barriers" (McGavran and Wagner 1990, 163). As a pastor in our own study explains, "In the Christian community we call it the homogeneous principle: . . . people want to worship with people who are like them." This is part of the broader sociological principle of what sociologists refer to as homophily—the idea that "similarity breeds connection," that ties between similar individuals are more binding, or more proverbially, that "birds of a feather flock together" (McPherson, Smith-Lovin, and Cook 2001, 415; Duncan, Featherman, and Duncan 1972; Marsden 1987; Park and Burgess 1921). Following these patterns of group association, 1.5- and second-generation Korean American pastors are creating their own faith communities, spaces of worship that uniquely resonate with today's SGKAs.

Their Own Homophily

Second-generation congregations provide a religious space that is attuned to the unique cultural upbringings of SGKAs and other second-generation Asian Americans. Jimmy, a SGKA, noticed how his cultural upbringing influenced the way he interacts with others:

> I went to a drug rehab at Saddleback Community Church [a mainstream megachurch in Southern California]. I was the only Asian in the group. I realized there that it's difficult to find people who can relate to both your addiction and your cultural background. I was very shy in the group. A lot of Asians are quicker to not speak and to listen as opposed to just blurt out your two cents. People were sort of raising an eyebrow at me because I wasn't saying a thing. They were probably thinking, 'Why is that Asian guy sitting there being defiant?' . . . But it's not defiance; it's just the way I was raised.

Jimmy currently attends a Korean American–led Asian American church and has started a drug-rehabilitation ministry for Asian Americans, which he hopes will be a safe and culturally sensitive environment for healing and recovery for addicts. SGKAs are attracted to such churches because they offer ministries and an environment where their culture is understood and incorporated into their spirituality.

The new churches also fill the void and longing for a more intimate and supportive family among the second generation. Second-generation churches provide for the English-speaking population, as first-generation churches do for the immigrant generation, a sense of an integrative community in which individuals who would otherwise be isolated in impersonal environments become part of a family network of "brothers" and "sisters." At these congregations, they find a supportive community of like-minded individuals who have had a similar set of life experiences. Within this community, they can also find coethnic people to date and marry. A SGKA pastor explains to his church members,

> One of the best places to meet a mate is the church because you'll be meeting someone who has the same beliefs and values. If you're searching for a soul mate here . . . if a guy asks you out, ladies, please say yes at least the first time and especially if he has the character over the cosmetics. Give him a shot. You don't know how hard it is for a guy to ask you. Guys, you gotta ask. Don't be afraid to ask. Take the risk. . . . What do you have to lose? Ask many of them out. . . . One of them has to say yes.

Indeed, they may say yes and eventually get married. And once they get married and have children, SGKAs want to have a place where they can pass on selective elements of their Korean culture to their children. Since they expect that their children will get the generic "American" culture through school and the broader media, they want a place where elements of their "Korean" culture can be passed on. A SGKA explains why she wants her daughter to be involved in a Korean American church: "We're hoping to surround our daughter with Korean culture. We want her to understand who she is and embrace her cultural identity. The church is the best place for this to happen because she can associate with others who have the same cultural history and upbringing." This desire is also fueled by the expectation that their children will be incompletely accepted in the broader society, as "Korean" or "Asian"-looking people. Because racism and ethnic divisions persist, SGKAs believe that later-generation Koreans who have no understanding or connection with their Korean culture will be rootless and homeless.

They too will be in their own cultural limbo. Consequently, SGKAs believe that U.S.-born Korean Americans should embrace their cultural heritage, as one explains: "No matter how much I try to disconnect from my culture, in this country, my ethnicity and culture will always matter at least to outsiders; that is . . . racial minorities, are defined by their ethnicity, so it's no advantage to us to deny our ethnic heritage. We might as well embrace it." SGKAs are thus turning to the new churches where they, along with their present and future children, can find their own homophily, cultural refuge, and identity development.

Hybrid Congregations

Within these newly developed churches, the ministers hope to create a hybrid second-generation spirituality by appropriating and fusing together elements of Korean Protestantism and expressions of American Evangelicalism. The leaders of these new churches want to adopt what they perceive to be essential beliefs, symbols, and practices from diverse sources and to reanchor them in their newly formed churches. Their goal is not simply to disassociate with the religion of their immigrant parents and realign themselves with mainstream Evangelicalism. The majority of the churches do not want to be replicas of the most successful white evangelical churches. Rather, they want to carve out a hybrid third space that is uniquely their own.

An important aspect of the "Korean" Christian practice that they want to maintain is the "Korean" way of praying. Instead of praying individually or having one person simply pray for the group, as in most other evangelical Christian churches, Korean-immigrant churches practice a style of prayer in which the entire congregation passionately, intensely, and simultaneously prays aloud together.[5] A typical Korean prayer meeting goes like this: The pastor gives a brief message that reminds the members that God hears their earnest prayers. The people then kneel on the ground for a time of tong-song gi-do (unison prayer). Inside a dimly lighted sanctuary, members begin to passionately and emotionally cry out to God in prayer. Some weep, others pound the ground with their fists, and still others shout "Jesus!" and "Lord!" at the top of their lungs. The themes of "deliverance" and "blessing" resonate through most of the pleading, with members petitioning for spiritual breakthrough, physical well-being, and material provisions for themselves and their children. Within Korean and Korean-immigrant spirituality, there is a sense that the more earnestly and desperately you pray to God, the more likely he will answer you.

This perspective is embraced and communicated by the majority of Korean Christians both in Korea and in the United States. Korean Christians reject a laissez-faire, purely cerebral attitude toward prayer. Rather, prayer first and foremost "moves the hand of God," and second, it is a holistic exercise that involves the individual's body, emotions, mind, and spirit. This kind of prayer tradition is something that the second generation want to carry on.

While the prayer meetings at the second generation's gatherings are more passionate than what you would witness at mainstream evangelical congregations, they are noticeably less intense than what you would find at Korean-immigrant churches. Several Korean-immigrant pastors even comment that the second generation lack fervor and intensity in their prayer compared to the first generation. Nevertheless, one of the characteristics of Korean Christianity that SGKAs want to preserve is "the Korean prayer."[6]

While the second generation want to maintain prayer gatherings that mirror more of their parents' style of prayer, their worship services are like many other contemporary mainstream white evangelical congregations. The services usually start with several contemporary praise songs led by a band of musicians. A contemporary "Vineyard" style of worship is led by a band of musicians on electric guitars, drums, and synthesizers, with lyrics projected onto large overhead screens. For about 30 minutes or so, the worshipers stand up and sing, swaying their body to the upbeat contemporary praise songs that cater to today's postmodern generation. When it comes time for the sermon, the second-generation pastors interact with the congregation in a more egalitarian and informal manner and preach in a conversational and interactive way. The hierarchies of the churches are also not as rigid as the first-generation church, and Korean food and holidays are not celebrated. SGKAs' congregations thus fuse elements of Korean as well as mainstream contemporary Christian practices.

Hybrid and Inclusive

SGKAs are articulating a second-generation spirituality and identity that captures their ethnic, racial, and generational selves. What we find interesting, however, is that the SGKAs seek to do this as they evangelize and welcome "all people" into their congregations. They want to be inclusive without compromising their hybrid identities.

Even though many of the SGKA campus ministries are predominantly Korean American, they will say that the ministry is open to all people. Some have dropped ethnic-specific monikers to attract a broader audience. And indeed, it is not unusual to have non-Korean Americans, particularly other Asian Americans, take part in the gatherings. The same applies for second-generation churches. Approximately 35 percent of the second-generation church members in Sharon Kim's study are non-Korean Americans. About 25 percent are Asian Americans who are not Korean Americans, and 10 percent are non-Asians. These other groups are able to stay in the new churches because there are elements of the second-generation identity with which they too can connect.

One of the primary sources of commonality is simply the similarities that emerge from being college-educated and upwardly mobile professionals. For example, in Fruitful Church's population of 350 predominantly university students and professionals, 11 non-Asian members are undergraduate students, 9 are graduate students, and approximately 13 are professionals in law, business, art, education, and medicine. Like other studies on multiethnic congregations, class homogeneity matters (DeYoung et al. 2003; Emerson 2006; Jeung 2005). The majority of the non-Korean Americans in the second-generation congregations were introduced to the church by their friends on college campuses or in the workplace. Thus, besides a common faith, class homogeneity shared among people in their 20s and 30s provides a source of commonality.

The emerging churches also reach out to local communities. They have homeless missions, tutorial ministries, and big brother and sister programs for inner-city youth, predominantly African Americans and Latinos. They hand out flyers to people in their local communities and invite them to their congregations. Thus, beyond their own natural friendship networks that extend beyond the Korean American community, they reach out to a variety of other ethnic and racial groups that inhabit Southern California.

Being inclusive yet providing a hybrid space for the second generation is not an easy balance. In fact, as we see it, the comfort that SGKAs enjoy in the emerging churches mean that those who are not Korean American or Asian American will have to bear with some discomforts. It is not the perceptual markers of culture such as the sound of the Korean language or the smell of kimchi at church that those who are not Korean American have to deal with. Instead, the discomfort and unease may come from the implicit Korean American culture and norms of the church. The typical stories that will get shared in small groups, the jokes that may be told, the assumptions that may be made will have a Korean American imprint. However, according to several pastors, this reality is not something that Korean Americans should suppress or have to apologize for, because all churches have had, at some point in their history, discernible ethnic fingerprints. According to one minister,

"'Mainstream' Protestantism is not 'a-ethnic.' To see it as such is another example of white privilege. What we know today as mainstream Protestant- ism is very much flavored by European ethnic culture." Rather than having to choose Westernized Christianity over Koreanized Christianity, second-gen- eration Korean Americans today have chosen to embrace certain elements of Korean culture that they feel are compatible with their Christian identity. In so doing, they are beginning to reflect critically on the impact of their own cultural heritage and personal experience on their understanding and interpretation of the Christian faith. As one pastor succinctly pointed out, "Because I am Korean, the Korean culture is an important part of the DNA of my church." In short, the ministers desire a higher degree of reciprocity wherein their hybrid spirituality, flavored by their ethnic culture, can take its place in the landscape of "mainstream" Protestantism.

In a white church, a person of color will have to inhabit the white norma- tive culture. In the emerging hybrid churches, the normative culture will be Korean American. Given this, the emerging church leaders know that those who are not Korean American or Asian are more likely to leave than to stay in their church. Establishing a multiracial church with Korean American fin- gerprints is not easy, but it is an endeavor that the SGKAs will pursue. The SGKA churches, still in their growing stages, will continue to offer alterative religious spaces for SGKAs while reaching out to other ethnic groups. Time will tell how successful they will be, but they are here to stay.

Conclusion

There are growing numbers of SGKA-friendly campus ministries and churches in areas such as Los Angeles, where many Korean Americans con- centrate. Other cities, however, are also experiencing the growth of similar second-generation Korean and Asian congregations (Kim and Pyle 2004). One of the SGKA churches in Sharon Kim's study has planted over 15 second- generation churches in cities throughout the United States, including New York, Boston, and Berkeley. As more SGKAs come of age and as increasing numbers of Korean American seminarians go out into the religious market- place, these congregations will become more commonplace throughout the United States.

In these emerging second-generation congregations, SGKAs can find healing in a setting where their multiple identities are embraced and inte- grated. They are creatively picking and choosing aspects of their varied back- grounds as Koreans and Americans and living in multiracial America to cre- ate a spiritual community that is all their own. Thus, the choice is not simply between ethnic retention and assimilation—between the ethnically loaded immigrant church and the assimilated mainstream or multiethnic congregation. What is more, these religious communities are hoping to extend beyond their ethnic boundaries and to redefine conventional understandings of a "minority" and "mainstream" church.

Social scientists, in focusing solely on how American society has impacted immigrant groups, have neglected to study the ways in which ethnic groups have impacted mainstream America. The study of emerging second-generation congregations, particularly in its current period of transition, experimentation, and innovation, provides a colorful and intriguing case study of how ethnic minorities, rather than simply adopting mainstream Christianity, can and do transform the practice and institutional landscape of religion in America.

NOTES

1. The second generation is defined as those who are born and raised in the United States with at least one immigrant parent. 1.5 generation is defined as those who are not born in the United States but are raised and schooled primarily in the United States. The first generation is defined as those who were born and raised largely in Korea. We define a church as an independent second-generation church if the pastor is a second-generation Korean American, if over 50 percent of the congregation is 1.5- and second-generation Korean American, and if the church functions independently from financial support of the first-generation church or other mainstream churches.

2. There are additional submodels of ethnic church transition (e.g., Goette 2001; Mullins 1987), but for the sake of clarity and simplicity, we focus on the main models of ethnic churches.

3. The de facto church structure can include an immigrant-based church with a distinctively separate English ministry for the second generation. But it is also possible that a more U.S.-born, English-speaking ethnic church can have a separate Korean-speaking ministry for the more recently arrived immigrants (Goette 2001).

4. The five churches were selected for their large congregation sizes as well as the willingness of the church leaders to administer the surveys. The surveys were passed out during small group Bible studies and were collected immediately after they were filled out.

5. The Korean way of praying is a unique historical product of Korean Christianity that is marked by intense passion, fervency, and urgency. American missionaries introduced Christianity to Koreans during the latter half of the nineteenth century, and more so than in other Asian countries, Christianity was widely embraced by Koreans. This was due to the fact that during the years of greatest growth of Christianity in Korea (1895–1910), two major wars were fought in the country, there was a widespread famine in the land, and the country was forcibly annexed by Japan. In was in the context of national suffering that Koreans embraced Christianity and the hope of a God who upon hearing their desperate cries for help would put an end to their suffering. The Korean way of praying has its historical roots in the sufferings of the past.

6. According to one minister, the prayer life of the second generation has become "diluted because their lives are too comfortable, and they are highly influenced by Western Christianity." One immigrant church reasoned that this is because the second generation is a *"hanless* generation," which means that the second generation has not experienced suffering in the ways that past generations of Korean have. The term *han*, a uniquely Korean concept, refers to a sense of suffering and pain that Koreans have endured throughout history, such as Japanese colonization, the Korean War, nationwide economic hardship, and the struggle for democracy and independence.

REFERENCES

Alumkal, A. 2003. Asian American Evangelical churches: Race, ethnicity, and assimilation in the second generation. New York: LFB.

Chai, K. 1998. Competing for the second generation: English-language ministry at a Korean Protestant church. Pp. 295–331 in R. S. Warner and J. G. Wittner (eds.), *Gatherings in Diaspora: Religious Communities and the New Immigration*. Philadelphia: Temple University Press.

Chong, K. H. 1998. What it means to be Christian: The role of religion in the construction of ethnic identity and boundary among second generation Korean Americans. *Sociology of Religion* 59:259–286.

DeYoung, C. P., M. O. Emerson, G. Yancey, and K. C. Kim. 2003. *United by Faith: The Multiracial Congregation as an Answer to the Problem of Race*. Oxford: Oxford University Press.

Dolan, J. P. 1975. *The Immigrant Church*. Baltimore: Johns Hopkins University Press.

Duncan, O. D., D. L. Featherman, and B. Duncan. 1972. *Socioeconomic Background and Achievement*. New York: Seminar.

Ebaugh, H. R., and J. Saltzman Chafetz. 2000. *Religion and the New Immigrants*. Lanham, MD: AltaMira.

Ecklund, E. H. 2006. *Korean American Evangelicals: New Models for Civic Life*. New York: Oxford University Press.

Emerson, M. O. 2006. *People of the Dream: Multiracial Congregations in the United States*. Princeton: Princeton University Press.

Emerson, M. O., and C. Smith. 2000. *Divided by Faith*. Oxford: Oxford University Press.

Fishman, J. A. 1972. *Language in Sociocultural Change*. Stanford: Stanford University Press.

Goette, R. D. 2001. The transformation of a first-generation church into a bilingual secondgeneration church. Pp. 125–140 in H. Kwon, K. C. Chung Kim, and R. S. Warner (eds.), *Korean Americans and Their Religions: Pilgrims and Missionaries from a Different Shore*. University Park: Pennsylvania State University Press.

Greeley, A. M. 1972. *The Denominational Society*. Glenview, IL: Scott, Foresman.

Guest, K. J. 2003. *Religion and Survival in New York's Evolving Immigrant Community*. New York: NYU Press.

Herberg, W. 1955. *Protestant, Catholic, Jew*. New York: Doubleday.

Hurh, W. M., and K. C. Kim. 1990. Religious participation of Korean immigrants in the United States. *Journal for the Scientific Study of Religion* 29:19–34.

Iwamura, J. 2003. *Revealing the Sacred in Asian and Pacific America*. New York: Routledge.

Jeung, R. 2002. Asian American pan-ethnic formation and congregational culture. Pp. 215–244 in P. G. Min and J. H. Kim (eds.), *Religions in Asian America: Building Faith Communities*. Lanham, MD: AltaMira.

———. 2005. *Faithful Generations: Race and New Asian American Churches.* New Brunswick: Rutgers University Press.

Kang, Connie K. 2008. Korean churches growing rapidly in Southern California. *Los Angeles Times*, November 1.

Kibria, N. 2002. *Becoming Asian American: Second-Generation Chinese and Korean American Identities.* Baltimore: Johns Hopkins University Press.

Kim, H. H., and R. E. Pyle. 2004. An exception to the exception: Second-generation Korean American church participation. *Social Compass* 51:321–333.

Kim, R. 2006. *God's New Whiz Kids? Korean American Evangelicals on Campus.* New York: NYU Press.

Kim, S. 2009. *A Faith of Our Own: Second-Generation Spirituality in Korean American Churches.* New Brunswick: Rutgers University Press.

Kwon, H., K. C. Kim, and R. S. Warner. 2001. *Korean Americans and Their Religions: Pilgrims and Missionaries from a Different Shore.* University Park: Pennsylvania State University Press.

Logan, J., D. Oakley, P. Smith, J. Stowell, and B. Stults. 2001. *Separating the Children.* Report by the Lewis Mumford Center. May 4. http://mumford.albany.edu/census/Under18Pop/U18Preport/page1.html.

Marsden, P. V. 1987. Core discussion networks of Americans. *American Sociological Review* 52:122–313.

McGavran, D. A., and P. C. Wagner. 1990. *Understanding Church Growth.* Grand Rapids, MI: Eerdmans.

McPherson, M., L. Smith-Lovin, and J. M. Cook. 2001. Birds of a feather: Homophily in social networks. *Annual Review Sociology* 27:415–444.

Min, P. G. 1992. The structure and social functions of Korean immigrant churches in the United States. *International Migration Review* 26:1370–1394.

———. 1998. *Changes and Conflicts: Korean Immigrant Families in New York.* Boston: Allyn and Bacon.

———. 2002. *The Second Generation: Ethnic Identity among Asian Americans.* Lanham, MD: AltaMira.

Min, P. G., and J. H. Kim. 2002. *Religions in Asian America: Building Faith Communities.* Lanham, MD: AltaMira.

———. 2005. *Asian Americans: Contemporary Trends and Issues.* 2nd ed. Thousand Oaks, CA: Pine Forge.

Mol, H. 1976. *Identity and the Sacred.* New York: Free Press.

Mullins, M. 1987. The life-cycle of ethnic churches in sociological perspective. *Japanese Journal of Religious Studies* 14:321–334.

Palmer, H. 1972. *Land of the Second Chance: A History of Ethnic Groups in Southern Alberta.* Lethbridge, AB: Lethbridge Herald.

Park, R. E., and E. W. Burgess. 1921. *Introduction to the Science of Sociology.* Chicago: University of Chicago Press.

Steinberg, S. 1981. *The Ethnic Myth: Race, Ethnicity, and Class in America.* New York: Atheneum.

Tuan, M. 1998. *Forever Foreigners of Honorary Whites: The Asian Ethnic Experience Today.* New Brunswick: Rutgers University Press.

Wagner, P. 1990. *Church Planting for a Greater Harvest: A Comprehensive Guide.* New York: Regal Books.

Warner, S. R., and J. G. Wittner. 1998. *Gatherings in Diaspora*. Philadelphia: Temple University Press.

Warren, R. 1995. *The Purpose Driven Church*. Grand Rapids, MI: Zondervan.

Zhou, M., and C. L. Bankston III. 1998. *Growing Up American: How Vietnamese Children Adapt to Life in the United States*. New York: Russell Sage Foundation.

Zhou, M, C. L. Bankston III, and R. Kim. 2002. Rebuilding spiritual lives in the new land: Religious practices among Southeast Asian refugees in the United States. Pp. 37–70 in P. G. Min and J. H. Kim (eds.), *Religions in Asian America: Building Faith Communities*. Lanham, MD: AltaMira.

PART IV

Minority Religions and Family Traditioning

CHAPTER 10

Second-Generation Chinese Americans

The Familism of the Nonreligious

RUSSELL JEUNG

If anything, I think the part that I'd carry on is going to the cemetery. I think the whole respect thing is really important—you take care of your elders, whether it's your parents or your grandparents. Even if that means it's in the afterlife. I believe that there is a supernatural kind of aspect to everything. It's a sign that you are there to take care of them no matter what that afterlife is, whether it's a spirit or there is an actual life after death. It's that your thoughts are still with them at some point.
—Sophia Wong, second-generation Chinese American

Sophia, in the above quotation, discusses the Chinese tradition of visiting gravesites (jizu) to pay respect and offer foods to one's ancestors. She plans to maintain this practice, even if she does not fully believe that the foods feed actual spirits. Instead, the offering of food is a sign of respect, a sign of family sacrifice. She concludes, "They're a part of what made your world what it is now. I would have to take care of the people who took care of me. It's like feeding the karmic effect. You give and get what you deserve." While she claims no religion, she certainly holds spiritual beliefs and practices, especially ones related to Chinese popular religion.

In China, Taiwan, and overseas Chinese communities, Chinese popular religion is enjoying a revival (Clart and Jones 2003; DeBernardi 2006; Overmyer et al. 1995; Overmyer 2003; Teiser 1995). Extended families offer incense (baibai) at home and business shrines. Villagers and neighbors flock to local temples that have been rebuilt or restored. People consult fengshui masters to situate homes, offices, and burial sites. Despite political efforts in various nation-states to remove "superstitious practices," Chinese popular religion has proved to be so persistent in the face of modernization and political oppression that one anthropologist labeled its revitalization as a "miraculous response" (Chau 2006).

Yet one overseas Chinese community is notably religiously unaffiliated, according to survey reports. Among all ethnic groups in the United States, Chinese Americans are the most likely to identify as nonreligious. According to Pei-Te Lien and Tony Carnes (2004), 39% of Chinese Americans do not affiliate as religious or even as spiritual. Those who are aged 21 to 45 years old are even more secular (Saguaro Seminar 2000).[1] This religious nonaffiliation is even more curious when one considers that the United States is the most religious modern state in the world and that immigrant American communities tend to be even more religious than other Americans (Albanese 2006; Chen 2008; Warner 1993; Yang and Ebaugh 2001). Given the revitalization of Chinese popular religion and the teeming religious marketplace of the United States, why are Chinese Americans seemingly so nonreligious?

This chapter explores debates in the sociology of religion around popular religion and secularism as applied to Chinese Americans. While Will Herberg argued that Protestant, Catholic, or Jew became the primary group identity of Americans in the mid-twentieth century, religious identity does not seem to be a key component of identity for Chinese Americans (Herberg 1955). Instead, only 20% of Chinese Americans claim to be Protestant, and 3% identify as Catholic (Lien and Carnes 2004). Furthermore, affiliation with and practice of Chinese popular religion also seems to be on the wane.

Chinese popular religion, as conceived here, is the repertoire of religious beliefs and practices employed by common Han Chinese (Chau 2006; Sun 2007). As a distinctive and localized religion, it consists of specific modalities of practicing religion, in contrast to exclusive belief in deities and truths (Chau 2006; Feuchtwang 2001; Teiser 1995). Components of Chinese religious repertoires include (1) ritualized relationships with gods, ghosts, and ancestors; (2) acceptance of the spiritual efficacy (ling) of religious practices; and (3) assumptions about the role of otherworldly forces, such as ming/fate, karma, and qi/universal energy (Ahern 1981; DeBernardi 2006; Freeman 1974; Wolf 1974; C. Yang 1961).

In this pilot study, interviews with eight second-generation Chinese Americans who self-identify as "nonreligious" reveal the key influences of modernization and migration in the religious affiliation of Chinese Americans.[2] Outside of the localized and extended familial context of Chinese popular religion, it does not have the cultural or institutional support to provide a meaningful worldview or to offer spiritual services. Instead, Chinese Americans discard ritual practices that they deem no longer efficacious in their pursuits, whether this-worldly or otherworldly. I hypothesize that their seeming secularization is attributable to the lack of structural support for Chinese popular religion in the United States and to their rationalistic and postmodern worldviews. In particular, they adopt an individualism that is either utilitarian or expressive.

At the same time, this cohort of the new second generation continues to utilize the religious repertoire of Chinese popular religion to develop a unique, hybridized sensibility: Chinese American familism. In contrast to a broad, Confucian worldview or a Chinese popular religious practice, Chinese American familism selectively maintains aspects of both to provide identity and belonging. In Chinese American familism, the discourse of family sacrifice—exemplified by immigrant parents' offering of time, resources, and even downward mobility—becomes the central narrative around which respondents develop their deepest and most meaningful pursuits and endeavors.

Chinese Popular Religion: Persistence and Revival

Reported numbers of religious self-identification in China, Taiwan, Hong Kong, and other overseas Chinese communities indicate that more Chinese affiliate with Chinese popular religion than with institutionalized religions (i.e., Buddhism, Taoism, Christianity, or Islam). In China, 60% believe in supernatural beings associated with Chinese folk religions, as compared to the 14% who affiliate with state-recognized religions (Grim 2008). Likewise, "mainstream religious beliefs in Taiwan—represented by Taoism, various Buddhist sects, and other denominations that originated in mainland China—are largely polytheistic and syncretistic," according to the Taiwanese

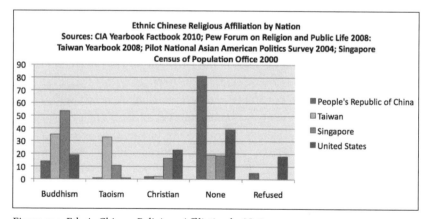

Figure 10.1. Ethnic Chinese Religious Affiliation by Nation

Government Information Office (Republic of China GIO 2008). The Central Intelligence Agency estimates that 90% of Hong Kong residents practice an "eclectic mixture of local religions" (CIA 2008). (See fig. 10.1.)

Unlike Western religious traditions, Chinese popular religion is not based on a formalized set of beliefs in particular deities. It has no sacred texts or religious doctrines, institutional organization, hierarchical priesthood, or rites that express particular beliefs (Dean 2003). Furthermore, Chinese rarely use the term religion for their popular religious practices, and they also do not utilize vocabulary that they "believe in" gods or truths (Goossaert 2006). Instead they engage in religious acts that assume a vast array of gods and spirits and that also assume the efficacy of these beings in intervening in this world. Given this conceptual problem of Chinese religious belief and the diversity of Chinese religious practices, earlier scholars of Chinese popular religion debated not only why they persisted but also whether they constituted a distinctive religion.[3]

Theories of Chinese popular religion have followed three trajectories. Early work utilized Durkheimian analyses and investigated how the beliefs and practices of Chinese folk traditions served as meaning systems that promoted social solidarity. With the revival of popular religious activity in Taiwan, and later the People's Republic of China, researchers examined the relationship of political opportunity structures and religious entrepreneurs. Research on overseas Chinese communities, however, highlighted the use of Chinese popular religion as identity movements to resist marginalization. These approaches that explain the persistence of Chinese popular religion in modernity, however, still generally assume a sociocultural context in which Asian religions are the majority.

Sociologist of religion C. K. Yang (1961) defined the form of Chinese popular religion as "diffused religion," in contrast to institutionalized religion. Found in the Chinese kinship system, in extrafamilial social and economic groups, in the community, and in the state, Chinese diffused religion persisted because it served to integrate Chinese culture. Yang wrote, in his functional and structural analysis, "The Chinese common people have always felt that, even with the utmost exertion, human abilities and efforts alone were not sufficient to guarantee physical well-being, economic success, or family harmony. There was always the profound feeling that success or failure in these respects was not entirely within human control, but needed the blessing of spiritual forces" (28). To secure the "blessing of spiritual forces," Chinese common people engaged in similar rituals that fostered both family unity and local community.

Anthropologist Arthur Wolf (1974) ranked the pantheon of these spiritual forces into gods, ghosts, and ancestors, each of whom blessed and protected the living. This tripartite division mirrored the bureaucratic land-scape of China: officials, beggars, and kin. Extending this imperial metaphor, Stephan Feuchtwang (2001) suggests that the rituals of Chinese popular religion enable historical identification with Chineseness. Both Wolf's and Feuchtwang's analyses argue that popular religion not only promoted social solidarity but also served as a meaning system rooted in the people's local context.

Chinese popular religion persists and grows, therefore, as its meaning sys-tems resonate with the historical moment. For example, Ole Bruun (2003) argues that the fengshui persists in China because it serves new generations of Chinese who continue to accept it as a "tradition of knowledge." As a means of native reflection, mode of thought, and cosmological knowledge, it helps adherents to understand and engage otherworldly forces operating in this world. As Chinese seek advantages in the pursuit of wealth, happiness, longevity, and procreation, they direct the flow of universal qi through space in their buildings.

In contrast to a focus on the meaning system of Chinese popular religion, Maurice Freeman (1974) focused on the political context that has enabled Chinese popular religion to flourish. He straightforwardly argues, "There is a Chinese religious system, both at the level of ideas and that of practice and organization. . . . There is some order—of a kind that should allow us to trace ruling principles of ideas across a vast field of apparently hetero-geneous beliefs, and ruling principles of form and organization" (20). This order and community of ideas, especially found among the ordinary people, reflects the political cohesion of China's dynastic empires. Concepts such as the power of Heaven and Earth to predetermine human history, yin-yang and the five elements, and the hierarchy of supernatural powers can be traced to a Chinese civil religion. It did not simply serve political interests but established a "common language of basic conceptions, symbols and ritual forms" (40). While Wolf and Freeman debated the unity of Chinese popu-lar religion, both scholars privileged the localized, sociopolitical context in which it developed. Similarly, more recent research examines the develop-ment of religious symbolic meaning systems in shifting political opportunity structures in both Taiwan and China (Bruun 2003; Clart and Jones 2003; Fan 2003; Jochim 2003; F. Yang 2007).

Besides emphases on the meaning system or political opportunity struc-ture of religion, other researchers focus on Chinese popular religion as a basis for identity and ethnic mobilization (Boretz 1995; Dean 2003). Particu-larly in sites where local Chinese make up a minority group, they organize temples and religious practices to set themselves apart from the mainstream.

Jean DeBenardi, for example, uses ethnography of the Hungry Ghost and Nine Emperors festival to illustrate how this revival and others were "social movements designed to create and sustain unity" in Malaysia (2006, 4). Similarly, Jonathan Lee concludes about the ritual practice of parading the goddess Mazu in the San Francisco Chinese New Year's Festival, "There is, therefore, the potential for American Mazu to function as a unifying symbol of Chinese identity for the various ethnic Chinese American groups in the United States" (2006, 250). These practices demarcate ethnic Chinese from their non-Chinese host societies and enable them to establish reactive solidarity in the context of racism and ethnic competition.

These three theoretical approaches to the revival of Chinese popular religion—as historically resonant systems of meaning, as responses to the political opportunity structure, and as ethnic mobilizations—each sheds light on why Chinese popular religion currently faces a decline, especially among the second generation. Chinese Americans do religion in very different cultural and political contexts, so that they utilize other religious and nonreligious resources to maintain meaning and a sense of belonging.

Instead of being a resonant system of meaning, Chinese popular religious beliefs make less sense to Chinese in the modernized and utilitarian culture of the United States. As voluntary migrants who often come on educational or professional visas, they pursue the material interests of the American Dream in very rational, calculated ways. With a large percentage coming from science and engineering backgrounds, these Chinese American households find rituals of Chinese popular religion often irrelevant to their day-to-day lives.

Furthermore, the American political context, especially that of freedom of religion, also ironically discourages the development of Chinese popular religion. Religious disestablishment encourages a competitive religious marketplace, in which congregations seek to attract spiritual consumers. Those congregations with greater institutional support, as well as cultural resonance, are more effective in marketing. Chinese popular religion, without a well-organized, professional hierarchy, is at a disadvantage in this setting. Instead, Chinese Americans are able to develop other ethnic symbols for identity and belonging. These factors—meaning systems, institutional support, and symbols of ethnic identity—are further explored in the research findings that follow.

Methodology and Sample

Chinese popular religion cannot be analyzed and categorized in the same way that Western religions are. Michael Syonzi summarizes the primary difference between Chinese understandings of religion and those of the West:

> Neither church attendance nor survey-based assessments of individual beliefs have much meaning for Chinese people, aside from Christians and Muslims. Practice ("doing," to use Chau's term (2006), meaning participation in individual and communal rituals, is a more defining element of Chinese religion. Here again we see the mismatch of the Enlightenment-derived definition of religion with the situation in China. (2009, 319)

To measure religiosity or its opposite, secularism, among Chinese Americans thus would entail an examination of the decline in religious practice and ritual participation. While others have examined secularism in terms of the privatization of religion or religious nonaffiliation, this research investigates instead how Chinese Americans do religion (Stark, Hamberg, and Miller 2005).

Another methodological problem raised by Chinese popular religious practice is that of religious identity. In China, the government and scholars consider popular folk practices as superstition (mixin; literally, confused beliefs) or excessive sacrifices (yin-si). Individuals, then, rarely identify as believing in or practicing such religions. In the United States, religious censuses and surveys do not offer categories for popular religious practices. Instead, mutually exclusive religious affiliations are listed, precluding the opportunity to identify with several traditions, as Chinese often do. Therefore, Chinese Americans may be more likely to mark "None" or "Don't Know" on these religious surveys.

To address these methodological issues of studying Chinese Americans, this research utilizes in-depth interviews to explore the religious practices of respondents, as well as their beliefs and meaning systems. To understand their worldviews and religious change, respondents were asked about their parents' religion, their own religious socialization, and their current moral frameworks, ultimate beliefs, and ritualized practices. In addition, questions about their ethnicity and race sought to ascertain how Chinese popular religion related to their identity.

Gained through purposive, nonrandom sampling to access this minority subpopulation, the respondents were second-generation Chinese Americans, aged 21–45 years old, who did not affiliate with any religion. By examining the second generation, religious change and secularization processes across generations are observed. This age cohort is the most secular of any age group in the United States, as they are undergoing life-cycle changes that are most conducive to religious change: being single, career transitioning, and having residential mobility. Furthermore, this age cohort of second-generation Chinese Americans make up the children of the "new immigrants," the largest influx of newcomers to the United States. As such, members of this second generation are still young adults and at the forefront of religious and racial demographic changes in the United States.

The eight respondents are all college-educated, with four whose parents are from working-class backgrounds and four with parents from professional backgrounds. The parents of the former were from Guangdong or Hong Kong who came through family-reunification visas. The parents of the latter were Mandarin speakers from the People's Republic of China or Taiwan and obtained advanced degrees in science while on student visas to the United States. Three were male and five were female, and they grew up throughout the country.

Findings
Parental Religious Repertoires: "Translating It and Carrying It Along"

The Chinese American immigrant community is bimodal in educational and class background. Like earlier Chinese immigrants who entered before the 1965 Immigration Act, Chinese who are from Guangdong province are more likely to be from rural, working-class backgrounds. In contrast, Mandarin-speaking immigrants who come from Taiwan through professional occupational visas are highly educated. Both groups are represented in this sample, and respondents reported that their parents practiced Chinese popular religion, but to varying degrees. Modernization theory, with the expansion of scientific worldviews, accounts for why some of the parents became more secular in outlook. Equally significant, though, was the fact that the practices and beliefs of Chinese popular religion do not have the same cultural support in the United States that they have in Asia.

The parents with scientific backgrounds tended to be atheistic and did not believe in supernatural intervention in this world. Cheryl Teng, whose parents both obtained doctorates, explained, "I would characterize [my parents] as nonreligious because they've never shown anything that would be otherwise. They're both practical people, and they're both scientists. It would go against their practical mind-set. I guess they need evidence and proof of something to believe it." She adopted a similar mind-set, and as the following quotation illustrates, she used biology as an exemplar for her paradigm of the world. Even in regard to the problem of suffering and the nature of reality, Cheryl shared their scientific viewpoint: "I've always thought that's the way things are. That's nature; [suffering and death are] going to happen sometimes. That's the nature of life—people live and die; it's biology. Consulting a higher being seems a little weird. Reality makes sense—that bad things happen." The others who were raised in scientific households held similar rationalistic and scientific models of thinking.

Cheryl's quotations reveal key aspects of this worldview. Her parents require "evidence and proof" for belief, which exemplifies their rationalistic and deductive perspective toward the nature of reality and their engagement with the world. In relation to suffering, her theodicy is simply to accept the natural course of life and death. The material world is all that exists, so she seeks to maximize her time here. Likewise, other Chinese Americans with scientific or engineering backgrounds are likely to be religious "Nones."[4] For those who come from such households, religion may not be necessary as a coherent system of belief and meaning, since science takes its place.

While the respondents often claimed that their parents were nonreligious, they also maintained that their parents practiced rituals of Chinese popular religion. As this chapter has argued, their belief in the religion may not be as relevant as their continued use of Chinese religious repertoires, that is, the range of rituals and resources used for different purposes (Jeung 2009; Sun 2007). Beliefs, symbols, and objects utilized in festivals and rituals such as Lunar New Year and ancestor veneration reveal how Chinese popular religion operates to maintain identity, to promote solidarity, and to help one relate to one's social context.

For example, each of the eight respondents reported that their families maintain Lunar New Year customs. Those who spoke Mandarin maintained simple family reunions over meals, but those from Guangdong adhered to much more elaborate tradition keeping: extensive decoration, eating special foods, and taboo rituals to ensure good fortune. Sophia Wong, who grew up in San Francisco in a Cantonese household, described her family's annual customs:

> Chinese New Year is always big. I remember when we were younger, it felt a lot more strict in terms of the traditions and things like that. I would say we pretty much kept most of the tradition. It felt more strict when we were younger: the whole thing about bad luck, good luck, during Chinese New Year. [You] can't drop your bowl, can't drop your chopsticks. You have to wash your hair, clean, and do all these things before the New Year.

Dropping items brings bad luck for the year. Washing hair would rinse away one's fortune. Sophia calls these traditions "superstitious," but she continues to avoid hair washing and haircuts during the New Year. She reasons that her parents are strict about their adherence because they were raised to believe in the efficacy of these rituals: "I think they do believe [the customs]. I don't think they do it just to do it. I guess they're superstitious. If anything, that's the way they were brought up. So they're just translating whatever they were taught, and they're carrying it along." Whether the parents believed in the power of a new year's tradition to bring luck, all the families "carried it along," translated it, and continued one form of the tradition in the United States. However, because such traditions did not belong to any clear-cut, institutionalized religion, the respondents did not know how to classify their parents' beliefs or practices. While Chinese in Asia may be able to identify and understand these practices, Chinese Americans such as Sophia are more likely to recognize them as "superstitions."

In one case, Steph Woo, who was raised in Prince George's County, Maryland, explained how her teacher counted her as Christian simply because her family put up a Christmas tree:

> In first grade, we went around the room and asked what religion did they have. And I didn't know what to say when they got to me. I'd say, "I don't know, I don't think I have one." And they'd say, "Well, do you celebrate Christmas? Yeah? Well, okay, then you're Christian." I'd say, "Okay!" I was sort of confused but also pleasantly surprised that I was suddenly accepted into the majority.

On the one hand, because her family celebrated Christmas with a tree and presents, Steph was easily categorized as a Christian. On the other hand, her family believed in and practiced Lunar New Year traditions but had no name or way to categorize themselves religiously. Consequently, others labeled her childhood religious affiliation as Christian and not with Chinese popular religion.[5] Later negative experiences with Christianity, however, predisposed Steph to avoid religion. Like six of the eight interviewees, she felt uncomfortable with the evangelical culture in her environment, disliked being judged and condemned to hell, and chafed against the morality and rules. Consequently, respondents did not feel the need to convert.

Often, whether the parents practiced Chinese popular religion depended on their context. Michele Li, who grew up in a suburb of Pennsylvania, returned regularly every three to five years to visit family in Taipei. She recalls that her parents did not practice any Chinese religious traditions while in the United States but actively participated when they were in Taiwan. Her grandmother's funeral service stood out in her memory because of her parents' unusual engagement in rituals:

> [My parents] don't practice anything. But I did notice recently, when my dad's mom passed away, that the funeral opened up all these different practices that I didn't know about. We all had to fold a billion different little paper boats and throw them in the burner because all the incense was going to go up with her. We had to make a shrine and pray to her, do incense and all these chantings. I don't think they were Buddhist. They might have had a Buddhist influence. It kind of felt a little Buddhist. I don't really know. That was the first time I realized, "Oh, my family does these ritual custom things."

Because she never saw such practices in the United States, Michele did not even know what to call them and equivocated as to whether they were Buddhist or not.

Michele explained that her parents, who retired in Taipei, now more often engage in these rituals of ancestor veneration despite their skepticism of them. The family's funeral rituals created tension between her family and her relatives in Taiwan, because of her parents' opposition to the high cost of the funeral, their lack of belief in these rituals, and their lack of understanding about the exact nature of the rituals. Nevertheless, in Taiwan, her uncle insisted that these religious practices were the taken-for-granted norms: "My uncle was like, 'This is normal. This is what you do.' So my parents were like, 'Okay, whatever makes you happy.' But I don't think they personally believe in any of the things. I don't know if they understand everything." Despite the family stresses over funeral arrangements, her parents agreed to the rituals and the costs because of family obligations. For the sake of family unity, they participated in the elaborate rituals. Michele herself found that the funeral connected her with long-lost relatives:

> But in general [the funeral ceremony] just brought us all together. We have a couple of uncles in China, and it was the first time our uncle in China and our other uncles were all together. So it was a nice family event. But it was really nice because all the cousins got together. My sister flew back. We all held the paper things together. When else are we going to come together, like these four brothers?

What made the ceremony special for Michele was the way it reunited the extended family from across the globe and provided her a ritual practice that tied her with her cousins.

Now that Michele's parents live in Taiwan, they continue to engage much more in the religious culture there. In that context, Chinese popular religion resonates more fully with local and household environments than it does in the United States. They regularly visit the grandmother's tomb, sweep it, and offer food there. They also have a shrine with the grandmother's photo in their home. Michele explained how the changes in the religious environment shaped her parents' resurrected spiritual practices:

> We never had a photo up or a shrine or incense. But now that they're back, they're more into it. Or, it's like a family event; everyone is going, so they just go along. [Their newfound practice of ancestor veneration] makes sense to me. When they're away in [the United States], they didn't really believe in it; they had their own little life in America. Now that they're back, it's such a big change. In general, they're so involved with the family. I think they're just back, and they're in that environment.

The behaviors of Michele's parents offer insights into how the cultural context shapes the practice of Chinese popular religion. In Taiwan, participation in religious rituals is a family obligation for which abstention would bring about social censure. In contrast, such practices are more privatized in the United States, in one's "own little life." Consequently, their continuance is more optional, and they are more likely to be dropped. These immigrant parents, in employing their religious repertoires from family and community, ward off misfortune and support their ancestors in the afterlife, as well as strengthen family harmony and preserve their Chinese heritage. Carried along to the United States context, however, these repertoires become uprooted from both their meaning systems and their original functions. Translation is difficult, as the parents do not have the language, religious categories, or institutions to effectively pass on these repertoires. Considered superstitions by the second generation, Lunar New Year traditions and ancestor-veneration rituals no longer have the broader cultural resonance or institutional support in the United States. The parents had these repertoires instilled in them as commonsense ways of life—"as the way they were brought up." However, second-generation Chinese Americans recount very different ways of religious socialization in the United States.

The Religious Socialization of the Second Generation: "We Never Talked about Why"

Even though the immigrant parents maintained Chinese religious practices, none explained the traditions or explicitly trained their children about them.

The second generation were often brought along to temples for observation when they were younger, but by adolescence, their religious obligations loosened. The second generation could only discuss their parents' religions in vague terms. Instead, the respondents expressed that they were highly unlikely to keep most of these traditions because of their lack of knowledge of the practices and their meanings. Indeed, the religious marketplace in the United States fails to supply requisite training, religious professionals, or institutional spaces for the development of Chinese popular religion.

Living about one hour from San Francisco, with its large Chinese American population, Rodney Shem's parents have been able to preserve several of the traditions from their religious upbringing in Hong Kong. He reports that they keep shrines in their study and that they strategically place fengshui symbols to protect rooms and the house. The parents even visit a temple fairly often and had a monk bless Rodney with a Chinese name. Despite their devotedness, Rodney understands little of his parents' religious and spiritual sensibilities because his father conducts rituals privately and his mother teaches him little. He elaborates, "My dad has in his office a Buddha statue and fengshui mirrors outside of the front door. He lights incense. Every morning he bows three times in front of it. He has a picture of his mom—she's deceased. He tells me he does, but I don't see him." Rodney's father even put up a Chinese inscription above Rodney's bedroom door frame, but again both parents failed to explain why: "He did put Chinese—it looked like a scripture—in my room above my wall and above the door. I don't know what the translation is. He didn't tell me what it was, and I didn't ask what it was. It's in red. I asked my mom about it. She said it's just for good luck. She didn't really elaborate on it." While preserving these practices was important enough to Rodney's parents for them to practice daily, they did not deem them important enough to explain them to Rodney.

Similarly, Laura Chan's Toisan-speaking mother brought her to a Chinese temple when she was in grade school outside of Boston, Massachusetts. She remembers that she simply followed her mother around and observed but did not participate much. By Laura's teen years, her mother visited the temple much less frequently because of the distance. Laura observed, "They go to the temple, and we used to go to the temple. They used to do it—back then it was like once a week, and eventually they stopped. It was a half-an-hour to 45-minute drive. I've been like twice. I followed my mom around. I didn't bow or anything. She'd talk to Buddhist monks, and I was just there. I remember standing near the gift shop or where they have beads and have donations." That visits to the temple were infrequent because of its inconvenient distance exemplifies the lack of institutional and community resources to support Chinese popular religion in the United States. Without the easy access, Laura's parents were less likely to pray and make offerings, as they did in Toisan.

Laura's statement "I was just there" reveals her passive attendance at the temple. While the visits could have been colorful or even exotic to her, her memories were nonvivid and disinterested. Since Laura did not receive training or explanation about her parents' practices, she feels that she could not continue Chinese traditions even if she desired to do so. She explained the difficulty in preparing special dishes for Lunar New Year's:

> I think it would be hard only because I'm not familiar with cooking food the specific dates, the new calendar versus the old [Chinese lunar] calendar. I'd celebrate it and have family dinner, but I'm not sure how traditional it could get. I don't know how to make the dishes. My mom tells me, "Go buy yourself a mooncake. Have at least one." I'd say, "It's okay. I don't need one." It's hard for me to keep those traditions because I don't know how to cook the food.

Instead, these Chinese traditions have become ethnic options for her.

Like Laura, Sophia does not know the traditional times to hold the festival or the ingredients to prepare the special dishes. She complains,

> That's the thing: they never explained why we do the things we do. We never talked about why. You do it because you're supposed to do it. When you go to cemetery or when my mom will make the zong,[6] she doesn't say why or what part of the calendar it lands on or why she's making it now. I come home one day, and she's in the kitchen, and the whole kitchen table is covered with all these ingredients to make it. So then I know it's that time of the year. I keep saying I need to learn how to do these things, but at the same time I never really get around to doing it. Part of it is the language. You can't just go to any old supermarket and say, "I'm looking for this." I would know what it looked like, but it would be kind of difficult.

Again, the lack of institutional support in the United States, such as being able to purchase Chinese food products easily, deters Sophia from participating in these traditions.

Since the Chinese religious repertoires are unexplained, these second-generation Chinese Americans consider them as "slightly superstitious or slightly silly," as Michele said. They especially doubted the efficacy of these practices, although three continue to uphold taboos and use fengshui concepts. Since these practices lack much meaning for the respondents, they instead adopt other worldviews that are more salient in the United States. In general, they adopt rationalistic, scientific approaches to reality and to mastering their environment. Laura shared the scientific perspective that all the second-generation respondents held about healing: "For example, my brother is diabetic, and he was having a sugar spell. My dad took this yin-yang thing, a spider-web-like octagon with a mirror. He started using it and rubbing ointment on his head. I'm like, 'That is not gonna do anything. He needs a glass of orange juice.'" Rather than utilizing Eastern holistic healing principles, the second generation prefer Western medicine and believe in its efficacy.

Thus, in the pluralistic religious marketplace of America, Chinese popular religion loses adherents due to lack of coherence and meaningfulness. Without an institutional base, professional staffing, or translated teachings, it cannot transmit traditions to the second generation.[7] Even though the immigrant parents practice customs and traditions of Chinese popular religion, they do not require or even expect their children to learn them or uphold them.

Yet the religious repertoire of Chinese Americans did not simply vanish as the second generation became acculturated. Instead, the values and ideals of Chinese popular religion transformed and developed into what I term Chinese American familism. Although their parents were not very strict with religious socialization, they did expect their adult children to take care of them and to respect their forebears. Their children learned to maintain this ethic regarding family responsibilities but combined it with distinctly American mind-sets of utilitarian and expressive individualism. The result is a hybridized form of Chinese popular religion, with very selectively retained elements.

Chinese American Utilitarian and Expressive Individualism:
"You Might as Well Work Hard for Yourself"

Bellah et al. (1985) identify two current forms of American individualism, utilitarian and expressive, that have arisen in the past half a century to supplant the biblical and republican traditions of communitarianism. Utilitarian individualism involves the pursuit and maximization of one's own self-interests. Expressive individualism, on the other hand, privileges the search for personal autonomy, fulfillment, and expression. Indeed, Americans now affiliate with religious traditions based on their own choice, which Roof and McKinney coined the "new voluntarism" (1987). They also can construct their own patchwork of religious references and practices, which Bellah et al. typified as "Sheilaism" (1985). This individual approach to spirituality often parallels a rejection of organized religions as too dogmatic and intolerant. Secularization theorists suggest that such religious "bricolage" is another indicator of institutional religion's decline.[8] In this American context of individualism, second-generation Chinese Americans are free to choose their own religious affiliations and practices. In contrast, in Asia, religious affiliation is more of an ascribed identity. Also, Chinese Americans who are non-religious do not need religion as a source of meaning or belonging but have found more individualistic ways to find purpose and values.

The lives of the college-educated, 20-something-year-olds in my survey revolved around their individual interests, whether their careers, their desires for more experiences, or their relationships. Overall, their purposes in life were this-worldly objectives that were generally attainable. Two men, Ben Hao and Peter Hsieh, illustrate utilitarian and expressive individualism, respectively. Ben Hao grew up in Seattle, Washington, where both his parents got graduate degrees in the sciences. They focused on his education, and he was able to enter the University of Washington as a 16-year-old. He obtained a degree in computer science but then entered an elite law school and became an attorney for start-up companies in Silicon Valley. Planning to quit soon to begin his own start-up, he explained that his choices center around gaining skills that will enable him to start his own business and reap the rewards of his own hard work: "I actually want to start a company. I'm writing a Facebook application, and maybe there will be something there. On a personal level, I don't really like working for other people. Mostly because the profit doesn't all go to me. If you're already working hard, you might as well work hard for yourself." He explained that he wanted to make a product that people would enjoy or would make their lives better, which seems altruistic. He went on to elaborate, however, on his assumption that personal consumption and commodities "make lives better":

BEN: Computer science has given me a lot of satisfaction. You're making something or doing something that a lot of the people are enjoying or makes their lives better.
INTERVIEWER: You want to create something that the rest of the world would enjoy?
BEN: Yeah. Something that's useful for the world.
INTERVIEWER: So Facebook apps? Is that the kind of thing?

BEN: Yeah. Pretty much any software that makes money. By definition, people are paying money for it; therefore, people place value in it. It's a broad definition "useful." Sort of the economic definition of utility. I want to do something that people are willing to pay for.

What people are willing to buy defines a commodity's usefulness. At this stage in Ben's career, he is aiming to utilize his degrees to earn as much profit as he can.

Peter is similar to Ben in that he, too, grew up in a scientific and non-religious household and he studied computer science. Having been raised in Naperville, Illinois, he moved to San Francisco after college, not only because of Silicon Valley but also because of the art scene there. He spends his off hours on his art and painting, through which he said he could make a living if he wanted. Rather than focusing solely on his computer career or his art, he pursues experiences to live life to the fullest:

There are more things I want to do—more art shows, work, making money, meeting a girl. . . . Our most important time is our time here. There's no point in saving up for karma; this is all we have. So I do things that make me happy: art, friends, family. I try not getting caught up in being compet-itive or overly ambitious. If I can take care of me and my own, I'm happy. I still want to travel, explore, and learn.

Peter's expressive individualism is structured by his atheism. Since he does not believe in any afterlife or karma, he aims to maximize his time here through whatever makes him happy.

These second-generation Chinese Americans were similar in their pur-poses in life. They generally wanted to be happy on this earth through career accomplishment, learning new things, and taking care of family. Being non-religious, they primarily framed the purposes of their lives in individualistic terms, with less regard to changing the world, improving society, or help-ing others. When a few did discuss helping others or effecting social change, they focused on how they can make small differences by having "good hearts." Cheryl Teng, a student at UC Berkeley, asserted, "I feel as long as there's an attempt to make a positive impact, that's okay. For me, it gives life more meaning." Even Cheryl's altruistic perspective is limited to her individ-ual intentions and not to actually helping others or creating a good society.

In contrast to Chinese in Asia, those in the United States are freer to choose their own, individualized sources of identity and purpose, given America's freedom of religion and its religious marketplace. In contrast to

Herberg's thesis, they do not need religion to establish a sense of identity or to assimilate. Neither do they need religion for a sense of their ethnic identity.[9] What distinguishes these Chinese Americans, though, from other typical American individualists is their particular relationship to their families, especially their parents.

Family Sacrifice: Narratives and Rituals of Belonging

When the respondents were asked what gives them purpose and meaning, all raised the idea of supporting and caring for their families. The value of filial piety, based in Confucianism and Chinese popular religion—respecting one's elders and taking care of those younger—permeated their worldview and significantly affected their individual choices about career, marriage, and residence. Their immigrant parents deeply impressed these values on the second generation through their own example of hard work, time usage, and personal sacrifice. By observing their parents' own behaviors, and from hearing their stories, the second generation developed a very keen sense of responsibility to care for their elders and to invest in raising their own children.

C. K. Yang (1961) argued that the function of Chinese ancestor veneration is to teach filial piety, and the Chinese Americans in my survey certainly learned their lessons. When Sophia Wong visited her parents' ancestral village in China, she went to visit her grandfather's and great-grandfather's gravesites. Her extended family joined her on a long trek to the site, bearing incense, drinks, and even a whole pig to offer. She recounted,

> The first time I ever went back to China was a couple years ago. We actually went up to the gravesite of my grandfather. It was the first time that we went to the tombs. They went all out in terms buying all the food: they bought a whole pig. They carried all these things to these gravesites. They're not like cemeteries here. You would hike like probably half a mile to a mile through hills and unmarked roads. I joke about it sometimes, but when we go to the cemetery here, we still call it "seung saan," like "walk up a mountain."[10] I used to be like, "Why do they call it that?" And now I'm like—I understand. Because they are literally going up through the hills and up through the brush. You're actually walking through.

The effort the family made to fulfill their filial duties made a deep impression on Sophia. In Chinese, sao mu (sweeping ancestors' graves) is the regular ritual of visiting the gravesite, cleaning the tomb, and making offerings (ji zu). When Sophia was asked whether she felt that these rituals held spiritual significance or were simply cultural customs, she recognized that they had more transcendent meanings for her. In fact, they were both a moral obligation and a way of being: "I think it's a very respectful thing. Back there it's the way it is. I guess in a way to me it's not just like a custom. It's like something you should do; it's something you're supposed to do." As "the way it is" and "something you're supposed to do," Chinese popular religion makes up Sophia's ethical and metaphysical framework.

Sophia does not firmly believe that offering food will benefit actual spirits, but she claimed that she will still continue the practice of visiting the cemetery. It is, in fact, her way of demonstrating family unity and love: "I feel like there is an afterlife. What it is, I don't know. But I think that [going to the cemetery] creates a stronger family bond. A lot of times, a lot of Chinese families aren't very affectionate or very close knit like you would see in an American family. This is not really an affectionate [way of relating], but it's, like, a thing you should have." Sophia is "spiritual, not religious" in that she does not affiliate with any institutional religion, but she carries on spiritual practices. Three of the eight respondents in my sample may be categorized in this way. They continue to utilize the religious repertoire of Chinese popular religion, even though they may not identify with it or fully believe in it.

The Chinese parents of these second-generation respondents, beyond making their children observe and participate in sao mu, also share stories and make pointed remarks to inculcate Chinese American familism. For example, Laura Chan shared how her father joked with her about visiting the gravesite:

My father did say, "If I ever die, I expect money in the afterlife." He says it jokingly. It's always kind of like an odd topic, like, "Oh, when I die, and you come see me, I expect you to do the same as what I'm doing for my father." Like burning the fake money, bowing, and burning incense—there's even fake clothes that you can burn that goes into the afterlife. They don't expect me to go to temple, have a Buddha statue, but they do expect go to the cemetery.

She said that although she plans to visit the cemetery after her parents pass away, she probably will not do all those traditions. On the other hand, Sophia is very willing to be financially responsible for her parents. Even though she moved to San Francisco for career opportunities, she offered to return to the East Coast to physically take care of them. She noted that this "expected" norm distinguishes Chinese Americans from other Americans:

I was going to move back to keep them company. There was an empty nest. They were always alone, so I said I was going to move back after two years. I think that's what they expected. I think that's the difference between American culture and Chinese culture: the kids are always expected to take care of your parents. I would take care of them if my brother didn't step up. I'd do my best to alleviate their stress.

Familism, in the form of taking care of the elderly and being responsible for children, is the ethnic symbol that Chinese Americans employ to demarcate them from other Americans. This value in and of itself, not the range of rituals of Chinese popular religion, serves to be sufficient to maintain ethnic identity.

What tempers the individualism of the second-generation Chinese Americans is the discourse of family sacrifice. To immigrate, their parents made great sacrifices and worked hard to support their families. The second generation feel a great indebtedness to them and hold a collective, group orientation that privileges family needs over their own individualistic ones. Ben Hao is very driven to maximize profits and his own use of time. When asked why he is so driven, he expressed, "Ultimately giving my parents like a good rest of their life, I guess." He reasoned that their commitment, especially his mother's sacrifice of the career that she loved, ought to be reciprocated: "I think my mom definitely loves medicine, but she sacrificed that to raise me and my sister. For example, we never had a baby sitter. She said many times that medicine is her true love. And so I think there's something about human nature makes me want to repay that." Just as Sophia asserted that ancestor veneration is "something that you should do," Ben has the conviction that "human nature" makes him "want to repay" his parents' love, support, and sacrifice. Not all American children have this same impulse to repay their parents, yet Ben believes that such reciprocity is his highest value.

The moral imperatives of familism thus provide these second-generation Chinese Americans a meaningful system of values that provides both identity and belonging. Their practice of traditions from Chinese popular religion has waned. But they continue to adhere to some of their religious repertoires, including values of reciprocity, symbols of family unity, and practices of respect.

Conclusion

Given the small sample size on which this chapter is based, only a few tentative conclusions can be made. These second-generation Chinese Americans identify as nonreligious because they do not belong to any established religious tradition. Instead, they hold scientific worldviews, as well as individualistic perspectives that undermine viewpoints from religious authorities. They also profess not to believe in God or divine beings, although they do not discount the possibility of their existence. Most are agnostic about life after death and doubt the efficacy of offering sacrifices to ancestors.

Yet defining religious affiliation by one's belief system or one's institutional membership fails to account fully for the spiritual and religious experiences of Chinese Americans. Three of the eight are "spiritual but not religious" and engage in spiritual practices such as ancestor veneration and fengshui. Even more significantly, perhaps, is that these Chinese Americans continue to adhere to a hybridized form of Chinese popular religion, which I term Chinese American familism.

Chinese American familism is more than simply valuing family and obeying one's parents, as it creates an ultimate meaning system that offers identity and belonging. When combined with American utilitarian and expressive individualism, this religious repertoire consists of values, symbols, and rituals cohering around the Chinese American family. The second generation find depth of meaning in working hard, with the end of supporting their family. They gain firm identity and belonging—expressive needs—by participating in rituals, such as simply visiting the cemetery or celebrating Lunar New Year, to promote family unity and harmony.

Because these needs for identity and belonging are fulfilled in these ways, they do not need to participate in more elaborate traditions of Chinese popular religion, including offering sacrifices to the ancestors or preparing special New Year's dishes. Although these traditions may have similar functional purposes of promoting family solidarity as they do in Asia, their symbolic meanings are increasingly lost in the United States.

Certainly, the degree to which these individuals adhere to Chinese American familism varies, as two do not even plan to have their own children. Yet they all agree that they feel a greater responsibility to their parents and siblings than other Americans do and that family loyalty supersedes their individual concerns. Their sense of loyalty and responsibility does not extend to other responsibilities to community, however, so they cannot be labeled as cultural Confucians (Sun 2007).

Other variations that may be seen as trends include differences in class background, ancestral region in China, and gender. Those whose parents were scientists were much more likely to be atheistic, while those from working-class backgrounds continued to practice fengshui. The Cantonese and Toisanese families had more elaborate Lunar New Year customs, and their children had a higher probability of continuing these traditions. In general, the men adopted more scientific perspectives, while the women were more open to existence of divine beings, spirits, and supernatural forces. Future research should investigate these emerging patterns.

Albeit exploratory, this study of second-generation Chinese Americans demonstrates that those who identify as nonreligious still make use of the religious repertoires of Chinese popular religion. As a result of their upbringing, they are each willing to make great family sacrifices.

NOTES

1. Among college students, 28% of Asian Americans have no religious preference, compared to 8% of African Americans and 17% of whites (Higher Education Research Institute 2005).
2. These initial in-depth interviews are part of a larger project on Chinese American popular religion and secularization.
3. Max Weber (1951) described Chinese popular religion as magic and as a "chaotic mass of functional gods." Quoted in C. K. Yang 1961, 20.
4. Indeed, with 52% claiming no religion, scientists are three times more likely than the general public to adopt a secular identity (Ecklund and Scheitle 2007). Almost half of Asians (47.3%) earned bachelor's degrees in science and engineering, in contrast to 31.6% of all Americans (Babco 2005).
5. Christian privilege structures how religion is conceived, practiced, and even experienced. For example, Khyati Joshi (2006) identifies how Western conceptions of religion—as doctrinal, congregational, and voluntary—shape how Asian Indians adhere to Hinduism in the United States. Although Joshi argues that her subjects do practice "lived religion," they themselves claim no religion, as they employ Eurocentric notions of religion.
6. *Zong* is glutinous rice steamed in bamboo leaves, traditionally eaten for the Dragon Boat Festival.
7. Similarly, ethnographic studies comparing ethnic Christian and Buddhist congregations indicate that the Buddhist temples have much fewer resources for religious training and youth programming than do the Christian ones. They thus lose adherents too (Chen 2008; Chai 2001).
8. From one perspective, secularism involves the decline of institutional religion and its importance in society. Religious bricolage, the combining of religious beliefs, indicates the privatization of religion and the lessened significance of institutional religion (Casanova 1994; Chaves 1994; Saroglou 2006).
9. Cavalcanti and Schleef (2005) found that second-generation Latinos (14%) were also more likely to be nonreligious than were their immigrant parents (8%). Furthermore, these nonreligious Latinos were very adapted to the dominant institutions of the United States, indicating that they did not need religion to belong or assimilate.
10. Sophia here uses the Sze Yup dialect. When individuals die, they are said to *shang shan*, literally, "climb up the mountain" to heaven.

REFERENCES

Ahern, Emily. 1981. *Chinese Ritual and Politics*. Cambridge: Cambridge University Press.
Albanese, Catherine. 2006. *America: Religions and Religion*. Belmont, CA: Wadsworth.

Babco, Eleanor. 2005. *The Status of Native Americans in Science and Engineering*. New York: Commission on Professionals in Science and Technology.

Bellah, Robert, Richard Madsen, William M. Sullivan, Ann Swidler, and Steven M. Tipton. 1985. *Habits of the Heart: Individualism and Commitment in American Life*. Berkeley: University of California Press.

Boretz, Avron. 1995. "Martial Gods and Magic Swords: Identity, Myth, and Violence in Chinese Popular Religion." *Journal of Popular Culture* 29 (1): 93–109.

Bruun, Ole. 2003. *Fengshui in China: Geomantic Divination between State Orthodoxy and Popular Religion*. Honolulu: University of Hawai'i Press.

Cavalcanti, H. B., and Debra Schleef. 2005. "The Case for Secular Assimilation? The Latino Experience in Richmond, Virginia." *Journal for the Scientific Study of Religion* 44 (4): 473–483.

Casanova, Jose. 1994. *Public Religions in the Modern World*. Chicago: University of Chicago Press.

Chai, Karen. 2001. "Intra-ethnic Religious Diversity: Korean Buddhist and Christians in the Greater Boston Area." In Ho Youn Kwan, Kwang Chun Kim, and R. Stephen Warner, eds., *Korean Americans and Their Religions*, 273–294. University Park: Pennsylvania State University Press.

Chau, Adam. 2006. *Miraculous Response: Doing Popular Religion in Contemporary China*. Stanford: Stanford University Press.

Chaves, Mark. 1994. "Secularization as Declining Religious Authority." *Social Forces* 72:749–774.

Chen, Carolyn. 2008. *Getting Saved in America: Taiwanese Immigration and Religious Experience*. Princeton: Princeton University Press.

CIA. 2008. *World Factbook*. https://www.cia.gov/library/publications/the-world-factbook/fields/2122.html?countryName=China&countryCode=ch&regionCode=eas&#ch (accessed October 31, 2010).

———. 2010. *CIA Fact Yearbook*.

Clart, Philip, and Charles Jones, eds. 2003. *Religion in Modern Taiwan: Tradition and Innovation in a Changing Society*. Honolulu: University of Hawai'i Press.

Dean, Kenneth. 2003. *Taoist Ritual and Popular Cults of Southeast China*. Princeton: Princeton University Press.

DeBernardi, Jean. 2006. *The Way That Lives in the Heart: Chinese Popular Religion and Spirit Mediums in Penang, Malaysia*. Stanford: Stanford University Press.

Ecklund, Elaine Howard, and Christopher Scheitle. 2007. "Religion among Academic Scientists: Distinctions, Disciplines, and Demographics." *Social Problems* 54 (2): 289–307.

Fan, Lizhu. 2003. "Study of Religious Beliefs and Practices in Contemporary China: Case Study of Popular Religion in Shenzhen." Ph.D. diss., Chinese University of Hong Kong.

Feuchtwang, Stephan. 2001. *Popular Religion in China: The Imperial Metaphor*. Richmond, UK: Curzon.

Freeman, Maurice. 1974. "On the Sociological Study of Chinese Religion." In Arthur Wolf, ed., *Religion and Ritual in Chinese Society*. Stanford: Stanford University Press.

Goossaert, Vincent. 2006. "1898: The Beginning of the End for Chinese Religion?" *Journal of Asian Studies* 65 (2): 307–336.

Grim, Brian. 2008. "Religion in China on the Eve of the 2008 Beijing Olympics." Pew Forum on Religion and Public Life. http://pewresearch.org/pubs/827/china-religion-olympics.

Herberg, Will. 1955. *Protestant, Catholic, Jew*. Chicago: University of Chicago Press.

Higher Education Research Institute, UCLA. 2005. *The Spiritual Life of College Students: A National Study of College Students' Search for Meaning and Purpose*. Report of "Spirituality in Higher Education" survey.

Jeung, Russell. 2009. "The Use of Religious Repertoires in Asian America." In Asian American Studies, eds., *At 40: Asian American Studies at San Francisco State*. San Francisco: SFSU Asian American Studies Department.

Jochim, Christian. 2003. "Carrying Confucianism into the Modern World." In Philip Clart and Charles Jones, eds., *Religion in Modern Taiwan: Tradition and Innovation in a Changing Society*, 48–83. Honolulu: University of Hawai'i Press.

Joshi, Khyati. 2006. *New Roots in America's Sacred Ground: Religion, Race, and Ethnicity in Indian America*. New Brunswick: Rutgers University Press.

Lee, Jonathan. 2006. "Contemporary Chinese American Religious Life." In James Miller, ed., *Chinese Religions in Contemporary Societies*, 235–256. Santa Barbara, CA: ABC-CLIO.

Lien, Pei-Te. 2004. "Pilot National Asian American Politics Survey." Inter-university Consortium for Political and Social Research. Available online at http://prod.library. utoronto.ca/datalib/codebooks/icpsr/3832/cb3832.pdf (accessed October 31, 2010).

Lien, Pei-Te, and Tony Carnes. 2004. "The Religious Demography of Asian American Boundary Crossings." In Tony Carnes and Fenggang Yang, eds., *Asian American Religions: The Making and Remaking of Borders and Boundaries*. New York: NYU Press.

Overmyer, David. 2003. Introduction to David Overmyer, ed., *Religion in China Today*. Berkeley, CA: China Quarterly.

Overmyer, David, Gary Arbuckle, Dru Gladney, John McRae, Rodney Taylor, Stephen Teiser, and Franciscus Verellen. 1995. "Chinese Religions State of the Field: Living Traditions." *Journal of Asian Studies* 54 (2): 314–321.

Pew Forum on Religion and Public Life. 2008. "American Religious Landscape Survey."

Republic of China Government Information Office. 2008. *Taiwan Yearbook*. http://www.gio. gov.tw/taiwan-website/5-gp/yearbook/ch21.html.

Roof, Wade Clark, and William McKinney. 1987. *American Mainline Religion: Its Changing Shape and Future*. New Brunswick: Rutgers University Press.

Saguaro Seminar. 2000. "Social Capital Community Benchmark Survey." Available online at http://www.ropercenter.uconn.edu/data_access/data/datasets/social_capital_community_survey.html (accessed October 31, 2010).

Saroglou, Vassilas. 2006. "Religious Bricolage as a Psychological Reality: Limits, Structures and Dynamics." *Social Compass* 53:109–115.

Singapore Census of Population Office. 2000. "Census of Population 2000." http://www. singstat.gov.sg/pubn/papers/people/censustaking.html (accessed October 31, 2010).

Stark, Rodney, Eva Hamberg, and Alan Miller. 2005. "Exploring Spirituality and Unchurched Religions in America, Sweden, and Japan." *Journal of Contemporary Religion* 20 (1): 3–23.

Sun, Anna. 2007. "The Chinese Religious Repertoire: A New Approach to the Classification of Chinese Religions." Paper presented at "The Nature and Components of Religion" session at the annual meeting of the American Sociological Association, August.

Syonzi, Michael. 2009. "Secularization Theories and the Study of Chinese Religions." *Social Compass* 56 (3): 312–327.

Teiser, Stephen. 1995. "Popular Religion." *Journal of Asian Studies* 54 (2): 378–395.

Warner, R. Stephen. 1993. "Work in Progress toward a New Paradigm for the Sociological Study of Religion in the United States." *American Journal of Sociology* 98 (5): 1044–1093.

Weber, Max 1951. *The Religion of China*. New York: Free Press.

Wolf, Arthur. 1974. *Religion and Ritual in Chinese Society*. Stanford: Stanford University Press.

Yang, C. K. 1961. *Religion in Chinese Society: A Study of Contemporary Social Functions of Religion and Some of Their Historical Factors*. Berkeley: University of California Press.

Yang, Fenggang. 2007. "Oligopoly Dynamics: Official Religions in China." In James Beckford and N. J. Demerath III, eds., *The Sage Handbook of the Sociology of Religion*, 635–653. Los Angeles: Sage.

Yang, Fenggang, and Helen Ebaugh. 2001. "Transformations in New Immigrant Religions and Their Global Implications." *American Sociological Review* 66:269–288.

CHAPTER 11

"I Would Pay Homage, Not Go All 'Bling'"

Vietnamese American Youth Reflect on Family and Religious Life

LINDA HO PECHÉ

At my parents' house, we have two altars: one for my maternal grandparents, one for my paternal grandparents. On the altars, there are pictures of my grandparents, red candles, and an incense burner. When we buy fruit, we must place the fruit on the altar as an offering and wait two days before we can eat it. The altars are simple in appearance but let us know that our ancestors are watching over us.

—Olivia, second-generation Vietnamese American

Many Vietnamese American families maintain a rich domestic religious life. Families often maintain home altars (ban tho) to venerate or memorialize Buddha, Jesus, saints, spirits, or ancestors. These spaces are often focal points in Vietnamese American homes, as the most respected domestic spaces. These cultural, familial, and religious practices maintain spiritual connections between this world and the spiritual world and also create meaningful ties to Vietnamese cultural identity. The immigrant first generation primarily maintains these folk practices. As the younger 1.5 and second generation comes of age, will these youth continue to maintain the religious practices of their parents?[1]

In this chapter, I explore some narratives about religious life among a select number of second-generation college youth who were born in the United States and a 1.5-generation couple who was raised here. The following narratives give an insight into the participants' views about religion and domestic folk practices—that is, those practices that are learned and passed down orally or informally. What these narratives reveal is a religious life that is intimately tied to a dynamic and adaptive family life and folk tradition. The following reflections also illuminate the range and diversity of religious participation among the Vietnamese American second generation, from informants who consider themselves "very religious" to those who identify as "not religious at all." I contend that a focus on popular religious practice can reveal the dynamic and adaptive nature of the social and spiritual roles of families and the religious establishment. Furthermore, the following personal narratives reveal the development of an autonomous spiritual orientation among several second-generation practitioners.

I focus on a discrete sample of Vietnamese youth who are enrolled in or just graduated from college and one couple beginning to raise young sons. For the participants on the verge of graduating college, this is a particularly interesting liminal time. Many of them are reflecting for the first time on the customs of their natal homes, formulating their own unique ideas about spirituality and the religious traditions they find relevant to their own lives. Their interpretations of family-based religious life offer valuable insights into what religious practices may look like for the next generation of Vietnamese Americans. I first outline a brief overview of the diversity of religious beliefs that have historically come to shape the religious orientations of Vietnamese Americans. I then outline some scholarly approaches to studying the second generation and then move on to the main focus of the chapter: reflections and narratives about religious life among these participants.

Religious Orientations

Although Vietnam is generally considered a Buddhist country, scholars agree that most practitioners, especially in the rural areas, adhere to a locally specific, kinship-based form of ancestor veneration.[2] The formal religious practice of Buddhism is based primarily in the urban centers and was introduced to Vietnam during one thousand years of Chinese colonization beginning around 200 BC (Rutledge 1985; Rambo 2005, 92). Despite countless pagodas and temples, most Buddhist-related practices remain informal and integrated into various domestic ancestral veneration practices. Roman Catholicism, a much more organized religious institution, gained influence with the upper-middle class during the French occupation in the 17th century, and Roman Catholics make up about 10 percent of Vietnam's population (Rutledge 1985). Historically, the Catholic institution has been scrutinized and persecuted in Vietnam, possibly for "its strong and cohesive organization, its wealth, its self-conscious militancy and above all, its foreign origins and identification with Western colonialism" (Rambo 2005, 90). As a result, a large number of

Catholics have sought asylum in the United States and constitute a large proportion of the Vietnamese American community.

Two native religions, Cao Dai and Hoa Hao, have added to Vietnam's religious diversity. Cao Dai is a blend of Buddhism, Confucianism, Taoism, and Catholicism. It is a relatively new monotheistic religion, officially established in 1926. Hoa Hao began in 1939 in Vietnam as a form of Buddhist "Protestantism." It has more than 1.5 million followers and is located predominantly in the Mekong Delta; it emphasizes a highly disciplined personal prayer life and has no temples or formal liturgies (Rutledge 1985). There are also smaller populations of Muslims among the Cham ethnic minority, Christian Protestants, and Taoists.[3]

In addition to these types of formal religious participation, many Vietnamese households subscribe to a tacit obligation to practice filial piety—informally encouraging members of the subsequent generation to care for their parents in their aging years and singling out the eldest son as the caretaker of the ancestral altar following the parents' deaths. These practices are often associated with the formal philosophical tenets of Confucian philosophy, which support the idea of obedience to one's superiors and respect for one's ancestors. These basic practices or philosophies have been adapted and integrated into the domestic religious practices of Vietnamese families across many religious beliefs, including Buddhism and Catholicism, among others.[4]

In a classical approach to studying religion, it is common to describe a community's religious life through the doctrines and precepts set forth by religious institutions and literatures. Moreover, there is a tendency to focus on the place of worship to determine degrees of religious participation (for example, Ebaugh and Chafetz 2000). However, this approach may overlook a number of meaningful cultural and religious practices taking place outside of the church or temple. Folklorists and many other scholars remind us that there is a range of popular religious beliefs and practices that work in tandem with institutional doctrine (Primiano 1995; Park and Ecklund 2007). For example, for many Vietnamese, religious life may also include reading signs, divination, spirit possession, and "luck." It is also not uncommon to find religious practitioners who subscribe to what some scholars refer to as a popular Vietnamese "spiritual orientation," that is, a common acceptance of a range of spiritual entities including Buddhas, ancestral spirits, saints, and other deities (Lee 2003; Padgett 2007). Some practitioners placate and/or venerate these spirits through offerings and prayers in altars located in a range of spaces including homes, restaurants, and schools. Thus, Vietnamese religious life is varied across a range of religious beliefs within and outside of religious institutions. All these religious influences have given Vietnamese communities in the United States enormous religious breadth and richness.

Across the Pacific Ocean in the United States, Vietnamese American religious practitioners inherited this rich and diverse religious history that is associated with a wide range of folk religious practices and formal religious belief systems. Most Vietnamese identify as Buddhists or practice a folk-traditional form of ancestral veneration; Vietnamese Catholics constitute about 20 percent of the total Vietnamese American population (Rutledge 1992, 47; Lien and Carnes 2004, 41). In Houston, Texas, there is a more even distribution; about 40 percent of the Vietnamese American population identify as Roman Catholic, and 44 percent identify as Buddhists (Klineberg 2004, 252).

The religious lives of Vietnamese living abroad, or Viet Kieu, are deeply rooted in this rich religious history. Even so, religious practices are in no way static. Religious practices and beliefs are continually reshaped and tailored to new lifestyles and to a new generation of Vietnamese Americans. Most of the aforementioned cultural and religious traditions are primarily maintained by the first generation of immigrant parents or grandparents. However, what about their children and grandchildren? Will the second generation continue the cultural and religious values and practices of their parents? In the next section, I briefly outline some of the scholarly approaches to studying religion and ethnic identity among the second generation.

The Second Generation

In the early 20th century, sociologists were very interested in the religious identity of the children of European immigrants. They concluded that the second generation maintained an immigrant culture at home but then encountered a "more valued" English-speaking culture outside of the home. According to these decidedly dominant-culture assimilation theories, second-generation youth internalized an "Americanized" identity and ended up rejecting their immigrant roots, assimilated, and supposedly became more successful and upwardly mobile as a result (Park 1928; Herskovitz 1938; Gordon 1964). Furthermore, according to Herberg (1955), religious identity replaced ethnic identity, and this is what purportedly ensured an easy transition to Americanization for early European immigrants.

However, such theories oversimplified the "Americanization" of immigrants of the past and overlooked a number of the race-based exclusions faced by those from eastern and southern Europe (Hing 2003). Furthermore, although variations of these assimilation theories are still popular in some scholarly circles today, these approaches do not necessarily account for similar race-based discrimination faced by a new post-1965 cohort of immigrants from Latin America and Asia (Ngai 2005). Some communities have found predominantly White churches to be racially exclusionary and ill equipped to attend to the needs of recent immigrants (Iwamura and Spickard 2003). In response, monoracial churches have arisen throughout the United States to serve as cultural and social services institutions, as well as places of faith, for immigrants (Yoo 1996). Unlike a majority of the second and third generations of European immigrants who have been subsumed under the racial category of "White," today's second generation does not have the option to assimilate easily into the normative White Protestant Christian milieu because of the racial identity ascribed to them (Joshi 2006). Rather than becoming irrelevant factors that are "shed," ethnicity and race are part and parcel of the religious lives of many of today's immigrants and their children. Moreover, instead of rejecting their immigrant roots, member of today's second generation overwhelmingly consider parents and family to be their primary source of cultural and religious influence (Park and Ecklund 2007).

The rest of this chapter explores the experiences of a select sample of 1.5-generation and second-generation Vietnamese Americans. They are among the most recent post-1965 second generation to come of age. The following written narratives and interview quotations examine their spiritual and religious views, including their reflections on family-based religious tradition and Vietnamese religious institutions. Far from a pathologized relationship of "intergenerational conflict" represented by the previously described assimilation theories and in popular psychology, their narratives describe close familial ties when it comes to cultural and religious customs (Maira 2002). In fact, members of the second generation overwhelmingly cite their parents as the primary source for informal religious and spiritual teaching, foregrounding the importance of cultural tradition and family-oriented forms of folk religious practice.

The Interviews

Five out of seven participants interviewed for this chapter were college students in 2008 living in Austin, Texas, and were former students in a course that I taught on Vietnamese American studies at the University of Texas at Austin. Of the seven participants, two of them, whom I interviewed in 2010, are a 1.5-generation couple raising two children. All participants were interviewed between one and three times for a total of two to six hours in their homes or on the college campus. Although all participants were encouraged

to share stories about their religious lives in the broadest sense, most participants chose to focus their reflections on family and domestic religious life.

All the participants have nuclear families living in Austin, Houston, or
Dallas, Texas, and identify with the beliefs of Buddhism, Catholicism, or
ancestor veneration. Olivia's family lives in Houston and has extended family in Dallas.[5] The family identifies its belief system as ancestral worship
or ancestral veneration. Vivian's household is multireligious. Her father is
Roman Catholic, and her mother is Buddhist. They lived in Dallas most of
her childhood and recently moved to the state of Virginia. Kevin's family is
from the Houston area; his family identifies as Roman Catholic. Lee's hometown is Houston; he identifies as Christian, and Linh comes from a Roman
Catholic family. Jennifer and Thanh are raising two sons in Austin, Texas,
and subscribe to a more general spiritual orientation that combines elements
of ancestral devotion and folk religious belief.

At the time of the interviews, all participants lived in Texas, a state that
hosts the second-largest Vietnamese American community, after California.
Surprisingly, until rather recently, little scholarly work has been published
specifically about Asian American experiences in this state (Klineberg 2004;
Bretell 2005; Dhingra 2007; Tang 2008). Texas is home to the emerging
immigrant gateway cities of Houston and Dallas, two of the largest points
of entry to the United States (Ebaugh and Chafetz 2000). According to U.S.
Census Bureau estimates for 2006–2008,[6] Harris County (including Houston) hosts the fourth-largest Vietnamese population in the country, with
67,413; Dallas County hosts 26,137, and Travis County (including Austin)
hosts approximately 11,804. Not surprisingly, Vietnamese is the third-most-
spoken language in Texas after English and Spanish.[7]

Furthermore, what little has been written about Asian Americans in Texas
tends to eschew the topic of religious practice altogether. More generally,
some scholars dismiss religion as an element of "ethnic nostalgia" that will
fade over the generations (Maira 2002). And yet, in a 2002 public opinion
survey conducted in Houston, religion was noted to be "very important" to
a majority of Asians, including Vietnamese (Klineberg 2004). By focusing
especially on members of the second generation during the liminal point in
their lives between college and adulthood, these narratives provide an insight
into what Vietnamese American religious practices may look like in future
generations and also contribute to an overlooked area of scholarship.

This work is one part of an ongoing project that examines Vietnamese
American religious practices across a broader spectrum of religious, generational, and socioeconomic backgrounds.[8] It is not meant to create a holistic
picture or generalize all aspects of the religious lives of second-generation

Vietnamese Americans. Instead, I explore a few common threads across a select range of religious affiliations and life experiences. This is a personal reflection as well as an academic analysis, based on my own background as a relative native "insider" second-generation child of a Buddhist Vietnamese father and Catholic Mexican mother. The following analysis inevitably incorporates both my personal experience and my academic training in anthropology to gain insight into the domestic realm and religious lives of these particular Vietnamese Americans.

Family Life and Folk Tradition

It is generally agreed that Vietnamese American religious life is intimately tied to family life and folk tradition, that is, those elements of religious practice and belief that are informally passed down from generation to generation. In many Vietnamese American homes, home altars function as sacred spaces to meditate, memorialize, and/or mediate between the mundane and spiritual worlds. General prescribed rituals and taboos govern the proper maintenance of an altar but are oftentimes adapted to meet each family's needs. Most altars are permanent fixtures in a home and are arranged in living rooms or rooms especially designated for religious prayer. They may be embellished for New Year's celebrations, death anniversaries, or weddings or may be constructed temporarily in another space, such as funerary homes or Buddhist temples, and then disassembled and moved to the household. Other altars are placed in transitional or liminal spaces, by windows or doors, and are meant to placate wandering spirits that could harm the family.

Altars that are dedicated to ancestors are often constructed on a shelf or piece of furniture or in a cabinet and frequently include incense, a photograph of a deceased relative, and/or offerings in the form of small cups of water, fruit, and fresh or silk flowers (Truitt 2008). In addition to photographs, incense, and flowers, an ancestor may be honored on the altar with fruit, candy, or cigarettes, according to the ancestor's past preferences. All informants spoke about the importance of keeping the altar scrupulously clean, a job, they agree, that usually falls to the matriarch of the family. On a daily basis, the fallen incense is swept up and returned to the urn, which is never emptied.

There are certain tacit rules and taboos for the proper maintenance of an altar. For example, Olivia explained, "When [women] are on [their] menstrual cycle, you cannot pray at the altar. I've always wondered about [that]. I've asked my mom, but she did not give me a straight answer." The answer that she received from her mother was, "It's just not respectful."

Anthropologists have pointed to the fact that the creation of the "sacred" is often only possible in relation to a binary opposite (Douglas 1966)—in this case, ideas about female "pollution" can reflect the opposite of "sacred" and reproduce a certain patriarchal social order that governs these gendered ritual taboos. Although these ideas have traditionally been passed down tacitly, it is noteworthy to point to Olivia's implicit dissatisfaction with not getting "a straight answer." This conversational account between mother and daughter points to the fact that the rules governing proper altar maintenance can establish and reflect certain religious and social orders—but not in an unchanging, timeless vacuum. Although Olivia does not openly challenge the taboo, this conversation can reveal that these tacit rules can also be epistemological sites of curious inquiry, negotiation, and possible contestation.

Altars in multireligious households—that is, homes where members of the same family follow different religious faiths—can also be sites of negotiation. Each family decides how to display the religious images of each belief system. Oftentimes, religious altars are set above an ancestral altar or on the highest shelf or cabinet in the room. A figurine of the bodhisattva Quan Am may make an appearance in a Buddhist household, or a statue of the Virgin Mary Duc Me could be displayed in a Catholic home.[9] Some families set devotional objects from different religious faiths on separate shelves. Vivian, who comes from a multireligious household, described the way that her parents negotiated the placement of the devotional items of their Catholic and Buddhist faiths: "We have a huge book cabinet; one side has [Catholic] paraphernalia—holy candles, holy water, rosaries, pictures of Jesus, and pictures of my dad's parents that passed away; the other side has all of my mom's pictures, [Buddhist imagery], and incense." Others might separate the religious altars from the ancestral altars and place them—as was the case in my natal household—in different rooms to avoid conflicts between the spirits or deities. Thus, each family negotiates proper placement of devotional items based on its own ideas about the proper reverence for an ancestral altar and the proper maintenance of religious practices.

In many households, fruit is first offered at altars before it is eaten. For example, ever since Vivian can remember, her mother, a devout Buddhist who also maintains an ancestral altar, would buy bananas and oranges on a weekly basis and place them on the altar on a dish in the same spot every time. The family would be allowed to eat the fruit only after it ripened and the ancestors were given a chance to partake.[10] Vivian and her siblings were encouraged to place the fruit on the altar, but Vivian's mother had a specific way that she liked to arrange the offerings. Vivian commented, "We tried to arrange it as best we could, but it always had to go through a last check with Mom. We were like, 'Man, it's just fruit,' but she would always change it just a bit." This comment illustrates how Vivian's mother feels deeply committed to maintaining her altar "just right." Not only does she pray periodically every week, but she also untraditionally places images of living relatives still in Vietnam alongside those who have passed away. For Vivian's mother, this is not only a place to venerate and petition those who have passed on but a special site to reflect and reminisce about family far away in Vietnam. Vivian, however, calls into question her mother's attentiveness to the aesthetic placement of the daily offering of oranges. Vivian's small complaint demonstrates how meaning can be constantly constructed and negotiated between family members through the active engagement of aesthetic tastes.

Other families set aside special spaces in their homes with photographs or mementos to memorialize deceased family members, but they may not necessarily call them altars. For example, Linh, who identifies as Catholic, described the space on her parents' bedside table,

> Unlike many Vietnamese families, my family does not really have an altar that is dedicated to honoring past ancestors. However, after my grandfather's death, my mother began keeping a small photo of him on our dresser, which she prays to every night when she gets home from work. It was our family's first experience of losing a loved one. My mother was very close to him.

In Linh's home, sacred spaces are demarcated through ritual action. They may not be called altars in the family's daily vernacular, but nevertheless these are profoundly meaningful spaces for prayer and meditation. Linh continued,

> Our altars are the places in the house where we gather to pray together as a family to bond. Every time I visit home, my siblings and I usually crawl into bed with my parents at night and together pray out loud before heading to bed. You have no idea how much I cherish those moments. I feel so safe and close to my family when we are in that room together. It makes me not want to leave back to Austin for school.

Although these are untraditional spaces for spiritual meditation, they are nevertheless meaningful ways in which families can experience religious devotion. The sacred space takes the form of a small photo at the bedside table and in the familiar routine of communal prayers before bed.

These narratives point to the diverse configurations of religious identity and ancestral reverence in multireligious homes as well as in traditional Roman Catholic and Buddhist households. Home altars are also the focal points during certain special occasions including the Lunar New Year, the celebration of the birth of a new family member, wedding rites, and the death anniversaries of ancestors. Everyone who was interviewed considers the Vietnamese Lunar New Year as the most important and joyous holiday of the year. This is a time when families gather, often for days, to celebrate the occasion; some pay homage to deceased ancestors to ask for luck and health for the coming year. Many Vietnamese families liken this holiday to celebrating everyone's birthdays, since traditionally it is not customary to celebrate an individual's birthday (although it is commonplace today). The family sets out a feast of special foods before the family altar as an offering and light incense, and the family waits to partake of the meal until the incense has burned away. In Vivian's household, one finds turkey, duck, stuffing, mashed potatoes, casserole, and pies as well as an array of traditional Vietnamese foods such as banh chung and pho.

All the participants also recall their families embellishing their ancestral altars to celebrate the annual death anniversaries of relatives. These special family gatherings—an dam gio, literally meaning "eating" event—constitute social rituals during which relatives reflect on, converse with, or petition their ancestors through the presentation of special foods and other rituals (Avieli 2007). Special foods are offered, such as fried spring rolls or pork paste, but food traditions and rituals can vary greatly from region to region and from family to family.

Many parents teach the second-generation youth to approach the family altar and light three incense sticks, carefully waft the flame to put it out (never blow, which is considered disrespectful), and place them in a bronze urn often filled with uncooked white rice. Olivia's family (which identifies with the practice of ancestor veneration) all come together on the anniversary of each of her grandparents' deaths. Each family member will light incense, pray, and bow deeply three times. She says, "We close our eyes and talk to them. We pray for them, for ourselves, for our loved ones, and wish for something that we want in life: good grades or happiness. We set food on the altar and wait for the first lit incense to burn down to the red stripe. Then we can enjoy the food."

These "death anniversary" days of remembrance provide a significant spiritual connection to ancestors and sustain social bonds with living kin. The establishment of a relationship between living kin and their ancestors begins with the funerary rites of a deceased loved one. In the event of a patriarch's or matriarch's death, families organize elaborate funerals where families line up in front of the funerary altar and dress up according to the family hierarchy to pay respects—the eldest son and his family line up first in order of age, and all wear a white band around their head and a white robe. These rites are dynamic, adaptive, and innovative. Depending on regional variation or personal taste, some families wear a white shirt or blouse and black slacks or wear different colors of head bands, depending on how close the relationship is with the deceased relative. Usually, a commemorative event is hosted in the home of the eldest son or a larger home of a close relative, if it is most convenient for visiting family members. The closest family members often pray together at the family altar for one hundred days past the death of a relative to ensure that the relative's spirit does not remain in the domain of the living.

Altars can also be embellished, moved, or temporarily placed in other spaces. In fact, altars are not considered permanent homes for ancestors or spirits but only meeting points from which the ancestors can "come and go" (Jellema 2007). For some Buddhist families, an image of a deceased relative is sometimes placed on an ancestral altar in a Buddhist temple. In time, the family may move it to the home of the eldest son. Lee (who identifies as Christian) explained,

> My parents are Buddhist and attend the Buddhist temple on a regular basis, but they have recently not been able to because of work. My grandmother's shrine used to be at the temple where we would visit and give offerings each year to pay our respects. My parents wanted to have her closer to home and decided to move her shrine to our home. The shrine itself is located in our kitchen. My mother would always tell me to ask my grandmother for a blessing because she is still around spiritually.

The Vietnamese American youth interviewed for this chapter cited their parents and family traditions as the primary source of informal religious teaching. For many, "being Vietnamese" is intimately tied to the devotional acts and traditional rituals surrounding the family altar. The rituals took on special meaning when they were performed in the presence of the nuclear and extended family during the Vietnamese New Year or during death anniversary commemorations. As is the case for most second-generation youth, Vietnamese American college students fit the pattern of citing these family-based rituals as the most important influences on the formation of their cultural and religious identities (Joshi 2006; Park and Ecklund 2007). Olivia explained, "I think about these [traditions] more than I did before.

Now that I'm older, family means a lot to me. I would hope that [when I have kids], they would keep their grandparents in mind when I pass away and my siblings pass away. [The tradition] has to stay." The next section offers a few reflections on the question of what religious life will look like for Vietnamese Americans in the future. As we will see in the next section, even those who did not identify with the institutional religion of their parents nevertheless identified the family as a conduit and reason for engaging in religious practice.

Not Going All "Bling"

The participants mentioned in the preceding section were either college students or recently graduated. It is generally accepted that the college years are a time for rebellious inquiry and self-absorption, but it can also be a time to reflect on and explore questions of transcendence, the divine, and the meaning of family. As such, this is usually the time in their lives when many youth of all backgrounds reflect on the familial traditions they may have taken for granted as children and begin contemplating their own meaningful beliefs and practices. All the participants reported that religious participation, both formal and at home, were mechanical and in some ways forced in their early years, but by the time they were in college or graduated (the time of these interviews), their reflections were both spiritually profound and critical of formal religion, which is also common in other youth communities (Maira 2002; Joshi 2006).

It is important to note that not all Vietnamese American college youth have a particular affinity for religious belief or practice. The following narratives illustrate the wide range and diversity of religious participation among Vietnamese American youth—from those who maintain only home-based practices tailored and suited to their social and spiritual needs to those who attend church institutions faithfully and frequently.

A few of the participants had a critical view of the highly ritualized nature of formal religious institutions. Vivian described her attitude toward attending Catholic Church this way: "My family [goes] to [the Catholic] church every Sunday, but I don't because I don't feel that I'm getting what I need. You can't express yourself—rules, rules, rules!" This critical view of the rigid rules of formal religious institutions was echoed by other participants. Lee commented that he visited the Buddhist temple and pagoda to socialize with friends, but it became so routinized that, he said, "my mind wasn't really there [spiritually]." So why do some Vietnamese American youth have such strong reluctance about attending religious services, especially in light of the first generation's commitment to such institutions? The different roles that religious institutions have played in the first and second generations may give us a clue.

Religious institutions played a central role in the social and spiritual lives of the first generation of immigrants. For example, in the 1970s and 1980s, churches and temples were important to recently arrived immigrants because it was difficult for them to build extensive social networks; this was mostly due to the U.S. government's early efforts to disperse the refugee communities all across the nation (Zhou and Bankston 1998, 45–48). Olivia's family, for example, lived in the southwest Bellaire area of greater Houston, which was populated by mostly White and African American residents until the 1990s.[11] Due to the growing concentration of Vietnamese families and the affordability of housing, it has now become one of Houston's largest Vietnamese enclaves. As the immigrant community grew, temples and churches were among the first institutions to be collectively funded. Often, religious institutions are among the first organizations to attend to specific immigrant community needs, including language courses for the second generation (Iwamura and Spickard 2003). Indeed, many Vietnamese religious institutions serve to promote language preservation as well as faith-based teachings.

The second generation does not seem to have such a commitment to the religious institutions of the first generation, despite the fact that Vietnamese parents continue to send their children to the temple or church for both religious teachings and linguistic and cultural formation. Kevin, Vivian, and Lee were all strongly encouraged by their parents to attend language classes in their local parishes. As Kevin explained, "Every Saturday afternoon or Sunday morning we had to go to Vietnamese-language classes to study and take religious courses. You have to go. It was a very structured system when I was younger. I dreaded going."

Despite these efforts at linguistic education, members of the second generation—especially younger siblings—are not very fluent in Vietnamese. Vivian and Kevin have siblings who attend church classes regularly but speak Vietnamese minimally or not at all. This may foreshadow a move away from the importance of Vietnamese-language religious institutions for future generations of Vietnamese Americans. In fact, some youth feel exclusion and discrimination from other Vietnamese Americans when attending church or temple. Vivian remembers being picked on by some of her Vietnamese-speaking colleagues: "[They would say], 'You're so whitewashed!' I was coined that way. It didn't help that I didn't know Vietnamese. That's because it was pretty diverse [where I lived]. I had a lot of friends from different backgrounds." Vivian has since ventured to other nondenominational religious institutions to fulfill the need for a more diverse spiritual experience.

While religious institutions continue to be central social and spiritual centers for Vietnamese parents, the second generation does not seem quite as committed to continued participation in Vietnamese religion and language classes. In fact, although second-generation youth do socialize with their Vietnamese peers, they are also finding social and spiritual comfort outside of Vietnamese religious institutions, in some cases trying to construct their own unique sense of spirituality. For example, Kevin explained, "When I first came to college, I was very good about coming to church, out of guilt. I felt that going to church was more forced. It was systematic and mechanical instead of spiritual. Now, I make a distinction between religiosity and spirituality. I pray every night in my own personal, authentic way—how I speak to God is the way I speak to God." Kevin carefully constructs an identity that is deeply implicated in a sense of religious and ethnic identity, while creating an autonomous space for his own unique sense of spirituality. He went on to say, "I pay . . . attention to the sense of community—generations of Vietnamese grandparents, children, and grandchildren who still hold on strongly to the sense of identity. It reminds me that Catholicism is a sense of who I am. . . . But I don't say [I am] Catholic Vietnamese American; it sounds silly to me. I'm unorthodox Catholic." Kevin also feels the need for a more open and inclusive space in which his sexuality will be accepted: "It is hard being a Vietnamese American and identifying as gay because it is in opposition to everything that is preached in the Bible and fundamental beliefs. So which one do I choose? How do I function?" Kevin has found a way to reconcile this challenge by continuing to attend church sporadically and also by joining a social organization on the college campus that is accepting of his sexual identity: "I feel much more comfortable and accepted in the Filipino Student Association, where homosexuality is actually celebrated. I can be myself. This is who I am; I encompass all these different identities. They clash, but I am all of them. I don't reject it or deny it."

While the parents of these second-generation Vietnamese Americans were part of the generation that built and maintained Vietnamese religious institutions as places of political, spiritual, and cultural refuge, some members of the second generation seem to be creating an autonomous sense of religious and spiritual orientation not totally reliant on Vietnamese religious institutions. Home-based practices remain an important aspect of their spiritual lives, albeit adapted to their own spiritual sensibilities. When I asked Kevin if he would continue the practice of maintaining a family altar, he responded, "I would pay homage and respect, not go all 'bling.' First, I would place pictures of my grandparents and my parents [on the altar]. A crucifix, of course, would have to be there, and saints, . . . and a Bible that I could pick up to read." Kevin's earlier comment about the distinction he makes between "spirituality" and "religiosity" is not a simple syntactic substitution. This conscious act points to the complex ways in which he and others like him are finding new approaches to experiencing and interacting with religion in daily life. This new approach rejects "bling"—that is, the ostentatious and, to Kevin, a superficial treatment of spiritual life. This idea is reflected in other religious youth communities (Carnes and Yang 2004, 5).

Likewise, Olivia will continue in the ancestral beliefs and traditions of her parents. Olivia explained, "Now that I'm older, family means a lot to me. As far as God, they say he created everything, but it's hard for me to believe because I can't see that. I believe in my ancestors though, because my grandfather created my dad, and my dad created me. With my family, I do know how that started, and that is easier for me to believe in." She plans to maintain an ancestral altar despite the difficulties of navigating a multiracial and multireligious household. Olivia believes that she will continue the rituals in the same manner that her family taught her and hopes that when she has children, they will continue to memorialize their grandparents in the same way. She admits that this will be particularly difficult since her spouse is a Catholic of Mexican/Spanish descent who does not necessarily support the idea of maintaining an ancestral altar, but nevertheless she feels committed to continuing the practices that have become a meaningful part of her spiritual life.

Jennifer and Thanh also have a more general spiritual orientation not tied to a particular religious institution. They are part of the 1.5 generation of immigrants who arrived in their formative years, in this case, at seven and eight years old. They are now in their late thirties and early forties raising two young boys in Austin, Texas. They identify as Buddhists through family tradition, although they are skeptical of what they refer to as "organized religion" and self-describe as "less religious, more spiritual." They describe a spiritual orientation that combines elements of ancestral devotion, karma, and folk religious beliefs including divination, reading signs, and concepts of feng shui. They maintain an ancestral altar above the fireplace along with incense, a clay pot from a trip to Greece, small glass containers of water, and an abstract painting of a Buddhist monk painted by Thanh.

Jennifer is often visited in her dreams by a particular ancestor, her uncle, who provides her with advice or warnings. Thanh remembers being awoken by the spirit of his favorite aunt at the moment that she passed away, when he was thousands of miles away studying in Europe. These profound experiences remain an integral part of their spiritual understandings. Jennifer has placed framed photographs of the most senior ancestors of her family, her grandparents, in her sons' rooms. She explained to them that "these are wise spirits to be respected. They are people that we love and respect." They are critical of institutional religion, although they remind their children to "be respectful of other people's religion." In fact, they do not visit the Buddhist temple or subscribe to any regimented or prescribed form of religious practice. Like many practitioners of ancestral veneration, Jennifer and Thanh's spiritual practices are a combination of folk tradition and their own unique set of spiritual interests. This could be a signal for future researchers that we may have to look beyond temples and churches to have a more nuanced understanding of religious practices in this community.

Nevertheless, there are some second-generation Vietnamese Americans who have continued participating in their religious institutions in addition to maintaining domestic religious practices. Linh, who previously described her family's prayer rituals in her parents' bedroom, explained, "My family and I are very devoted Catholics; we go to church every Sunday, and ever since I was a little girl, I have always said a little prayer before going to bed."

These personal reflections illustrate the wide range and diversity of religious participation among the Vietnamese American second generation. In general, family-oriented folk religious rituals remain an important influence for Vietnamese Americans. Most of the participants in my survey seem to have developed a preference for a more general spiritual orientation, with some voicing apprehension toward organized religion. Most of the criticisms of religious institutions were centered mainly on the rigid and formal structures of religious institutional practice and its social conservatism. It may very well be that the second generation is informed by the American values of individualism, equality, and informality, as is the case in the broader youth community (Carnes and Yang 2004, 5). As Kevin related in the quotation earlier, not going "all bling" demonstrates a certain informal approach to the ancestral altar tradition, an informality that is in some ways antithetical to the first generation's carefully guarded conscription of appropriate filial duties based on institutional or traditional norms. As Nazli Kibria (1993) predicted almost twenty years ago, the second generation has renegotiated and redefined identity and religious practice in response to a shifting set of challenges and circumstances. Vietnamese American youth are being informed by American values; all the while they are also reshaping the landscape of American religious life.

Instead of dismissing Vietnamese American youths' ideas as youthful impressions, the narratives contained in this chapter reflect the ways in which they are formulating complex and profound ideas about belief, practice, tradition, and inclusiveness within their families and with their ethnic religious communities. For this generation, the sacred is perceived to take on a more fluid and unconventional form, all the while actively constructing and contesting various intertwined notions of filial piety, religious belief, and cultural identity. The preceding narratives also reflect the diverse ways in which Vietnamese American youth are articulating their sense of self in the context of the cultural and language politics of the broader ethnic community.

As I continue this research, I hope to contribute more broadly to the growing literature on religion in second-generation communities, particularly how they have constructed and continue to construct their worldviews in light of their religious commitments. This analysis offers only the beginning of an insight into yet another chapter of Vietnamese—and American— religious history. Further research will illuminate what Vietnamese American religiosity may look like in future years, across a broader spectrum of different institutional and folk religious practices and beliefs.

NOTES

1. According to Sucheng Chan, the 1.5 generation are immigrants who come to the United States at a young age and have the ability to mediate culturally and linguistically between the immigrant first generation and their American-born peers (2006, xiv). According to Doug Padgett (2007), the use of the term *1.5 generation* highlights the importance of the age of arrival as opposed to the year of arrival.

2. Many scholars refer to this practice of veneration as "ancestor worship," although Jonathan Lee (2003) aptly points out that this connotes a Christian-centered understanding of altar practices. Ancestor "veneration" may be a better alternative to express the mutual respect and relationships maintained between the living and the dead through the ancestral altar.

3. Taoism encompasses a variety of philosophical and religious traditions that emphasize a return to the simplicity of nature. Everything, including humans and spirits, exists through the dynamic interaction of two forces, the yin and yang.

4. In 1968, the Vatican officially allowed Vietnamese Catholics to practice ancestral veneration.

5. All names are pseudonyms to protect the confidentiality of participants.

6. U.S. Bureau of the Census, "American FactFinder," http://factfinder.census.gov/.

7. This is according to the Modern Language Association, "MLA Language Map," http://www.mla.org/map.

8. Although social class is not a focus of this study, its association with religious identification merits mention. In the Vietnamese community, religious identification is closely correlated to specific immigration circumstances. For example, in Houston, Texas, 40 percent of the Vietnamese population are Catholics who arrived in the 1970s as part of the affluent class seeking refuge after Vietnam's civil war; 44 percent are Buddhists who arrived more recently and are generally working class (Klineberg 2004).

9. Quan Am Thi Kinh, or Quan Am, is the Vietnamese name for a bodhisattva or goddess also commonly known as Guan Yin in Chinese. She is one of the most common
representations on Buddhist altars, along with the original Buddha. In some households, this figure is conflated with Duc Me, the Blessed Mother Mary in the Catholic
tradition (Lee 2003, 14). Some people consider them to be different manifestations of
the same deity.

10. In general, Vietnamese Buddhists believe that ancestors and spirits can and do partake
in meals, bestow luck, or cause conflicts. Vietnamese Catholics, in general, do not
believe that spirits come back, and they place fruit and flowers on the altars for their
own aesthetic enjoyment.

11. Houston was designated a refugee resettlement area (Rodriguez 2000). When Vietnamese families encouraged extended kin and friends to move once again to join
them, the community grew considerably.

REFERENCES

Avieli, Nir. 2007. Feasting with the Living and the Dead: Food and Eating in Ancestor Worship Rituals in Hoi An. In *Modernity and Re-enchantment: Religion in Post-revolutionary
Vietnam*, edited by P. Taylor. Singapore: Institute of Southeast Asian Studies.

Bretell, Caroline. 2005. Voluntary Organizations, Social Capital, and the Social Incorporation of Asian Indian Immigrants in the Dallas–Fort Worth Metroplex. *Anthropological
Quarterly* 78, no. 4 (Fall).

Carnes, Tony, and Fenggang Yang. 2004. *Asian American Religions: The Making and Remaking of Border and Boundaries*. New York: NYU Press.

Chan, Sucheng. 2006. *The Vietnamese American 1.5 Generation: Stories of War, Revolution,
Flight, and New Beginnings*. Philadelphia: Temple University Press.

Dhingra, Pawan. 2007. *Managing Multicultural Lives: Asian American Professionals and the
Challenge of Multiple Identities*. Stanford: Stanford University Press.

Douglas, Mary. 1966. *Purity and Danger: An Analysis of Pollution and Taboo*. New York:
Routledge.

Ebaugh, Helen Rose Fuchs, and Janet Saltzman Chafetz, ed. 2000. *Religion and the New
Immigrants: Continuities and Adaptations in Immigrant Congregations*. Lanham, MD:
AltaMira.

Gordon, Milton. 1964. *Assimilation in American Life: The Role of Race, Religion, and
National Origins*. New York: Oxford University Pres.

Herberg, Will. 1955. *Protestant, Catholic, Jew: An Essay in American Religious Sociology*.
Garden City, NY: Doubleday.

Herskovitz, Melville J. 1938. *Acculturation: The Study of Culture Contact*. New York:
Augustin.

Hing, Bill Ong. 2003. *Defining America through Immigration Policy*. Philadelphia: Temple
University Press.

Iwamura, Jane Naomi, and Paul R. Spickard. 2003. *Revealing the Sacred in Asian and Pacific
America*. New York: Routledge.

Jellema, Kate. 2007. Returning Home: Ancestor Veneration and the Nationalism of Doi Moi
in Vietnam. In *Modernity and Re-enchantment: Religion in Post-revolutionary Vietnam*,
edited by Philip Taylor. Singapore: Institute of Southeast Asian Studies.

Joshi, Khyati Y. 2006. *New Roots in America's Sacred Ground: Religion, Race, and Ethnicity in Indian America.* New Brunswick: Rutgers University Press.

Kibria, Nazli. 1993. *Family Tightrope: The Changing Lives of Vietnamese Americans.* Princeton: Princeton University Press.

Klineberg, Stephen L. 2004. Religious Diversity and Social Integration among Asian Americans in Houston. In *Asian American Religions: The Making and Remaking of Borders and Boundaries,* edited by Tony Carnes and Fenggang Yang. New York: NYU Press.

Lee, Jonathan Huoi Xung. 2003. Ancestral Veneration in Vietnamese Spiritualities. *Review of Vietnamese Studies* 3 (1): 16.

Lien, Pei-Te, and Tony Carnes. 2004. The Religious Demography of Asian American Boundary Crossings. In *Asian American Religions: The Making and Remaking of Borders and Boundaries,* edited by Tony Carnes and Fenggang Yang. New York: NYU Press.

Maira, Sunaina Marr. 2002. *Desis in the House: Indian American Youth Culture in New York City.* Philadelphia: Temple University Press.

Ngai, Mae M. 2005. *Impossible Subjects: Illegal Aliens and the Making of Modern America.* Princeton: Princeton University Pres.

Padgett, Doug. 2007. Religion, Memory and Imagination in Vietnamese California. Ph.D. diss., Indiana University.

Park, Jerry Z., and Elaine Howard Ecklund. 2007. Negotiating Continuity: Family and Religious Socialization for Second-Generation Asian Americans. *Sociological Quarterly* 48 (1): 26.

Park, Robert E. 1928. Human Migration and the Marginal Man. *American Journal of Sociology* 33 (6): 881–93.

Primiano, Leonard N. 1995. "Vernacular Religion and the Search for Method." *Western Folklore* 54:37–56.

Rambo, Terry, A. 2005. *Searching for Vietnam: Selected Writings on Vietnamese American Culture and Society.* Kyoto: Kyoto University Press.

Rodriguez, Nestor. 2000. Hispanic and Asian Immigration Waves in Houston. In *Religion and the New Immigrants: Continuities and Adaptations in Immigrant Congregations,* edited by H. R. Ebaugh and J. S. Chafetz. Lanham, MD: AltaMira.

Rutledge, Paul. 1985. *The Role of Religion in Ethnic Self-Identity: A Vietnamese Community.* Lanham, MD: University Press of America.

———. 1992. *The Vietnamese Experience in America.* Bloomington: Indiana University Press.

Tang, Irwin. 2008. *Asian Texans: Our Histories and Our Lives.* Austin, TX: The It Works.

Truitt, Allison. 2008. Offerings to Kings and Buddha: Vietnamese Ritual Activities at Chua Bo De. Louisiana Folklife Program. http://www.louisianafolklife.org/LT/Articles_Essays/offeringskingsbuddha.html.

Yoo, D. 1996. For Those Who Have Eyes to See: Religious Sightings in Asian America. *Amerasia Journal* 22 (1): xiii–xxii.

Zhou, Min, and Carl L. Bankston. 1998. *Growing Up American: How Vietnamese Children Adapt to Life in the United States.* New York: Russell Sage Foundation.

CHAPTER 12

Religion in the Lives of Second-Generation
Indian American Hindus

KHYATI Y. JOSHI

After nearly half a century of immigration being open to predominantly
Protestant Europeans, the Immigration and Naturalization Act of 1965 is one
of the main reasons for the racial, ethnic, and religious diversity we have in
the country today. The post-1965 wave of immigration—the largest in U.S.
history—is challenging traditional understandings of the so-called straight-
line assimilation theory of ethnicity and the normative place of Judeo-Christian traditions in society and religious scholarship. For example, the growth
in immigration from South Asia, particularly India, has increased the presence of Hindus.

A racial and a religious minority in the United States, Indian American
Hindus illustrate how ethnicity, race, and religion all play a substantial role
in their identity development. This is true not only because of Indian Americans' status as a racialized minority in the United States but also because of
the interconnectedness of Hinduism and Indian American ethnic identity.
The purpose of this chapter is to show the various ways in which religion
is present in and affects the lives of second-generation Indian American

Hindus, including in the development and maintenance of ethnic identity. The data show that Indian American ethnicity does not "fade into the twilight" (Alba 1985) and that Hinduism plays a part in the maintenance of ethnic identity in the Christian-dominated milieu of the United States. The data also show that Hinduism has multiple roles in the lives of the second generation, including not only worship and spiritual expression but also the maintenance of Indian culture and of transnational connections to India. This chapter also discusses the existence within the second-generation Indian American population of two cohorts that are similar in some respects and different in others and considers possible trajectories for the Indian American Hindu experience in the second generation.

Commonalities and Distinctions among Second-Generation Indian American Hindus

While there are nuances to the definition of the new second generation, in this chapter I use Zhou's (1997) definition, in which second-generation Indian Americans are those individuals born in the United States or those who arrived to the United States as young children, below the age of five. This limits the definition to those who spent their "formative years" of childhood and adolescence in the social and cultural milieu of the United States.

The second generation of this post-1965 population thus encompasses individuals between the ages of 18 and 44, a very wide range. This population includes substantial differences in experience between those older members who grew up in the 1970s, when few Americans could find India on a map, to the present day, when Hindu temples abound and the annual Diwali shows are sold-out events at colleges and universities. Elsewhere I have identified these cohorts as "Second Generation A" and "Second Generation B" (Joshi 2006). While many earlier studies explored the experiences of Second Generation A (e.g., Asher 2002; Fenton 1992; Joshi 2006), some recent studies focus on Second Generation B (Brettell and Nibbs 2009; Kurien 2005; Shankar 2008), and others have included members of both groups (Dhingra 2007; Maira 2002; Purkayastha 2005).

The distinction between Second Generations A and B is important as scholars and practitioners set policies and combat presumptions about educational achievement. Collectively, these distinctions and the related life experiences of each cohort mark a substantial and pervasive cleavage within what might otherwise be described merely as "the second generation" (Joshi 2006). Three distinctions between A and B are sufficiently important to the topic of this chapter to warrant separate discussion: the characteristics of their parents' immigrant cohort, attributes of the mainstream culture encountered outside the home, and distinctions in collegiate experiences.

First, members of Second Generation A, who came of age in the 1980s and early 1990s, were the children of the first wave of immigrants from India that arrived between 1965 and 1976. The educational background of this immigrant cohort, and their resulting relative privilege with respect to socioeconomic class, has affected the lives of their children The United States did receive a cross-section of Indians; it got a cross-section of professional Indians (see Prashad 2000)—in particular, an overwhelming number of immigrants with MDs and PhDs (Chandrasekhar 1982; Takaki 1989). Most members of Second Generation A succeeded academically, not only because a premium was placed on education in their households but also because of the socioeconomic characteristics and educational backgrounds of their parents. Members of Second Generation B are the children of the second wave of Indian immigration to the United States, which lasted from about 1977 to 1986 (Seth 1995).

The second salient distinction between cohorts A and B of the Indian American second generation relates to the U.S. social context with which they interacted and by which they and their peers were influenced. Here, we see how India's place and, more broadly speaking, South Asia's place on the global stage—in terms of culture, religion, regional politics, religious violence—can affect how members of the second generation are perceived by dominant society, as well as how they see themselves.

The social, cultural, and historical contexts are the ground in which identity is embedded. Experiences of the second generation may vary across space (e.g., south versus northeast, urban versus suburban) and time (e.g., the 1970s versus the 1990s) and may be affected by events of global and local importance. For Second Generation A, salient global events included the Iran hostage crisis of 1979–1980, the first U.S.-Iraq war in 1991–1992, and the denouement of the Cold War between the United States and the Soviet Union. National events and political disputes and local upheaval over issues such as school integration and court-ordered busing all brought to the second generation's attention their status as racial and religious minorities. At the same time, India and South Asia were largely unfamiliar to the mainstream.

Second Generation B came of age and was in college between 1995 and 2008. During these years, Indian culture and South Asian geopolitics came more toward center stage in the media. India and Indian Americans appeared in different facets of mainstream and popular culture. While Second Generation B was growing up, Bill Clinton issued the first ever White

House Proclamation recognizing Diwali and made a highly publicized trip to India in 2000, the first presidential visit to India since 1978. For Indian American Hindus in Second Generation B, the September 11 attacks on the World Trade Center and the Pentagon in Washington, DC, and the events that followed—including "backlash" attacks in the United States and the wars in Iraq and Afghanistan—are another defining moment.

Second Generation A grew up during a time when the only images of India were of rural villages and those straight out of National Geographic. The only time India was mentioned in school was if teachers talked about Gandhi. The only other appearance of India in popular film was in *Indiana Jones and the Temple of Doom* (1984), in which Indians were shown eating monkey brains and live snakes and engaging in human sacrifice and child enslavement. In the mainstream media, the only Indian character was a cartoon: Apu, the convenience-store clerk in the animated series *The Simpsons*.

Unlike Second Generation A, Second Generation B could see facets of their lives reflected on television shows, in magazine advertisements, in movies, and even on Broadway. Movies such as *Monsoon Wedding* (2001) and *Bend It Like Beckham* (2003) enjoyed big-screen success in the United States. Prime-time television shows such as ER featured sympathetic Indian American characters in major roles. Indian themes also made appearances, such as when a 2006 episode of *The Office* was built around the occurrence of Diwali. Jhumpa Lahiri's novel *Namesake* (2003) became a film in 2007 and was adopted as required, recommended, or summer reading in high schools and colleges. Indian cultural phenomena such as henna "tattoos" and the forehead bindi have been adopted by popular entertainment figures. These positive portrayals and expressions of mainstream interest were a very different sociocultural backdrop for Second Generation B.

Third, one can identify an important demarcating line between the collegiate experiences of Second Generation A and Second Generation B around the years 1993–1995. Prior to those years, second-generation Indian American college students (the A cohort) had not yet developed to the level of a critical mass; while present, they were not highly visible and did not generally arrive on campus to find student organizations or many courses that reflected their background. Many members of Second Generation A reported building such organizations and pushing for the availability of such classes. Even where the universities had Indian or Hindu student organizations, the mid-1990s was a period when the population of such organizations shifted from being predominantly international students to predominantly members of the Indian American second generation. The B cohort, arriving after 1995 up to the present, finds organizations ready and waiting, with resources available and a tradition of visibility on campus. Coursework on India, Indian Americans, and Hinduism is more likely to be available than it was for Second Generation A.

Lived Religion in Indian America

Religion has been characterized by some scholars as a dimension of ethnicity that fades over time. Maira (2002) calls religion an element of "ethnic nostalgia," something that helps the second generation think about the essence of "Indianness" but that, she implies, is not genuinely "religious" and will fade over time. Kurien (2005) suggests that religious involvement among second-generation Indian American Hindus indicates reactive ethnicization due to a sense of racial marginality, which can sometimes lead to the embrace of puritan or even radical strands of religion. The notion of "symbolic ethnicity" (Gans 1979) or "symbolic religiosity" (Gans 1994) is certainly a part of the experience for some Indian Americans, particularly Hindus. In reference to second-generation Indian American Hindus, Fenton observed that approximately one-third of Indian American students who take his undergraduate course on Hinduism are "culturally Hindu," which "is equivalent to the customs of the ethnic group accompanied by broadly Hindu or Indian moral principles. Hindu ritual survives for them as a second-hand celebration of ethnic heritage and as festival (fun and games)" (Fenton 1992, 263). To some extent this is no less true in any religion: the concept of performing a ritual "as it has always been done" carries importance among people of all faiths, and the line between religion and culture frequently blurs.

For Indian American Hindus, the concepts of Indian ethnicity are intertwined with Hinduism. While some may identify distinctions between "Indianness" and "Hinduness," many second-generation Indian Americans use Indian and Hindu synonymously. For example, when participants in my study (Joshi 2006) were questioned about their cultural background, most responded with an answer that referred to religion—practices, tenets, or mores associated with the respondent's home religion. This reflects the conflation of ethnicity and culture and religion that is so commonplace among Indian Americans. It also reflects the remarkably high salience of religion among factors affecting ethnic identity among second-generation Indian Americans of all religious backgrounds. Religion is present in a myriad of ways in the lives of second-generation Indian American Hindus—including those who describe themselves as "religious" and those who say they are not, those who have grown up with a strong ethnoreligious community and those who have not, and those who self-identify in adulthood as atheists.

However, the assertion that reactive ethnicity is the only reason why second-generation Indian American Hindus take an interest in their religion trivializes the place and the many roles of religion in the lives of many. The data reveal that there is substantially more than nostalgia going on as second-generation Indian Americans approach Hinduism. Many facets of the lived religious experience include experiencing Hinduism through acquisition of knowledge, ritual, and transnational connections (Joshi 2006). Religious practice is situational; it may mean one thing during high school and something very different in adulthood—and it may do so without being inconsistent or diminishing the depth of meaning respondents feel toward their religious practices and identities. Categorizing religious identity or practice as merely a response to external factors, or as an element of ethnic nostalgia, not only misses the point but also exhibits a narrow view of what it means to be Hindu. Smita, a member of the Second Generation A cohort, engaged in a ritual worship activity while away at college. "She performed aarti, a light offering to Hindu gods and goddesses, with a friend every week, in that friend's dormitory suite" (Joshi 2006, 85). Nirav, a member of Second Generation B, described how having a group of Indian Hindu friends in college spurred him to participate in religious worship:

> If we had a big exam coming up in the next couple of days, . . . we go and pray, and [we would pray about] other parts of life, what things to improve—whether you want a better grade or you try to do well in sports, as I used to do sports. In the beginning we go to pray for those kind of things. But we also tend to go for no reason. We'll go just to spend some hours with gods in the mandir.[1]

Nirav was clear that he attended for religious reasons and not social ones. He described the temple as being very quiet, something different from his experience growing up and going to temples with his family. Here Nirav and his friends were going for their own "religious reasons." For others in the second generation, Hinduism is experienced as rituals and practices that their parents do—and because they do not have the frequency of engagement in ritualized religious observance, they often view themselves as less "religious."

Upon closer examination, Hinduism goes far beyond texts, traditions, and rituals; it is present as "lived religion" in the everyday lives of second-generation Indian Americans. There is religious practice and knowledge taught to the second generation; but there are also the principles and unspoken tenets internalized through interactions with parents, grandparents, and others who represent piety. These facets intersect to shape and constitute the individual's self-understanding as a religious (or irreligious) person. Second-generation Indian Americans experience religion in a variety of other ways as well: as an element of the experience of community, culture, and family; as knowledge and the pursuit of knowledge about Hinduism; and as a moral compass. Second-generation Indian American Hindus also experience religion through transnational experiences, particularly travel to India, and through experiences of religious oppression in the United States (Joshi 2006).

Navigating Two Worlds

For the second generation of both cohorts, doubt, denial, and discovery are all elements of "negotiating religion," as is the backdrop of the Second Generation A's cognitive development and their evolving relationship with "religious" ideas and opportunities. Second-generation Indian American Hindus of both A and B cohorts grew up in a society that presented them with a competing religious worldview. They were raised with steeples on the horizon or megachurches on the corner. There were school holidays at Christmas and Easter, while they had to miss a day for Diwali or other Hindu holidays. The entire vocabulary and imagery of "religion" in the United States was, and is, profoundly Western and Christian in nature. Most of the participants in my study reported feeling different from their classmates and from U.S. society in general, because Christianity is omnipresent and hegemonic and because of its contrasts with their home religion. For example, when asked about feeling different as a child growing up in Massachusetts, Second Generation A member Anila's experience reflected the experience of many in her cohort: "Not going to church was something. People talked about going to church, and I did not go to church."

Second-generation Indian Americans experience bicultural conflicts in which they feel out of place both at home and at school (Asher 2002; Gibson 1988; Maira 2002). The bicultural conflict is omnipresent, but changes in the broader society in which the Indian American community has existed, described earlier in this chapter, have meant that the experience of bicultural conflict has had different qualities for Second Generations A and B. Individuals in both cohorts expressed feeling that sense of not "fitting in." Most reported keeping their ethnic and religious lives private by not sharing information about their home life with school classmates.

One half of the "bicultural conflict" was the school environment and the general American social milieu, described earlier. The other half was the home environment. Second-generation Indian American Hindus were often embarrassed about their Indian culture and aspects of Hinduism as children and adolescents, mostly because it was either invisible or ridiculed or both in the school and the wider society. At the same time, they were absorbing American sensibilities and took note of their families' (i.e., Indian culture's and Hinduism's) status as outsiders to the American mainstream.

This "differentness" of their religious identity was manifest in various ways as social contexts varied. Some second-generation Hindus in my study reported feeling different because they did not attend church, prayed to different god(s), and prayed in a different manner. Some felt different when engaged in the "constant story of explanation," having to explain themselves and their families' tradition to their non-Indian peers and others around them. The K–12 educational environment played a significant role. It was largely during the school day that research participants reported experiences that caused alienation and isolation from their peers and classmates, from their neighbors, or from dominant society generally. For example, many of the Hindu research participants reported being told their gods looked funny and being teased in school for not eating beef during elementary- and middle-school years. For example, Bhrugesh, a male Hindu in Second Generation A, discussed at length about the way kids in school and others would treat him differently because he was not of the same religion as everyone else in school: "Some of the kids wanted to learn, and for some, since it wasn't their religion or their background, and so they thought it was stupid." He recalled several classmates asking him, in a hurtful manner, why his god (Ganesha) had an elephant's head or why his goddess has eight arms. Likewise, Suhas reported why he felt different: "the fact that we don't believe in Christ and that kind of thing, and that made me stand out."

A common response of the participants to experiences such as these was to seek more knowledge about Hinduism from their parents. But while many described growing up in a home where religion was practiced devoutly, through daily rituals and prayers, they could rarely get what they felt was a satisfactory explanation of these practices or the tenets of Hinduism. For example, Sina, a Hindu woman, described her father as "a very religious man" who taught "Sunday school" at the temple. Yet Sina also reported that she "never really knew what Hindu meant as a religion." If she had had what she felt was "enough" knowledge, Sina implied, then she would have been able to cope better with the harassment or to provide educational information to teachers and classmates. Demonstrating the normative power of Christianity in the American religious dialogue, Anita, another woman in Second Generation A, said she grew up wishing someone would tell her "the Ten Commandments of Hinduism" (Joshi 2006, 27).

The conflict between two worlds of home and school/society also involved gender expectations, social pressures, conflicting cultural norms, and parents' coping with new experiences, including unfamiliarity with the school environment that their second-generation children were attempting to negotiate without incident. All these factors interact in dynamic, cross-cutting, and contradictory ways across the life span.

The meaning and impact of the bicultural gap varies across the second generation in both cohorts. Overall, it depends on how dramatic or extreme the difference between home and school is. Even as a member of Second Generation A, Avinash did not feel that different, in large part because he went to a diverse school in the Philadelphia area, where he was one of many Indian American young people. Others in that cohort, such as Monali in Kansas, dealt with more extreme contrasts between home and school and therefore were more reticent about "being Indian" anywhere outside the home. Those who shared information about Hindu traditions and rituals with non-Hindu classmates did so in a context where the school environment was relatively diverse and welcoming. However, even though India was gaining wider exposure in society as Second Generation B matured, Hindus in that cohort also experienced marginalization or "outsider" status similar to Second Generation A.

Second-generation Indian American Hindus negotiated the home/school divide in part by retreating periodically to the company of friends who also felt out of place in the "two worlds," who shared both the anguish of being different from school peers and common complaints about parents' actions and expectations. This was a "third space," a physical, emotional, and social space where second-generation Indian American Hindus encountered people who shared their challenges and frustrations. This third space often existed within the context of the ethnoreligious community—the group of fellow Indian American Hindus, beyond the family unit, that the second generation encountered at temples and community centers.

Ethnoreligious Community

Religious experiences during the K–12 life period for Second Generation A Indian Americans was inextricably bound up with experiences within their families and ethnoreligious communities. As noted, ethnoreligious community provided the second generation with a third space, between the home and the dominant society. In this space, the second generation could encounter religion and express religious beliefs. During the K–12 years, ethnoreligious community functioned as a social safe haven and the first place second-generation Indian Americans could begin to develop a sense of their place within—and outside—the home and school worlds. For those second-generation Indian American Hindus who had access to such a community, it was a place where they felt physically, socially, and emotionally protected relative to their experiences in the wider world, while also liberated—at least to some degree—from what they viewed as the most restrictive elements of life at home. Anisa's remark is a typical illustration of this phenomenon:

> I went to Indian cultural school, which turned out to be my biggest outlet. Because I finally had peers who were not my family friends, who I could get to know and talk to. I was so happy. I had something to go to every weekend. So they taught us a lot. It was predominantly north Indian, so some of the stuff I could not relate. Given what I had, why not?! I started going when I was 15. I have learned a great deal, so much that I still know today. It was very, very valuable.

Anisa called the Sunday school she shared with other young Indian American Hindus her "social outlet." Anisa's experience is an example of one of the more ubiquitous elements of the second-generation experience, across geography and time: "Sunday schools." In Sunday schools, a teacher—a member of the immigrant generation—taught elements of Hindu belief and practice, along with Indian history and culture. Hindu holidays were celebrated, as was Indian Independence Day. When interviewed in early adulthood, many members of the second generation indicated that they did not retain much of the information taught at Sunday school. Nevertheless, they were influenced by a great deal of informal learning that occurred, with social mores and manners—such as reverence for elders—conveyed successfully.

For both cohorts, the ethnoreligious community was the space where second-generation Hindus expressed and were exposed to religious beliefs. For both Second Generations A and B, religion during the K–12 life period was something they had to do. Many second-generation Hindus were not interested in rituals or thinking about deities and belief. Instead they were interested in the social (read: fun) parts of coming together as a community with their coethnic peers. The interest in the "essence of God"—the phenomenon of religious belonging that includes nonobservable qualities such as belief and transcendence—comes later in adolescent development. Religious participation before adolescence, if it occurs, is merely didactic (at best) rather than spiritual. During the K–12 years, the phenomenon of the ethnoreligious community as a "safe space" was even more important than the religious function per se.

On the other hand, some members of the second generation expressed frustration with Sunday school, mainly because they felt it did not convey concrete information they wanted about Hinduism. Sila's and Anila's comments, described in the preceding section, are examples of this perspective. The presence of a dominant alternative theology—Christianity—and their academic exposure to Western rationalism, along with cognitive development and adolescent exploration, resulted in many Second Generation A and B individuals wanting to understand Hindu religious practices, such as different pujas (religious ritual), in order to participate in them. This is an example of Christianity's deep normative influence: being raised in the United States meant absorbing Western understandings of what constitutes a "religion" and what the societal function of a "religion" is meant to be. An important difference between immigrants and the second generation is that second-generation Indian Americans Hindus want to know why they should believe in Hinduism.

The experience of ethnoreligious communities also marks one of the most substantial differences between Second Generation A and Second Generation B. Second Generation A grew up at a time when Hindu temples were just beginning to appear on the American religious landscape. In many cases, it was their parents' involvement in cultural and religious organizations that led to the building of those temples, for religious and cultural maintenance and transmission (Fenton 1988; Joshi 2006). Before that, they had worshiped in the basement of their own or a friend's home or in worship space borrowed or rented from another religious group (including ISKCON, the predominantly White sect of Hindus better known as the Hare Krishnas) or from a secular community organization.

A Second Generation A female described the construction of Pittsburgh's Sri Venkateshwara Temple as a landmark in her life (Joshi 2006). For this individual, seeing her religion's temple literally take a place on the American map was to see herself and her community as "real" and "official"—a meaningful experience for a previously invisible religious minority. Coming of age 10 to 15 years later, members of Second Generation B, on the whole, have grown up within driving distance of a preexisting Hindu temple. Now there are third and fourth temples being built in some communities. Whereas early temples might have brought together devotees of different gods or Hindus from different regional or linguistic backgrounds in India, the proliferation of temples now means that there are temples dedicated to a certain guru, sect, region, or language (Waghorne 1999; Williams 1998). Also, whereas many early temples were in buildings that had the outward appearance of a house or community center, Hindu communities are now building architecturally grandiose facilities that mimic the greatest temples of India. Vasudha Narayan (2009) states that the rate of Hindu temple construction in the United States is only matched by the Hindu temple construction that occurred in Cambodia 1,000 years ago.

While this proliferation may make second-generation Indian American Hindus feel visible or "located" on the American map, most second-generation Hindus are not experiencing Hinduism, primarily or at all, by going to temples and worshiping there. For both Second Generations A and B, the temple is not a place for them; the rituals are in a language they do not know, and they often feel embarrassed by what they do not know or cannot remember from Sunday school classes. Thus, most of the young adults worshiping at Hindu temples in the United States today are new immigrants rather than members of the second generation.

College

For second-generation Indian American Hindus, college meant negotiations that were new and different from those of the K–12 experience in their ethnoreligious communities. They were still in a Christian-dominated social context and continued to experience feelings of marginalization and acts of proselytization and discrimination against them. Still, the college years were also the first time that most Second Generation A Indian Americans interacted with larger numbers of coreligionist and coethnic peers and on their own terms. College is a stage of life when most young people are pushing the boundaries of childhood rules and societal rules, as part of figuring out what they believe and who they are. In college, informal networks of coethnic roommates and friends took on functions similar to the aforementioned "third space." While they may not have shared a common language or religious rituals, due to the diverse languages used and traditions within Hinduism, they did share the experiences of being children of immigrants, such as ethnoreligious communities and parental boundaries. They concluded they were not alone in being raised by strict parents or, for young women, in being prohibited from sleepovers and dating while their parents "follow[ed] a don't-ask-don't-tell policy of freedoms for their male children, rationalizing these as 'Indian cultural norms'" (Purkayastha 2007, 87). Second-generation Indian American students shared in experiences of racialization, especially the experience of being treated as native informants for all things Indian. Among other results of their interaction with coreligionist classmates with different social or regional backgrounds, many discovered that their home religious practice was not the "only way" Hinduism was practiced: an experience of cognitive dissonance that often led individuals to ask even more questions.

Second Generation B member Nirav, whose collegiate prayer activities were described earlier, talked about how most of his friends during this phase of his life were Indian:

> I actually do a lot more Indian events, you know, like Holi or other events that we have that I never really participated in the past. I felt myself partic- ipating because some of my friends had more [of an] Indian background; [they] kept up with more Indian culture than I did, do more activities than I would. They started getting me more involved. So I occasionally did one or two things, [and then] I saw myself continuously doing [activities] throughout my four years—doing Holis, you know, because we have a big Indian community at Emory. I felt more people I related to. I felt more at home . . . with the Indian community.[2]

During the college years, deep thinking about matters of faith and tran- scendence is common among Indian Americans (Joshi 2006; Kurien 2005; Maira 2002; Shankar 2008). Smita, for example, had always kept her home and school lives strictly separated and had never spoken to her White high school classmates about her culture or identity. In college, she observed an Indian American friend cooking Indian food for and describing Indian cul- ture and traditions to her non-Indian roommates. Seeing her friend's expe- rience showed her (as, perhaps, it showed her friend) that Americans who were not Indian could still be curious and enthusiastic about Indian culture:

> Before, everything I did with my Indian culture was always kept behind closed doors, and it was always with people of my same background. My American friends stayed away, and I never let them in or never even asked them [to participate in any Indian event]. And for my friend to have done that—she had an American roommate. She was like, "This is Krishna," and just explaining to Evelyn, "This is what [ritual or prayer] I'm gonna do." That was a real shock for me. (Joshi 2006, 32)

This experience, of revealing her ethnic self and not being ridiculed or rejected for it, was surprising and encouraging to Smita. It opened a whole new set of thoughts in her negotiation and ultimately made her less reticent about being "openly Indian" (my words) in the company of non-Indians.

The college years are a life period when we can observe several salient distinctions between the experiences of Second Generation A and those of Second Generation B. As noted earlier in this chapter, 1993 to 1995 were the pivotal years of change. During those years, the number of Indian American college students grew substantially and achieved a critical mass on campus, which allowed them to create organizations, to command resources, and even to call for more academic attention to India, Hinduism, and related topics. This increase reflects the children who arrived in the United States before the age of five for immigrants arriving between 1965 and 1975. Around this time, either South Asian–based organizations started or existing organizations went from serving a population made up predominantly of Indian nationals (international students) to serving second-generation Indian Americans. Examples include the South Asian Student Association (SASA) and campus-specific groups. These organizations often become predominantly Indian or Hindu-focused, in part because a critical mass of Muslim and sometimes Sikh students was developing around the same time and forming separate religious student groups, whereas they might in earlier years have participated with Hindus and others in pan–South Asian groups. Even Indian American fraternities have developed, including Iota Nu Delta, founded in 1994 at Binghamton University (SUNY) and now with chapters on eight college campuses, and Beta Chi Theta, founded in 1999 at UCLA and now with chapters in nine states.

In the mid- to late 1990s, Hindu student religious groups, particularly chapters of the Hindu Student Council (HSC), arose on many college campuses. This increased the number of organizations in which Indian American Hindus could be involved. HSC chapters engaged in various activities, such as Gita study groups, interfaith forums, celebration of festivals, and presentations by various Hindu organizations whose roots are in India.[3] HSC is affiliated with the Vishwa Hindu Parishad (VHP), a right-wing political movement in India that emphasizes "Hindu nationalism." Many second-generation Hindu youth who are active in collegiate HSC chapters are unaware of VHP's political agenda (Mathew and Prashad 2000). Instead, they get involved because they are in search of their roots and a place to assert their Hindu identity in a safe way (Kurien 2005). Many join merely to socialize, while others want to use the organization to pursue a deep and intellectual expression of Hinduism. Two members of Second Generation B interviewed by Kurien (2005) expressed frustration when their peers in HSC would discuss and explain Hindu concepts and rituals using the Christian normative terminology and concepts. They wanted Hinduism to stand on its own and saw HSC—perhaps even more than their coursework—as the place to accomplish that goal.[4]

Second-generation Indian American Hindus in college also found themselves (most for the first time) in a position to engage with their Indian culture—which they began to define in terms separate from their childhood participation in an ethnoreligious community. In this context, Diwali quickly developed into the bellwether holiday for collegiate Indian Americans—including, but not limited to, Hindus. Diwali functions were among the first things nascent Indian and South Asian student organizations carried out. Some groups emphasized the religious aspect, even performing a puja; others focused on popular dance, cultural shows, fashion, and the like. Over the second half of the 1990s, the annual Diwali event grew from a club activity to a major campus function at many universities, often attended not only by a large number of Hindus but also by their non-Hindu classmates, faculty, and administrators. Thus, by the time Second Generation B member Hetal arrived in college in 2001, "there were a lot of South Asian things going on campus, both at Barnard and Columbia": "We do all these things: we get dressed up, we go to garba, we're doing all these Indian things. Like that was everywhere."[5]

In addition to social and cultural functions, college was a period when second-generation Indian American Hindus sought out information about Hinduism through their coursework, living Hinduism through the acquisition of knowledge. Most second-generation Indian American Hindus had very limited knowledge about the rationale for and practice of specific rituals in the home religion (Fenton 1988; Joshi 2006). They sought out courses to fill the gaps (Fenton 1992). Suhas, a Hindu in the A cohort, described how he saw classes: "as a chance to move towards understanding myself. . . . I wanted to explore myself. . . . I started taking a lot of different cultural classes. I took a South Asian geography course, I took a 'Religions of the World' course, I took several religion and philosophy classes, I took 'Ritualism in Primitive Cultures,' and I really tried to explore differences in people." These students took the opportunity to do projects on Hinduism and India-related topics in political science and international studies courses. Interacting with the coursework, even when it resulted in cognitive dissonance—such as when professors' descriptions of Hinduism did not square with the traditions students had learned in their home and ethnoreligious community as children—reportedly helped many people practice their faith and feel connected to it.

Members of Second Generation B arrived at college after a critical mass of Indian Americans had been noted in the study body and therefore have often had more academic opportunities to study Hinduism and related topics than did Second Generation A. Many of the Second Generation A research participants, who reported finding ways to fit research on India into independent study or projects in postcolonial literature or Asian history courses, would envy Second Generation B member Hetal, who described her coursework:

> We covered—actually I had some really great courses on that stuff: religion and human rights, I think we did Hinduism, Islam, Judaism, Christianity. We had a lot of text. That was a grad-level course as well. We read a lot of translations of religious texts and then try to compare the messages of love or what messages are being sent within those scriptures. I think we probably read portions of the Bhagavad Gita, maybe some. . . . But then I took "Nonduality of Indian and Tibetan Thought" course, which was specific to pretty much Buddhism and Hinduism, so we covered a lot of interesting things.[6]

Current and Future Trends

The experiences of both Second Generations A and B in adulthood, beginning at age 23, highlight some of the trends developing in American Hinduism. Adults in both cohorts live Hinduism in a variety of ways. While temples might be the most visible manifestation of Hinduism in America, they are not central in the lives second-generation Indian American Hindus. Instead, those who pursue worship or religious practice do so through reading Hindu holy texts at home with their families and performing pujas and fasting for specific holidays. Hinduism also continues to be experienced as difference, now in the workplace instead of school; as the pursuit of knowledge; and in other ways. Individuals in both cohorts are concerned about retention of culture and religion for transmission to the next generation, so they take actions that will help in the transmission process. Rituals are performed in the home with the children. For example, Nirav had "a mandir installed in the home," and he and his wife think and talk frequently about passing on culture and religion to their young children.

    In the public sphere, the presence of advocacy organizations marks one distinction between Second Generations A and B. Just as in college, Second Generation A has built structures from which Second Generation B—along with Second Generation A—is now benefiting. The Hindu American Foundation, a civil rights advocacy group created in 2003 by a group of Hindu Americans in Second Generation A, is one example. The presence of these activist organizations, the ability to intern with these organizations in college and or to be involved with them for the first few years postcollege, can have life-long implications for members of Second Generation B and subsequent cohorts. As these organizations exert more and more influence on Hinduism's place and the rights of Hindus in mainstream American culture, their effect on the second-generation experience will warrant further study. Other areas for further study include the effect of transnational experiences, the development of "American Hinduism" and how it responds to the different needs of second- and later-generation American Hindus and blended families, and the interaction among second- and later-generation American Hindus with the continual flow of new young families immigrating from India. There is also a great need for research on the religious lives of American Hindus that looks beyond temples, particularly for the second generation.

NOTES

1. Nirav (pseudonym), interview, Atlanta, Georgia, May 25, 2010.
2. Ibid. Here, Nirav is also engaging in the conflation of religion and culture described earlier, by referring to a Hindu holiday, Holi, as an "Indian" one.
3. HSC began in 1987. See www.hindustudentcouncil.org.
4. Several of the Hindus I interviewed (Joshi 2006) reported experiencing a sense of conflict or dismay when they took collegiate religious studies courses, because the Hinduism they were studying, they said, "doesn't look like my Hinduism." In the classroom—where they had gone seeking more information about their parents' stories and beliefs—individuals encountered *other* religious ideas and manners of practice, with which they were not previously familiar and which they found jarring. Some expressed skepticism about the person at the front of the classroom: the faculty teaching Hinduism or Indian history or even Indian languages were generally White and often Christian. Subconsciously, the research participants seem to have responded by saying to themselves, "How can he possibly know my religion better than I do? Who is he to be telling me these things I've never heard before about my own religion?"
5. Hetal (pseudonym), interview, June 21, 2010, Bloomfield, New Jersey.
6. Ibid.

REFERENCES

Alba, R. D. 1985. *Italian Americans: Into the Twilight of Ethnicity*. Englewood Cliffs, NJ: Prentice Hall.

Asher, N. 2002. Class Acts: Indian American High School Students Negotiate Professional and Ethnic Identities. *Urban Education* 37 (2): 267–295.

Brettell, C. B., and Nibbs, F. 2009. Lived Hybridity: Second-Generation Identity Construction through College Festivals. *Global Studies in Culture and Power* 16:678–699.

Chandrasekhar, S. 1982. A History of United States Legislation with Respect to Immigration from India: Some Statistics on Asian Indian Immigration to the United States of America. In S. Chandrasekhar, ed., *From India to America: A Brief History of Immigration; Problems of Discrimination; Admission and Assimilation*. La Jolla, CA: Population Review.

Dhingra, P. 2007. *Managing Multicultural Lives: Asian American Professionals and the Challenge of Multiple Identities*. Stanford: Stanford University Press.

Fenton, J. Y. 1988. *Transplanting Religious Traditions: Asian Indians in America*. Westport, CT: Praeger.

———. 1992. Academic Study of Religions and Asian Indian-American College Students. In R. B. Williams, ed., *A Sacred Thread: Modern Transmissions of Hindu Traditions in India and Abroad*. Chambersburg, PA: ANIMA.

Gans, H. J. 1979. Symbolic Ethnicity: The Future of Ethnic Groups and Culture in America. *Ethnic and Racial Studies* 2 (1): 1–19.

———. 1994. Symbolic Ethnicity and Symbolic Religiosity: Towards a Comparison of Ethnic and Religious Acculturation. *Ethnic and Racial Studies* 17 (4): 577–592.

Gibson, M. A. 1988. *Accommodation without Assimilation: Sikh Immigrants in an American High School*. Ithaca: Cornell University Press.

Joshi, K. Y. 2006. *New Roots in America's Sacred Ground: Religion, Race, and Ethnicity in Indian America*. New Brunswick: Rutgers University Press.

Kurien, P. 2005. Being Young, Brown, and Hindu: The Identity Struggles of Second-Generation Indian Americans. *Journal of Contemporary Ethnography* 34:434–469.

Maira, S. 2002. *Desis in the House: Indian American Youth Culture in New York City*. Philadelphia: Temple University Press.

Mathew, B., and Prashad, V. 2000. The Protean Forms of Yankee Hindutva. *Ethnic and Racial Studies* 23:516–534.

Narayan, V. 2009. Diasporas of Religion and Religions of Diaspora. Paper presented at the American Academy of Religion annual meeting.

Prashad, V. 2000. *The Karma of Brown Folk*. Minneapolis: University of Minnesota Press.

Purkayastha, B. 2005. *Negotiating Ethnicity: Second-Generation South Asian Americans Traverse a Transnational World*. New Brunswick: Rutgers University Press.

———. 2007. Anatomy of Second Generation "Indian" Cultural Events in the USA. In A. Singh, ed., *Indian Diaspora—The 21st Century: Migration, Change, and Adaptation*, 81–89. New Delhi: KRE.

Seth, M. 1995. Asian Indian Americans. In P. G. Min, ed., *Asian Americans: Contemporary Trends and Issues*. Thousand Oaks, CA: Pine Forge.

Shankar, S. 2008. *Desi Land: Teen Culture, Class, and Success in Silicon Valley*. Durham: Duke University Press.

Takaki, R. 1989. *Strangers from a Different Shore: A History of Asians in America*. Boston: Little, Brown.

Waghorne, J. P. 1999. The Hindu Gods in a Split-Level World: The Sri Siva-Vishnu Temple in Suburban Washington, D.C. In R. A. Orsi, ed., *Gods of the City: Religion and the American Urban Landscape Religion in North America*. Bloomington: Indiana University Press.

Williams, R. B. 1998. Asian Indian and Pakistani Religions in the United States. *Annals of the American Academy of Political and Social Science* 558:178–195.

Zhou, M. 1997. Segmented Assimilation: Issues, Controversies, and Recent Research on the New Second Generation. *International Migration Review* 31 (4): 975–1008.

CAROLYN CHEN is an associate professor of Asian American studies and sociology at Northwestern University. The author of *Getting Saved in America: Taiwanese Immigration and Religious Experience*, she has written extensively on religion, immigration, race, and ethnicity.

RHONDA E. DUGAN is an assistant professor of sociology at California State University, Bakersfield. She is the coauthor (with Janet S. Armitage) of "Marginalized Experiences of Hispanic Females in Youth-Based Religious Groups" (*Journal of the Scientific Study of Religion*, 2006) and author of "Gender Bias" (*The Encyclopedia of Social Problems*, 2008).

EDWARD FLORES is an assistant professor of sociology at Loyola University, Chicago. He received his doctorate from the University of Southern California.

JOAQUIN JAY GONZALEZ III is a professor of politics, Asian and Asian American studies at the University of San Francisco. He is the author of *Filipino American Faith in Action: Immigration, Religion, and Civic Engagement* (also available from NYU Press), *Diaspora Diplomacy: Philippine Migration and its Soft Power Influences* (2012), and other books and articles on migration, ethnicity, and globalization.

EDWIN I. HERNÁNDEZ is a senior program officer at the DeVos Family Foundations and a research fellow with the Center for the Study of Latino Religion at the Institute for Latino Studies at the University of Notre Dame. His publications include *Emerging Voices, Urgent Choices: Essays on Latino/a Religious Leadership* (2006).

RUSSELL JEUNG is an associate professor of Asian American studies at San Francisco State University. He is the author of *Faithful Generations: Race and New Asian American Churches* and coproducer of the documentary *The Oak Park Story* (2010).

KHYATI Y. JOSHI is an associate professor of education at Fairleigh Dickinson University. She is the author of *New Roots in America's Sacred Ground: Religion, Race and Ethnicity in Indian America* (2006) and other publications on race and religion in the U.S.

HELEN K. KIM is an assistant professor of sociology at Whitman College. Her research interests include race and ethnicity, gender, and intermarriage among Asian Americans.

REBECCA Y. KIM is an associate professor of sociology at Pepperdine University. She is the author of *God's New Whiz Kids? Korean American Evangelicals on Campus* (also available from NYU Press).

SHARON KIM is an assistant professor in the department of sociology at California State University, Fullerton. She is the author of *A Faith of Our Own: Second-Generation Spirituality in Korean American Churches.*

NOAH LEAVITT is a visiting assistant professor of sociology and general studies at Whitman College.

ELISE MARTEL is a freelance writer and researcher in Chicago. Her publications include "Yard Games: The Social, Symbolic, and Economic Logic of Exchange in a Scrap Metal Yard in Chicago" (*Research in the Sociology of Work*, 2009).

GERARDO MARTI is the L. Richardson King Associate Professor of Sociology at Davidson College. He is the author of *A Mosaic of Believers: Diversity and Innovation in a Multiethnic Church* and *Hollywood Faith: Holiness, Prosperity, and Ambition in a Los Angeles Church.*

JERRY Z. PARK is associate professor of sociology at Baylor University. He is the author of numerous peer-reviewed articles in the sociology of religion, race, and civic life.

LINDA HO PECHÉ is a doctoral candidate in the Department of Anthropology at the University of Texas at Austin. Her academic interests include transnational religion, material and expressive culture, and the politics of representation among immigrant and refugee communities in the United States and the Americas.

MILAGROS PEÑA is a professor of sociology and women's studies and associate for social and behavioral sciences at the University of Florida. She is the author of *Latina Activists across Borders: Grassroots Women's Organizing in Mexico and Texas*, which was awarded the 2008 Distinguished Book Award by the Latino/a section of the American Sociological Association.

R. STEPHEN WARNER is a professor of sociology, emeritus, at the University of Illinois at Chicago. He is coeditor, with Judith Wittner, of *Gatherings in Diaspora: Religious Communities and the New Immigration*.

INDEX

Jesuit, 101, 118
Jewish, 8, 12, 14, 102, 103; Americans, 69, 75;
    United Jewish Communities, 72; Jewish
    Federation system, 72; synagogues, 103
Jews, 13, 14, 17, 18, 69–87, 73, 88n7, 198; Asian
    American, 3
Jobs For a Future, 118, 120
Jobs Not Jails, 128
Judaism, 2, 11, 12, 14, 69–88, 256; American,
    74
Judeo-Christian, 69, 241

Korean American, 15, 135–149, 150n1, 164,
    176–190; Christianity, 190n5

La Gran Comisión, 33, 34
La Iglesia De Apostoles Y Profetas, 32, 33,
    34
La Posada, 107
La Raza: definition, 25
Latin American Bible Institute, 118
Latino gang ministries, 3, 113–129
Latino Pastoral Action Center, 97, 101, 102
Latinos/Latin American, 1–20, 25–42,
    46–66, 85, 93–110, 110n1, 113–129, 136,
    139, 143–147, 165, 188, 218n9, 226; immi-
    grant congregations, 31; labeling, 30;
    neighborhood, 182
liberation theology, 54, 111n5
Los Angeles, 27, 29, 34, 70, 75, 93, 96, 118;
    East, 26, 29, 34, 35, 113–129, 158, 166, 173,
    176, 179, 180, 189
Loving v. Virginia, 70
low-income: Asian Americans, 6; Latinos,
    6, 29
Lutheran, 51

Malaysia, 202
Manhattan, 95, 99, 100, 102, 103
Manila, 162, 163, 172
marginalization, 13, 15, 18, 20, 101, 142, 200,
    249, 252; socioeconomic, 106; racial,
    138, 139
Maryland, 206
Massachusetts, 209, 247
McManus, Erwin, 29, 35
mestizo, 30

Mexican American, 8, 14, 15, 25–42, 46–66,
    93–111, 123; Ethno-Catholicism, 15;
    migrants, 160
Mexican heritage, 15
Mexico, 36, 69, 122, 159
Miami, 96
middle class, 14, 30; Asian Americans, 6;
    Latinos, 6, 7; white, 6
Middle Eastern, 26, 27, 30, 59
migrants. *See* immigrants
minority, 125, 141; Chinese, 201; church, 190;
    ethnic, 47, 141; invisible religious, 251;
    neighborhood, 166; racial, 141, 149, 243;
    religions, 17; religious, 47, 243; status, 149
"model minority" stereotype, 85
modernization, 198; theory, 204
Mosaic Evangelical Church, 12, 25–41, 42n9
multicultural, 30, 107; educational policies,
    8; multiculturalism, 7, 8; religious com-
    munity, 149
multiculturalist: discourse, 8; viewpoints, 9
multiethnic congregations, 7, 35; Protestant,
    25, 26, 27
multiracial, 30; community, 12
Muslims, 3, 9, 13, 17, 46–66, 85, 129n3;
    African American, 48, 59; American,
    54, 55, 66, 143; Bosnian, 59; British, 55;
    Chinese, 203; Indian Americans, 254;
    North African, 85; North American,
    65; Pakistani, 1, 55, 59; South Asian, 13;
    Vietnamese, 224
Muslim: Student Association, 1, 50, 56, 57,
    59; Women's Association, 57, 59

National Jewish Population Survey, 72, 88n6
National Longitudinal Survey of Freshman,
    16, 142–147, 150, 151n11
Nation of Islam, Louis Farrakhan's, 48
Native American, 114, 118, 125, 126, 127
New Immigrant Survey, 150n3
new second generation, 3, 4, 5, 6, 7, 8, 12, 13,
    15, 18, 19, 20, 70, 84; Asian American, 4,
    5, 9, 12; Latinos, 4, 5, 9, 12; Mexican, 4
new voluntarism, 211
New York, 70, 75, 94–111, 118, 139, 158, 173,
    189
Nueva Esperanza, 1, 98, 102, 109